NEVER TURN
THE OTHER CHEEK

PADDY CRERAND

Never Turn the Other Cheek

HarperSport

An Imprint of HarperCollins*Publishers*

HarperCollins*Publishers*
77–85 Fulham Palace Road,
Hammersmith, London W6 8JB

www.harpercollins.co.uk

First published in 2007 by HarperSport
an Imprint of HarperCollins London

1

A CIP catalogue record for this book
is available from the British Library

ISBN 13 978-0-00-724761-5
ISBN 10 0-00-724761-3

Printed and bound in Great Britain by
Clays Ltd, St Ives plc

All photographs supplied courtesy of Paddy Crerand with
the exception of the following: Empics/PA Photos 1, 2 (middle
and bottom), 8 (bottom), 9 (bottom); Express Newspapers
15 (top); Getty Images 7, 8 (top), 11 (bottom), 15 (middle);
Mirrorpix 2 (top), 3 (top and middle), 5 (top), 9 (top),
14 (bottom); MUTV 15 (bottom); News International 14
(top right); Popperfoto 10 (top and bottom), 14 (top left);
Rex Features 13 (top); Topfoto 5 (middle).

Mixed Sources
Product group from well-managed
forests and other controlled sources
www.fsc.org   Cert no. SW-COC-1806
© 1996 Forest Stewardship Council
FSC

For my mother, Sarah,
who made me the person that I am

Contents

Acknowledgements ix
Introduction xi

1. Heart of the Gorbals 1
2. A Grand Old Team to Play For? 23
3. End of a Dream 41
4. South of the Border 56
5. The Making of Champions 74
6. Best Team in England 104
7. Champions of Europe 132
8. Cheated 173
9. Decline and Despair 190
10. Troubled Times 206
11. A Brave New World? 226
12. Red Eyed 252

The Crerand Career 278
Index 281

Acknowledgements

I'd like to thank all of the following people who helped with this book. Firstly, Andy Mitten, who put my thoughts into words. We spent a lot of time together and had a laugh, although I think he learned some words he won't have heard inside a football ground.

All of the following people helped directly: Brian Kidd, Joyce Woolridge, Tony Smith, Tony Veys, Billy McNeill, Steve Bower, Vinny Scarvey, Ray Adler, my sister Bridie and my children Patrick, Danny, and Lorraine. My wife Noreen chipped in, too, usually over an argument in the kitchen.

Thanks to Paul Moreton, the agent who brought the project together and to everyone at HarperCollins including: Tom Whiting (editor), Michael Doggart (publisher), Jane Beaton (publicist), Dom Forbes (cover designer), Louise Connolly (picture researcher), and Chris Stone (reader).

There are many individuals who have shaped and influenced my life. In years gone by it was people like my brother, Charlie Duffy, Jock Stein, Mick Jackson, Paddy McGrath, Ruben Kaye and then Matt Busby and the lads. These days it's my three children and my eight wonderful grandchildren. For the vast majority of my life Noreen has been there for me. I really don't know how you've put up with me for so long, but I'm glad that you have.

Introduction

Many people have approached me over the years to write an autobiography, but it wasn't for me until now. I don't feel comfortable talking about myself and never have. If you talked about yourself where I was from then you were seen as being big-headed. But I've had a good chat with my family and they've encouraged me to tell my life story. I've waited until I am 68 years old – so I have plenty to say. I played football for Celtic and Manchester United, the two greatest clubs in Britain – some might say, the world – and football has remained my life since I hung up my boots in 1972.

My vices are red wine and bad language. I've toned down the swearing for this book; those reading it will probably be able to see where. I speak as I find and there are many things which made me angry, and still do. My opinions can be as strong as my language.

Some people think of me as being rabidly pro-Manchester United. I am. And I'm proud of it. Proud to stand up for the club when so many people want to put us down. Manchester United has been a huge part of my life and Manchester has been my home for over four decades. I believe in standing up against injustice and always have.

I defended Eric Cantona after his infamous so-called 'kung-fu' kick in 1995 and got slaughtered for it in the media. That didn't bother me one bit as most of the people offering opinions knew nothing about football or United. And if I had been in Eric's boots when that idiot came at him from the stands, I would have done exactly the same; except I would have hit him hard enough to make sure that he didn't get back up. If someone attacks you then you have every right to defend yourself – you hit them hard and make sure it's a good one.

A BBC presenter from Northern Ireland had a real go at me for sticking up for Eric. A radio station called me for my opinion, and the presenter went on about how she was a United fan who had watched the incident on television with her two sons. She said it was the worst thing she had seen in her life, how it was a totally deplorable act. I wasn't having that.

'You work in the media in Belfast,' I said. 'And you're telling me that even with all the troubles that have affected your part of the world, that Eric Cantona kicking a complete idiot who deserved it is the worst thing you've ever seen? Who are you kiddin'?'

I wasn't naïve about Irish politics when I made that statement, as you'll see. At times I was more than an observer of The Troubles.

Standing up for what I believed in often got me into trouble as a player. I'd not been at Celtic long when we played a five-a-side tournament in Falkirk, then the most anti-Catholic, anti-Celtic town in Scotland. You were not allowed to pass the ball back in your own half in five-a-side, but this referee let a Falkirk player get away with it so I swore at him. He sent me off. Three Falkirk players came charging towards me and a fight followed which saw my mate Mick Jackson and me dismissed, leaving Celtic with two outfield players. I was fined, not just for being sent off, but for attacking a journalist who tried to speak to me about the incident after.

It wasn't the only time I was sent off in a career that spanned nearly 500 games for Manchester United and 120 for Celtic, and it wasn't the only time that I was involved in an argument with a journalist, but we'll come to that.

My life's philosophy was determined by my upbringing in Glasgow's Gorbals. I was a child of Irish Catholic immigrants and we led an impoverished, underprivileged existence – not that I knew it at the time. I became interested in politics at an early age and joined the Labour Party as soon as I could. There was a rumour that someone in the Gorbals voted for the Tories in the 1970s, but I don't believe it.

Principles formed in Glasgow still govern my life. I was taught to face problems head on, never to go down in a fight and never to turn the other cheek. I've made mistakes and I've got things right, but my life has seldom been dull. After reading what follows, I hope you'll agree with me.

Paddy Crerand
Manchester 2007

ONE

Heart of the Gorbals

My dad felt uneasy about going to work on the night of 12 March 1941. He wanted to be with my mum, who was about to give birth to their fourth child. He was also nervous because German bombs were being dropped around the ship-building yards on Glasgow's River Clyde with increasing frequency, but my mother reassured him that he would be fine and off he went.

Dad Michael worked for John Brown's Shipyard in Clydebank, one of the most famous shipbuilding yards in the world. In later years, the *Queen Mary* and the *QE2* liners were constructed there with the 'Clyde-built' seal of quality. Before the war, John Brown's built many notable warships and liners like the *Lusitania* and *HMS Hood*.

Eighteen months into the Second World War, the focus of the yard was *HMS Vanguard*, which was to be the biggest-ever British battleship. Dad was not a skilled ship worker but a recently arrived Irish immigrant who had ambitions of opening a grocery shop in Glasgow. He was on fire-watch when the German bombers flew along the Clyde and made several direct hits on the shipyard.

1

Dad was killed instantly by a Luftwaffe bomb. Several other people lost their lives that night, most of them Irish immigrants who had come to Scotland to make a living. Michael Crerand's name is etched into an obelisk that stands in Clydebank. I'd like to see it one day.

The day after my father's death, my sister Mary was born. Can you begin to imagine what my mother, Sarah, went through in those twenty-four hours? She never did speak about it. Mum became a widow with responsibility for four children, all of them under the age of four. My brother John was three and a half; I was two; and my sister Bridie was just a year old when my father was killed.

My parents were originally from County Donegal, in Ireland's beautiful north west. At 19, mum left the small town of Gweedore to work as a maid at the Baird Arms Hotel in Newtonstewart, County Tyrone, following in the path of some of her eleven sisters. Mum worked for next to nothing, but that she didn't have to pay for food and accommodation meant she was in a better position than many of her friends. The hotel owner was originally from Kilmacrennan, County Donegal, and she had two sons, one of whom, Michael, became my father. Dad worked in the hotel, too, and that's where he met my mum.

Dad was 15 years older than mum and his mother did not approve of the relationship, partly because of the age difference and partly because my mother was a maid, which she considered to be a lowly profession. Mum and dad were in love though and, unable to face the hostility from my dad's family, they eloped to Symington in Ayrshire, Scotland, where his brother John was a priest, the youngest in Scotland. My parents married at the beginning of 1937, but John couldn't conduct the service as he died from pneumonia in late 1936. When my grandmother heard of the marriage she hung a black bow on the door of her hotel, as was the custom in Northern Ireland when someone died.

My parents returned to Northern Ireland and opened a food shop in Plumbridge, County Tyrone. Poverty was rife and it was difficult to achieve a good standard of living if you were a Catholic because you were treated like a second-class citizen, no matter how hard you worked. The Catholics suffered extreme hardships under British rule. British imperialism meant Protestant landlords got the best land which they rented to Catholic tenants. This created deep religious animosity and the Catholics rightly felt persecuted. During the Famine of 1845–49, the British offered relief to the Catholics on the condition that they attend a Protestant church. It was no surprise that Irish nationalism gained momentum.

The British had no right to be imperialistic in Ireland, although the British media usually see it differently. They claim now, for instance, that everybody in Iraq who fights against the invading British or American forces is a terrorist. But what right do the British and Americans have to be in Iraq? If you invade someone else's country then you are wrong. I cringe at phrases like 'the sun never set in the British Empire'. That meant nothing to the ordinary man in the street who was used as cannon fodder so that the rich could get richer. The British conquered and exploited countries all over the world for centuries. Catholics had a very difficult existence under British rule, but it was seldom easier for the working-class Protestants either. They just weren't aware that the British were dividing and ruling. My family were deeply resentful of the British in Ireland.

My older brother John was born in Plumbridge, but the shop was not a success so he and my parents moved to Glasgow, with dad finding work digging the tunnels that were to form the Glasgow underground system. He always saw it as a temporary job and hoped to scrape enough money together to open another shop. It never happened.

I came along on 19 February 1939, my first breath taken in the family home at 260 Crown Street, in the heart of the tough Gorbals district just south of the city centre on the other side of the Clyde. I don't remember my father, but I was curious to find out about him as I grew older. I learned that he came from a staunchly republican family who had fought in the uprisings of 1916 and 1922. Most of his friends finished up in jail for being involved in the republican movement, and when he died mum received several letters of condolence from the jail in Belfast.

After his death, my granny Anabella in Newtonstewart who had been so disapproving of the marriage asked my mum and the kids to come and live with her. She had forgiven my mother for the crime of falling in love with her son, but mum decided to stay in Glasgow. Granny in Newtonstewart then disowned her, a strange situation as she deprived herself of seeing her only grandchildren.

Back in the Gorbals, neighbours and friends held a collection to raise money for my mother as there was no social welfare. Mum went back to work as a waitress in a city centre hotel in an attempt to scrape enough together to feed and clothe the four of us. She couldn't do it alone and my aunt Mary, who had moved to Glasgow, was a great help looking after us when mum worked. Our grandmother in Gweedore sent food parcels too. Mum's sisters would frequently come over from Donegal to help us out. We needed the support and the lack of money was always evident. Mum regularly used to dispatch me to the front door when the rent man came and I would tell him that my mum wasn't in so we didn't have to pay. Someone in London owned our property so I wasn't bothered about not paying them. It wasn't the fault of the rent man – he was just doing his job – but he was working for an absentee landlord who made fortunes out of the poor in Glasgow. Like many in the Gorbals, we felt that there was something inherently wrong with that. We'd delay paying the rent for as long as possible, our own little protest in the hope that we would make life awkward for the landlord.

Mum rented a room for us in the house on Crown Street, where five of us slept, ate and washed, sharing a communal toilet. Mum was used to hardship but she considered the conditions intolerable and we moved to a tenement building nearby at 129 Thistle Street. That had the luxury of a kitchen, which my mother slept in on a pull-out bed, leaving the four kids in the other room. With hindsight I realize that we lived in abject poverty, but at the time we didn't know any different and I never felt hard done by. We used to get our clothes from the church and even though we were desperately poor, we always tried to show otherwise. The church used to give us boots, big clumpy ones that would have lasted for a hundred years, but we tried not to wear them. We were never hungry and I was happy playing football all the time. Mum told me that from the age of three or four I would head a ball against the wall. Well, it was better than staring at it because there was nothing else to do.

Boredom was everybody's enemy. We had few toys and there was no such thing as a television, so the only thing to do was play football. You weren't allowed to play in the street, but we still did ... and ran every time a policeman appeared. The police got sick of us smashing the low windows of the tenement blocks and would stop us playing. They once chased me down a back alleyway. I thought I could get out at the other end but I couldn't and they caught me. 'You'll get a real kick if we catch you again', said one of them. I was petrified. I was only five.

My first school was St Luke's primary. I was in the school football team by the age of seven, alongside players three years older than me. I played against Frank McLintock as he was at a nearby primary school, St Bonaventures. Years later, in 1963, we would be on opposite sides in an FA Cup final.

School was just an extension of football as far as I was concerned. We played every day after school, in the light summer evenings, and Saturday mornings and Sunday too. I used to wake up at seven o'clock every morning, although school didn't begin until nine. My pals all did the same and we had a full-scale match in the playground before going into class. The playground was the only place we could have a game without breaking the law. It's a cliché that people of my generation started playing football with tennis balls or bundles of rags; we did see the occasional full-size football. The problem was that the lads who owned them were invariably useless and always last to be picked. So they would take their balls home. At lunch I would go home for food: soup and potatoes, or mince and potatoes. I never really saw fruit, unless I got an apple or an orange as a Christmas present. I'd eat as quickly as I could and then rush back to school to play football.

I played centre-forward for my primary school team, not because I was quick, but because I was strong and could kick the ball with both feet. I scored loads and loads of goals and played there until I was ten. Then they put me back in the middle of the park, again because I was so strong.

Football was our lives although we did occasionally play rounders or cricket, with the stumps marked in chalk against a wall in the street. The tenement building would stretch for 150 yards and there would be five or six football matches going on in front of it at a time. Nobody owned a car in the Gorbals and we only saw cars on the main roads, so they weren't a distraction.

We used lampposts as goalposts, only stopping when the man came to light them. Nobody wanted to play in goal – that's probably why Scotland is not renowned for its goalkeepers. If you went in net you were allowed to come out after letting two goals in, so that's why there were high scoring games. Because we were playing ten-a-side in a very enclosed area, players became very skilful.

If we weren't playing sports, we'd have a look around the middens – the place where the rubbish was kept. Rats were plentiful there. We'd search through the rubbish for 'lucks' – something which someone had thrown out that might be worth something.

A big day in my life came when I had my first holy communion aged seven. I was nervous and excited. People made a sandwich and wrapped it in paper. They would also slip some money between the paper and the sandwich which was a local tradition. I was given three or four pence and thought I was rolling in it.

It was at primary school that I learned the facts of Gorbals life, namely that there were two kinds of people in the world – Catholics and Protestants. You were either one or the other. There was no such thing as a neutral. That's what we were taught, but it wasn't totally true. The Gorbals had a significant Jewish population and I used to go to the houses of some Jewish families on a Saturday and offer to light their fires for a few coins, because they were forbidden from doing so. The Jews were kind to me and I liked them.

I am a Catholic, of course, one of many children from Irish families who settled in the Gorbals, partly because it was the cheapest place in Glasgow to rent a room and partly because they were likely to know people who had already moved there.

Poverty and other social problems like alcohol meant the Catholics fought a lot among each other. There were public houses on every corner and when men came out of these at night they stood around, argued and they fought. Not that they needed an excuse. They probably reckoned any kind of exercise was better than going back to houses that were darker and more overcrowded than the pubs they had left. They fought with fists, or bottles, hatchets, or knives. And this wasn't just in the evenings. I can vividly remember watching a hatchet fight at three o'clock on a midweek afternoon.

Since the adults spent so much time fighting it was only natural that the kids followed their example. We used to have mass battles twice a week with the boys at Adelphi Street, a Protestant primary school, over the road. It was harmless stuff – nobody really got hurt – but it seemed the proper thing to do. Benny Lynch, later a world champion boxer, was a Catholic who lived on Adelphi Street.

On the street, the rules were simple. If someone didn't like you then he hit you. And you hit him back whether he was bigger than you or not, because if you didn't hit back then the word went round that you were a sissy ... and then everyone in the neighbourhood had a belt at you. As you grew up you learned more about fighting – and I can assure you that nobody ever mentioned the Marquis of Queensberry. Punching, kicking, and spitting were all in the game and you had to give as much you got.

There were many wonderful people in the Gorbals, people who would give you their last penny and do anything for anyone in trouble, but there were some bad characters. The adults used to say that if someone asked you for a match in the street when it was dark, you didn't stop – you ran. Because that was a common trick of stopping people to slash them, and there were probably another couple of toughs hiding nearby in case you resisted.

There was an old Polish cobbler who had a shop in our street. We always played football near his shop because he didn't chase us away and we liked him. There was a spell when we didn't see him for weeks. I never forget how I felt when I saw him again. He had a scar which ran from his right ear to the side of his mouth and another from his mouth to his other ear. Someone had stopped him at night and taken the few shillings he had with him, and he needed eighty-five stitches.

The dark streets and even darker closes and stairways were made for crime. My mum was strict and wouldn't allow us out at night, but I still got into lots of fights as a kid. A lad called John Ferguson battered lumps out of me and bullied me a little bit. I knew that I had to have a go at him again and I did. I beat him; I knocked the daylights out of him in fact, but he became my pal then. There was another lad that I beat up who kept turning up at my door every five minutes to ask for another fight. I could have beaten him, but he would have kept coming back for more. I gave up in the end and said, 'You're too good for me.' He accepted that, because he had shown his courage. I was ten.

It didn't matter how big the fella was who hit you, you had to hit him back. If you didn't then your life was a misery. You got little fellas who would fight people ten times bigger than them just to show that they were not cowards.

It wasn't long before I discovered the library. It was an escape, a world away from the fighting and football, the only place I went to which was quiet. I had been a good reader at school and I would read through the newspapers a few times a week. I developed a love for books and although I was never really a fan of fiction, I loved *Treasure Island*. I would read about Ché Guevara in later years and be fascinated to learn that he had family connections with the west of Ireland. His real name was Ernesto Guevara Lynch De La Serna.

9

The Catholic Church kept a lot of people out of trouble. They paid for a Boys' Guild which had a gym where you could play crab football – where you sit on the floor and kick out with your legs – or snooker. They organized a football team and I used to play for them on Saturday, as well as my school team. Two games on a Saturday were normal for me and on Sunday I went to church partly through fear; it was a mortal sin if you didn't attend.

There were loads of lads who were better footballers than me in the Gorbals but they were distracted by drink and drugs in later years. They are the sort that sit at the bar telling everyone how good they could have been. My mother kept me away from all that. I'd get a belt from her across the back of my hand if I misbehaved.

Being Catholics, we always had fish on a Friday. A man used to come round with a barrow laden with every type you could imagine. You would pay a fortune for it today, but it couldn't be anything but cheap in the Gorbals because nobody had any money. For Christmas I'd get a bag of sweets, which was a big thing for me. They were wrapped in curly paper which made them more important.

It's funny how your memory works. I can't remember what I did yesterday and yet I have vivid recollections from childhood, like watching the communist marches each May Day. They were led by a fella called Andy Smith who lived on Thistle Street. He was a mad Celtic supporter who had a big poster of Stalin in his flat. Stalin was still alive and I was led to believe that he was a good person by Smith, who believed that we should all look after one another. Most people in the Gorbals agreed with the philosophy, even if they didn't see themselves as communists. People helped their neighbours out and always supported them. Maybe they could only offer milk and sugar, but they supported each other emotionally too.

For as long as I can remember, I have supported Celtic. If you were a Catholic and Irish then you supported Celtic. I can't even begin to explain why my brother John supported Rangers. Maybe it's because they were a better team or maybe it was because he wanted to be different and, if so, he certainly achieved that. I can remember him getting his Rangers scarf and going off to Ibrox by himself, which was a very brave thing to do if you lived in the Gorbals. I admired him for that.

Mum was a real Celtic nut. She went to lots of matches and her support of the team never wavered. She was lucky enough to attend three European Cup Finals in four years, the first in 1967 when Celtic triumphed in Lisbon, the second a year later between Manchester United and Benfica and the third in 1970 when Celtic lost in Milan.

Celtic's ground, Parkhead, was a twenty-minute walk away and I would go with my mates for matches and wait by the turnstiles until someone lifted us over. I never went to games with my mum, that wasn't the done thing. The ritual of being lifted over the turnstiles was one that every Glaswegian kid went through. It was accepted that if a man arrived at a turnstile with his boy he was allowed to lift him over and they both got into the match for the price of one. The turnstile attendant could hardly ask the man to prove that the boy was his son. Most supporters, therefore, were willing to lift a boy over if he asked them. So before any game you would see dozens of boys running alongside the grown-ups as they approached the turnstiles, shouting the immortal phrase: 'Gonny gie's a lift o'er, mister?'

Until I was too old, or too heavy, I had many a lift, and one of my earliest football memories is of getting into Hampden Park at the age of ten and seeing a fabulous Great Britain team with a forward line of Stanley Matthews,

Wilf Mannion, Tommy Lawton, and Billy Liddell beat the Rest of Europe 6–1. I can also remember seeing Tom Finney play for the first time in 1952 when England beat Scotland 2–1. Even though he was wearing the white of England, I knew I'd seen a great winger. The Scots didn't know what to do with him because, being so two-footed, he could beat them any way he wanted. Later I saw Finney play in quite a few internationals. I saw Stanley Matthews, too, but Finney was clearly the better of the two. The one thing I liked about Finney is that he bowed out at the top. Most good footballers refuse to admit when their best playing days are over, and they go on and play for as long as they can for the sake a few more pounds when they have already made a lot of money in their career. I think this spoils them in the eyes of the public because they are remembered as failures with an expanding waistline instead of the brilliant performers they were before. It says much that Finney was prepared to step out of the limelight when he had the slim build and was still in his prime.

I went to Parkhead for most of the home games. It was so huge that despite the big crowds it was rarely full to its 80,000 capacity. I don't think I ever had a penny in my pocket but I always got into the ground and stood on one of the vast sweeping terraces that made up three-quarters of the stadium.

Charlie Tully was a Celtic player who became my childhood hero after the war. He was signed from Belfast Celtic in 1948 in the hope that he would stop a decline at the club. He never trained well but he had so much ability. I loved him and he was a big star, just like George Best was to become. He once scored direct from a corner kick against Falkirk. The referee blew his whistle and made him take the corner kick again. Nobody could believe it when he re-took the kick and scored for a second time.

Playing for Ireland at Windsor Park in 1952, he scored from a corner again, this time in a 2–2 draw with England. However, he's more remembered for his pre-match chat with his marker Alf Ramsey that day.

'What's it like to be an automatic selection for your country, Mr Ramsey?' he asked him.

'It's an absolute privilege, Mr Tully,' Ramsey replied.

'Good, because you won't be one after today.'

Charlie, nicknamed 'The Clown Prince' because he used to torture opposition right-backs and make clowns out of them, was a cult hero in Glasgow. There was even a green flavoured ice cream called 'Tully'.

Celtic didn't win the league between 1938 and 1954 – Rangers were a much stronger team in those days – but they did win the 1951 Scottish Cup at Hampden against Motherwell 1–0 thanks to a John McPhail goal. I went to that game along with 131,392 others.

My memories are not just confined to football in Scotland. I remember listening to the 1948 FA Cup Final on the wireless. A family who lived near us had a radio and I was amazed at how it worked and how words could come out of it direct from Wembley Stadium in London. I listened to the game and I wanted Manchester United to win for two reasons. The first was because they were losing 2–1 at half-time and I liked the idea of a team coming from behind, no matter who they were. The second was because United had Jimmy Delaney, an old Celtic player, in the team. Yet if Blackpool had been losing 2–1, I'd have wanted them to win.

In later years, Duncan Edwards, the Manchester United great who died in the Munich air disaster, was a hero of mine. I liked half-backs. He scored the winning goal for England against Scotland at Wembley in 1957. I took an interest in Manchester United because they were such a young team. The

Busby Babes they called them. Most teams seemed to have an average age of twenty-eight – but the Busby Babes' was about twenty-two.

During the school holidays – Easter, summer and Christmas – we'd head back to Ireland to visit my grandmother in Gweedore. We'd get the Anchor Lines boat to Derry from the Broomielaw in Glasgow and I'd spend all my free time in Donegal. It always felt like home and I would cry my eyes out when it was time to leave. I've now lived in Glasgow for over twenty years and Manchester for over forty, but I consider Donegal home, even though I wasn't born there or have never lived there for more than four months. When I met someone in Glasgow, they would ask when I was going home for a holiday.

I was so excited when we travelled to Donegal. We'd get the boat at 5.30 pm and would arrive in Derry at 9 o'clock in the morning. The journey would be horrendous as the boat chugged along and we travelled third class. I can remember sitting there alongside cows, which travelled in the same compartment. There was a bar on the boat though. The owners knew what they were doing, keeping the masses half pissed that they wouldn't care about being treated like cattle.

The boat arrived in Derry and we had to cross the border between the six counties and the rest of Ireland, where the controls were very strict. We would try to bring chickens and eggs back from Ireland because they were scarce in the Gorbals. The B-Specials, who were a branch of the Royal Ulster Constabulary (RUC), would come onto the bus and treat us very badly because we were Catholics. They would get us off the bus and search it. When we re-boarded everything would be gone. If you said anything to them they would hit you with a rifle.

The situation made me very angry and I started to become more politically minded when I was a teenager. I read a lot about Irish history and formed the opinion that the British policy in the north of Ireland amounted to dividing and conquering. My father's side of the family had been hard-line republican. When revolutionary leader Michael Collins wanted to come to an agreement with the British for an Irish Free State in 1921, with the six counties in the north being worked out later, my family were against it and accused Collins of selling out. They wanted all of Ireland or nothing. They didn't want a Northern Ireland and didn't recognize the new border. The British, in their wisdom, knew that partition would split the republican movement and civil war ensued. Collins should be remembered as one of the greatest ever Irishmen, but I wouldn't have voted for him because he compromised and split the country. He did this because he believed he could make further progress with the British in the future. But he was killed in an ambush in August 1922.

Gweedore is officially the largest Irish-speaking parish in Ireland – Gerry Adams learned his Irish there – and, despite only having a population of 5,000, has some notable former residents. Vincent 'Mad Dog' Coll was born there and was related to my family. He left Gweedore at an early age and became an enforcer for the mafia in early twentieth-century New York City. He grew up on the streets of the Bronx, where he joined a street gang and befriended the gangster Dutch Schultz. As Schultz's criminal empire grew in power, he employed Coll as an assassin. During the 1920s, Coll developed a risky but lucrative scam whereby he would kidnap powerful gangsters at gunpoint and extort a ransom from his captive's associates before releasing them. He knew that the victims would not report it to the police, especially because, being criminals, they would have a hard time explaining to the authorities how they happened to have such huge supplies of cash in order to pay for their release. Coll is one of the villains depicted in the film *The Untouchables*.

Coll is distantly related to former Northern Ireland MP Brid Rodgers, who is also from Gweedore. She became the leader of the Social Democratic and Labour Party (SDLP) and was involved in the Irish Civil Rights Movement from 1965.

Another son of Gweedore is James Duffy, an Irish recipient of the Victoria Cross. He was 28 years old, and a private in the 6th Battalion of the Royal Enniskillen Fusiliers during the First World War, when he was awarded the VC for gallantry in Palestine.

The musical heritage of Gweedore is very rich. Clannad and Enya are from there. A lot of my friends from Glasgow moved back to Donegal and still live there. If I go to Glasgow these days I have to get a hotel room and that seems strange.

In 1949 there was a change in our family life. My mum got married again to a fella called Charlie Duffy. He was a great man who was also from Gweedore. It was a big burden for him to take on a woman with four kids. They went on to have another two girls. I used to see Charlie as my mate. He never hit me once in his life when it was the done thing to give a kid a smack if he stepped out of line. Mum would hit us and it never did me any harm, but Charlie didn't. I'd walk with Charlie on his way to work just so I could be with him. He would wind me up by pretending to be a Rangers fan.

Me and my brother John used to argue about Celtic and Rangers, too, but we were very close. We played together all the time and he was a good footballer. John told me that he wanted to be a priest. He became poorly when he was twelve with rheumatic fever and I went to see him in hospital. Everything seemed all right because he was talking to me.

But everything wasn't all right. I was sitting in the house one Saturday evening listening to the football results on the radio when we were told that John was dead. I couldn't understand it because I had been to see him a few days before and he seemed fine. I was too young to properly understand what death was, but my mother was heartbroken. You don't expect to outlive your kids and she was crying all the time. They brought the coffin to the house because there was nowhere else to take it. It wasn't a big coffin, just a small thing. He was buried in the Catholic cemetery next to Celtic Park, not in the Protestant graveyard behind the jungle stand (the name Celtic fans gave to the covered terrace where the most vocal Celts stood because they said it was full of animals). Billy Connolly used to joke about those graveyards. 'Why don't they get buried together? Are they going to get up and fight with each other?'

All the relations came over for John's funeral. A lot of drink was taken. It's an old standing Irish joke that the only difference between a wedding and a wake is that there is one less drunk at the wake. It's a great way of getting over things and I think the drink helped the adults.

I missed John terribly. When I wanted to play with him he wasn't there. I missed talking to him about football and helping mum do household chores with him. I cried a lot and felt very alone. The adults could speak about it, but I couldn't. When I did try to talk about it with mum she said that John wouldn't be coming home again. The mood in the house was awful, but the adults tried to be normal with me.

When you are that young you can be resilient to almost anything and you adapt quickly. You just do. I had so many friends that before long I was immersed in football again and life continued as normal, only John wasn't there. I never spoke to my mum about John in later years. I find death very hard to accept and I think she did too. My sister Bridie lost her husband when he was quite young and then lost her son in a car crash. He was returning from a Simple Minds concert in Dublin and driving back to Donegal. So what happened to my mum also happened to my sister.

Not long after John died, I did well in my exams and attained a very high pass mark to go to Holyrood, a school with a good reputation. They had their own red shale football pitches. Scottish international Alan Brazil went there, as did Eddie Gray who played for Leeds United. One of my schoolteachers, Mr Murphy, was the announcer at Celtic Park. Our school had a good team and we won the final of a schools' competition at Hampden Park in 1955.

I read newspapers a lot more as I entered my teenage years and became very left wing. I still am today, but I'm much milder than when I was younger. I started becoming more politically aware in 1951 when Churchill got into power again. The war had been over quite a while but there was still rationing for people who had no money.

The political situation in Ireland was always pertinent for me. I came from a family that wanted a united Ireland and I still believe in that. I have never accepted the violence and, hopefully, we have seen the last of The Troubles. I'm pleased that there has been a lot of political progress in the last decade. People have realized that you get progress by talking and not by shooting each other and I'm more optimistic about the future of Ireland now than I have ever been.

The problems affected football as well of course. I was indifferent to Glasgow Rangers until I was about thirteen when I found out that they didn't sign Catholics. The discrimination enraged me, yet it was something Catholics were used to.

I never had a girlfriend. If you had one aged fourteen in Glasgow then you had to fight everybody because you were considered a softie. Besides, I couldn't go out on a Friday night because I always played football on a Saturday morning.

As I got older, I'd cross the River Clyde with my mates and go into the centre of Glasgow. It was an adventure going into town and seeing different types of people for the first time in my life. I looked in the windows of shops and marvelled at all the things that people could buy and we couldn't. Plenty of my mates went stealing but I was never tempted. I had that Catholic mentality in my head that if I committed a sin then I'd go to hell. That, and the prospect of having to face my mother, who would have killed me.

On the football field my life was progressing well. Up to the age of fifteen I was a prolific centre-forward. I was stronger than most of the other players and found scoring goals easy. I wasn't quick, but I could brush players off and I had a hard, accurate shot. My reputation was growing locally and I was approached by a man called Hugh Wiseman. He ran a football team called RanCel, short for Rangers and Celtic. He wanted to get Celtic and Rangers fans closer together and asked me to play in his team on a Saturday afternoon. But I just wanted to watch Celtic, especially as I had just joined a Celtic supporters' club and travelled on a bus with them to matches. They used to subsidize the travel for the young fans and that meant I could go to away games, loving the experience of travelling with my friends. My mother got the needle with me and told me that I couldn't let Mr Wiseman down. Everyone knew him because he used to keep the toilets clean on Cumberland Street. So I didn't let him down and played. He got me my first pair of football boots. Mr Wiseman encouraged me to play in midfield rather than up front. I could hit the ball a considerable distance accurately and he thought that I was better suited to playing in the middle.

After playing with RanCel, I was told that Duntocher Hibs, one of the junior sides, wanted to sign me. I was still just sixteen, but within the space of a few weeks I went from going to watch Celtic to playing in front of 3,000 most Saturdays in Duntocher, close to Clydebank where my dad had a job.

I still needed to work, and while I'd done well at school it was hard getting a job with the blatant sectarianism that existed. Newspaper adverts declared: 'No RC (Roman Catholics) or Irish may apply.' There was always a feeling that the Irish immigrants were taking jobs away from the home-bred Scots.

I got a job in Fairfield's shipyard on the River Clyde, where I was taught to prepare the steel plates for the welders. I was up every morning at six to catch a lorry which came by Gorbals Cross half an hour later. We'd stand in the back of the lorry in all weathers and started work at ten to seven. I earned £2 10 shillings a week, but I loathed every minute of it. You were outside all the time, it was cold and miserable. I used to ask myself, 'What am I doing here?' It wasn't living, it was surviving, but rather than becoming disillusioned, it made me determined to get out and be a footballer.

The best thing about work was the great camaraderie among the workers, but there was always a divide between Celtic and Rangers supporters, a real 'them' and 'us' mentality. If someone said that they supported Partick Thistle we thought that was just an excuse for being a Rangers fan. It was ridiculous. Men were working together, helping each other make the same ship, yet basically hating each other because they supported different teams. You never knew when an argument might get out of hand. I became a target for the Rangers followers because in their eyes Duntocher was just a junior Celtic team. In the yard, as at home, I had to be ready to hit back. It was a return to the law of the streets.

My week would come alive on a Saturday. I'd catch a red bus from Glasgow to Duntocher. The standard of football at Duntocher was very high, the games ultra competitive. I loved every minute playing for that club and stayed for two years. A lot of people who lived in Duntocher were Catholics who had come from Donegal. All the top scouts were constantly coming to watch us. When Duntocher Hibs became defunct Drumchapel moved into their ground and they have stayed there to this day. The Drum are still one of the top amateur teams in Scotland and many big names in professional football have started out there, including Sir Alex Ferguson, David Moyes, Andy Gray, Archie Gemmill, Asa Hartford, and John Robertson.

I got to know a lovely man called Jimmy Smith at Duntocher. He had been a great player for Rangers before the war and was acting as a scout for them after it. He frequently said to me, 'I'd love to sign you for Rangers, Paddy.' But he couldn't because I was a Catholic. Again, I considered that ridiculous. Jock Stein, when he became Celtic's first Protestant manager, was asked in his first press conference: 'If there was a Catholic and Protestant of equal ability, which one would you sign first?' Jock replied straightaway: 'The Protestant. Because it would stop Rangers getting him. And then I'd get the Catholic anyway.'

My football was going well and the papers began to talk of senior clubs being interested in me. In fact, I think the Manchester City scout was the most persistent but Jimmy McLean, who ran Duntocher, never allowed any of them to speak to me because he knew that one team dominated my thinking.

It was a bright summer's day in August 1957 when I found out that Celtic were keen on me. Jim, a Rangers supporter, met me coming off the pitch at Ashfield away one day. He kept laughing and saying, 'You're going to enjoy this.' We went through the dressing room, then into a side room where he introduced me to a complete stranger.

He was Teddy Smith, Celtic's chief scout, but I didn't know that until he asked, 'How would you like to sign for Celtic?' I remember those were his exact words. A pretty ordinary sentence, but to me they were the greatest words in the world. I was stunned and just said, 'Yeah.' He told me to go to Celtic Park the following Monday evening. I went home straight-away, my head buzzing and full of thoughts. I ran into our house and told my mum. She put her arms around me and hugged me tight. I felt like the proudest man alive. As I pulled away, I saw that mum was crying. It was the best present I could have given her.

TWO

A Grand Old Team to Play For?

Had anyone asked me on the tram car from Gorbals Cross where I was going, I could have answered, 'To sign for Celtic.' Nobody did, but that didn't diminish the excitement I felt. The occasion was a game between the first team and the reserves, and while I wasn't playing, I was there to sign a youth contract.

I wasn't alone. Billy McNeill and a lad named Andy Murphy also turned up to sign. Billy had already met the reserve team manager, Jock Stein, because Jock had been to his house. Jock told Billy's parents that he wanted their son to sign for Celtic and when they agreed he said, 'If he's cheeky, can I skelp him one?'

I met Jock for the first time after the game. He was a former miner and someone I warmed to, just as I had done as a player. I'd watched Jock play as a no-nonsense centre-half many times as a fan. He used to knee the ball a lot when others kicked or headed it instead. He could knee the ball as far as some players could kick it. In 1953, Jock captained Celtic to Coronation Cup success, Celtic surprising many by beating Manchester United, Arsenal, and Hibernian to

23

become unofficial champions of Britain. He was still captain a year later when Celtic won their first league championship since 1938 and their first League and Scottish Cup double since 1914. I had travelled to Easter Road to see Celtic win the league against Hibernian and I'd watched them beat Aberdeen in the cup final.

An ankle injury, which left him with a limp, forced Jock to retire from football in 1956, aged 34. He was then given the job of coaching the reserve and youth players at Celtic. But he was far more than a reserve team coach. He persuaded the Celtic board to purchase the Barrowfield training ground, because he realized the importance of preparation.

Jock came out with many sayings over the years which became famous, among them: 'Football is nothing without fans,' and 'Celtic jerseys are not for second best, they don't shrink to fit inferior players.' There were no grand speeches for me that day. He shook my hand firmly, wished me luck and said he hoped that I had a career as a professional foot-baller.

I was given a provisional contract until the end of the 1957/58 season, so I still played some games for Duntocher and some for Celtic's reserve teams, while all the time working at the shipyard.

I soon realized that Jock was far superior to any of the other coaches I'd worked with. This was no surprise because I hadn't played at a professional level, but I'd still say that he was well ahead of his time. He'd used his experiences in foot-ball well – always watching and learning. During Scotland's performances in the 1954 World Cup Finals, he'd witnessed the shambolic preparations and, like Roy Keane in Saipan in 2002, he didn't like what he saw.

Jock also studied foreign tactics, particularly the Hungarians who were revolutionizing the game. As a man he was sometimes as complex as the tactics he talked about, capable of sympathy and understanding, yet also very hard when he needed to be. He was one of the few people at Celtic with a car and he used to regale us with football stories as he gave us a lift home. My only regret was that I lived so close to the training ground because I wanted to stay in his company for longer.

As a manager he started implementing his ideas. In training, he would place chairs at different positions around the pitch. To make your passing more accurate, you had to hit the chairs from distance. It doesn't sound revolutionary now, but training at Celtic before then had amounted to long runs and practice matches. Jock would work on set plays and encourage me to hit free-kicks towards Billy McNeill's head. We'd repeat this in the games with success. Jock employed formations that no team in Scotland had used. But he would also issue simple advice, like telling you to keep your head up all the time. He was a visionary who would use players in different positions so that you could appreciate what it was like to play from the perspective of others. The players adored him and the excellent team spirit he generated lifted a talented group of young players, many of whom were local lads, so that they were good enough to go on to become European Champions with Celtic in 1967.

Crowds of up to 10,000 would watch Celtic reserves when the first team were away and in 1958, we won the second XI Cup with an 8–2 aggregate triumph over Rangers. That was Jock's first success as a manager. I was fortunate in that my arrival at Parkhead coincided with Jock's managerial career taking off. There was a feeling that he was special because when we played the first team in practice matches we would often beat them because of Jock's organization and tactics.

Other people at the club began to notice me and were pleased with my progress. Celtic offered me a professional contract worth £9 a week at the end of the 1957/58 season. It was far more than I had been earning at Fairfield's Shipyards, but the money didn't matter, I just wanted to leave that place as much as I wanted to play football full-time.

I started the next season still in the reserves but I was soon called up to train with the first team. The difference was that the reserve players could be identified by the red marks on their necks caused by the rubbing of their rough old jerseys, whereas the first team's kit was newer. We used to run through the streets around Parkhead during training sessions most days and nobody paid us much attention. Back then if folk wanted to see a star they went to the cinema. Footballers were not stars, but seen as part of the community. If you became big-headed you would get slaughtered.

I made my debut against Queen of the South on 4 October 1958. We won 3–1 and I did all right. The first team manager Jimmy McGrory told me that I was in the first team on the Friday morning before the game. I was very excited and quickly told my mum, who rang all the family in Donegal. They dropped everything they were doing and travelled to Derry for the night boat to Glasgow to watch me.

Jimmy was a Celtic legend and still holds the records for the most goals scored for the club in a season and overall. He was a nice man, but he should never have been a football manager. He was an old school type who wore a cap and smoked a pipe. 'Find the corner flag,' that's all he ever said to me before my debut and in subsequent games. His thinking was that there was a winger out there somewhere and if I hit the ball towards the corner flag then hopefully the winger would get it.

We had a party in the house on Thistle Street after the game to celebrate, with family and friends in attendance. There were about thirty or forty people in the house which was usually full with four people, but the night did not pass off without incident. A fight broke out near my house. It was nothing to do with us, but a few of the more curious ones including me went to see what was happening. The police turned up and arrested me. They took me to the police box on the corner of Crown Street and Cumberland Street, which was like a telephone kiosk. I was quaking with fear, but people gathered outside and protested that I had done nothing wrong. The police realized the strength of feeling and let me go.

I kept out of the gangs who divided the Gorbals into territories. It seemed to me they had nothing else to do than fight each other, while I had my football. I was never a drinker either. I never had a single pint in a Gorbals pub, despite knowing most people in them. I didn't drink because I thought it would impair my football ability, but on a Saturday night I would go to a pub where they played Irish music with my mum and her pals. They played republican and rebel songs like 'James Connolly' and you'll still hear them sung in Glasgow now.

My second Celtic game was against Falkirk and they beat us 4–3, largely thanks to a lad they had just signed from Alloa called John White. English and Scottish scouts had watched him many times at Alloa and usually went away saying that he was too frail. Falkirk went for him and they got a brilliant player whose greatness lay in his ability to drift into spaces without the opposition realizing it. He was always in space and that made it easy for team-mates to find him with a pass. However, people never really understood this ability and tended only to notice his inch perfect passes which would split open a defence and lay on a scoring chance for someone else. Maybe the fans and the journalists didn't see it, but as an opposition player I'll tell you that he destroyed us that day. The scouts carried on watching him, unable to make their minds up until Tottenham signed him in 1959. It was no coincidence that Spurs became a great side with White. He was an ever present in the double-winning side of 1961, scoring 18 goals.

The word Falkirk always seems to be associated with negative things in my career. I'd not been at Celtic long when we played a five-a-side tournament at Falkirk. Those tournaments were big in the 1950s, all of the main clubs would enter a team, and large crowds would watch. Back then, Falkirk was the most anti-Catholic, anti-Celtic town in Scotland and we used to get horrendous sectarian abuse, far worse than we ever got playing against Rangers.

You were not allowed to pass the ball back in your own half in five-a-side. This referee let a Falkirk player get away with it so I called him 'a f***ing wanker'. He sent me off. Three Falkirk players came charging towards us so me and my mate Mick Jackson punched them. Mick was dismissed as well, leaving Celtic with two outfield players. Outside the changing room, a journalist from a Sunday paper had a go at me. I was raging with anger and charged towards him, something he wasn't expecting. He looked terrified and with every justification. I had completely lost the plot. I was suspended for that and also fined by Celtic for something I wasn't proud of.

Even though I wasn't playing in the first team every week, I was delighted to be around heroes of mine like Charlie Tully, Bertie Peacock – who was great with the young lads – and Bobby Collins. Billy McNeill and I used to watch and listen to how the senior players operated. My cousin Charlie Gallagher played at Celtic, too. He was about a year younger than me. Charlie was a great passer of the ball with either foot – it must run in the family. Passing was my greatest skill, that and fighting.

But it wasn't long before players started to drift away from the club. In May 1959, Charlie Tully moved to become player manager of Cork Hibs. Earlier that season, Bobby Collins had gone to Everton when he was at the peak of his game and Willie Fernie went to Middlesbrough. Celtic made a statement about the players being 'dissatisfied'. If they had added 'with the chairman' that would have been the truth. There was another reason why Celtic sold Collins and Fernie. They needed money to install floodlights at Parkhead and to fix holes in the roof of the jungle stand.

Another great player, Bobby Evans, left Celtic after 535 games for the club and joined Chelsea in the summer of 1959. He had been the first Celtic captain to lift the League Cup in 1956 and he famously helped defend it a year later against Rangers in what will forever be know as the '7–1' game. Celtic cited 'personal reasons'. There were suspicions at the time of Bobby's departure, whispers of games not being right and strange goings on. I never saw Bobby do anything wrong, but looking back I'm convinced that games were being fixed. I was a kid who was oblivious to the politics and I didn't want to ask awkward questions, but I was present at one meeting in Glasgow with some of the senior players. I was only on the periphery, but there was talk of games being fixed. On one hand I could understand why players were being tempted not to be totally honest. Players were frustrated that the crowds were high and the wages were low. There was a lot of loose talk and allegations about where the money was going, but none of it could be substantiated. I wasn't comfortable with what I was hearing in that meeting and left. Stories of match fixing were investigated by journalists in Glasgow, but a lack of concrete evidence meant that they were never published. For his part, Evans said that the manager had no influence over team decisions or tactics, but that the orders came from the directors' box and were passed to the pitch by a trainer. In that sense Evans was right. I saw orders myself being given from the likes of Bob Kelly.

Bobby's departure created a space for me in the team. We went on a tour of Ireland in the summer of 1960 and I played in every game, doing well for a large part of the tour. Billy McNeill had got into the team just before me and there was a feeling that a new wave of home grown Celts were coming through. It was exciting to be part of it, but success would take some time coming.

Some of the press bought it and coined the phrase 'the Kelly Kids'. One journalist even suggested that we would surpass the fame of the Busby Babes, eight of whom had lost their lives at Munich two years before. You might have thought that with a headline like that Kelly, not Jimmy McGrory, was our manager. Bob Kelly was the Celtic chairman, yet such was his power at the club that he picked the team, too. And that was the crux of the perennial problem at Parkhead.

Unlike at Old Trafford, Celtic had no Matt Busby-type figure with a long term plan. At Parkhead, there wasn't the quality among the trainers or the ambition from the board to spend money when it was needed. Jock Stein had the talent, but he was looking after the reserves and Jimmy McGrory wasn't really football manager material.

And while Matt Busby let players serve an apprenticeship and blooded them when they were ready, Celtic did not. Players barely out of junior football were expected to play in Celtic's first team and cover for the experienced men who had left. Worse, they were played in different positions to cover for deficiencies. Jock had done that in the reserves because it made your game better and there was room to experiment. You couldn't take chances like that in the first team, but Celtic did. Billy McNeill played right-half, right-back, and centre-half. He was a great footballer, but it was too big an ask for most of the young lads. Young players were naturally full of promise, but they were also vulnerable to losing self-confidence when things didn't go right. At Old Trafford, United had the correct strategy of mixing youth and experience. It also didn't help that the team changed every week at Parkhead. In the first four months of that season, Celtic used six different outside-rights, four inside-rights, four centre-forwards, four inside-lefts, and three outside-lefts.

While some of the media talked up the Kelly Kids, by the turn of the year in the 1959/60 season Celtic were 11th in the league. After one 3–2 defeat by Dundee at Parkhead, watched by a crowd of just 10,000, the Glasgow *Evening Times* wrote: 'Tonight the unpalatable fact is this – Celtic are being deserted by hosts of their fans. They believe the *SS Celtic* is in trouble and they have no great desire to stand on the deck of a sinking ship.'

The fans booed us off the pitch after that game and had a go at Kelly and the other directors. Legend has it that one fan, upon hearing 'Off to Tipperary in the Morning', over the public address system, shouted: 'If they give me the fare I'll not wait until the morning. I'll be off on the Irish boat tonight.'

Supporters realized that Kelly ran the club from top to bottom, that McGrory was merely his puppet and they rightly criticized the chairman. Kelly's response to his critics was to tell them to stay away and come back in two years when we'd have a good team. Yet such was the belief, a few good results and we'd get 50,000 back at Parkhead.

Even though I was playing more and more for the first team, I was dismayed when Jock Stein was allowed to leave the club to manage Dunfermline in 1960. I think he felt that as a non-Catholic, he would be overlooked as a future manager of the club. It was one of the few times he was wrong. Jock wanted me to go with him but I didn't want to leave. I hoped that he would do well at Dunfermline before returning to Celtic to become first team manager. Jock's first game at Dunfermline was against Celtic. They scored after 15 seconds and his good start proved to be no fluke as he helped them avoid relegation and created a side that were difficult to beat. Almost every week we had had the bittersweet feeling of reading how well Jock was doing.

I was a Celtic first-teamer, but my life didn't change much away from football. I used to hang around with the same mates outside one of the pubs. The pubs shut at 9.30 pm and the saying was that you took the pavements indoors at that time because nothing was safe when people spilled out of the pubs.

Players couldn't be seen in a pub. I was never a beer drinker, but thanks to the Gorbals' grapevine if I'd have had one pint it would have been reported as ten by the time I got to training the following morning. There were no nightclubs at that time, although there was the Locarno dance hall where me and my pal Eddie Duffy sometimes went on a Saturday night until it finished at 11 pm. There was no booze in the place and you would get searched for alcohol before going in. The music was great – Sinatra and Dean Martin and big dance bands.

There were about twelve or thirteen of us who used to hang around on the street corner and they were all mad Celtic fans. The next day's *Daily Record* – or 'Daily Ranger' as we called it because we thought it was biased towards Rangers – would come in about 11 pm and we would discuss the stories. Even though I played for Celtic, one lad used to take the mickey out of me for my ability. He kept saying that I couldn't run and claimed that he was a faster runner than me. I used to laugh it off, but one night I said, 'F**k it, do you fancy a race then?'

32

He said yes. I absolutely destroyed him and was back with my mates before he had got halfway. He couldn't believe how quick I was. What did he expect? I was a professional foot- baller, as fit as anything. He never did mention my pace again. I was criticized for my lack of speed but I could run 100 yards in 11 seconds. You don't have to run that far in a game – runs of two or three yards are common – and I was a tackler and a passer, not a winger. And anyway, my brain worked quicker than other players.

I felt confident and despite the team not doing particularly well, the fans took to me. If things were going badly I would still want the ball and fans appreciated that. They saw that if your midfield players have control of the game then you will win. It's a team game, but the midfield players are so impor- tant. It's easy to destroy, far harder to create.

Financially, I was earning enough money to rent a house in a more middle-class area of Glasgow, but I never thought of leaving the Gorbals because I would have hated people to think that I had changed.

As I became better known I started to receive letters from fans. One guy sent me a series of diagrams showing me how to take successful penalty kicks. Another sent me a genuine mourning card – made out to me and edged in black. I guessed that must have been from a Rangers fan. A Glasgow girl called Moira Gallagher, who was originally from Gweedore, used to post me a good-luck greetings card before every single game. She was a bus conductress and was so dedicated to Celtic that she applied for a permanent night shift so that she never missed a match. I saw a newspaper article that showed she had a shrine dedicated to me in her house which consisted of press cuttings pasted on the walls. The journalist asked her if she had a boyfriend and she replied, 'The men in my life are the 11 boys in green and white. What better could I find?'

We had a tight relationship with supporters and they often kept us amused. At Broomfield, the home of Airdrieonians, my team-mate Bobby Carroll, who wasn't the thinnest of players, went to take a corner from the right. Suddenly there was a movement in the crowd – and a giant black pudding came sailing through the air and landed at his feet. At the same time, a voice cried out: 'There you are. That makes two of you.' Every player was convulsed with laughter and play was held up for about a minute.

My first Old Firm match was on 9 May 1960 in a Glasgow Merchants' Charity Cup semi-final at Ibrox. It was actually a low key affair as only 14,500 turned up, but I was still delighted to score in a 1–1 draw. I was less happy that Rangers went through to the final on the toss of a coin.

Now I was a first team regular, there was a growing expectation that I would soon receive a full international call up. But my relationship with the Scottish selectors was always fraught. Sectarian bigotry and, later, the bias against selecting 'Anglos' (Scottish players at English clubs) ensured that I made only 19 appearances for Scotland.

I played one game at Under-23 level at Ayresome Park, Middlesbrough, in 1960 when we beat an England side containing Bobby Moore. My full debut came in May 1961 in a World Cup qualifier against the Republic of Ireland at Hampden, a game which we won 4–1. It was one of the proudest moments in my career, but coming from an Irish family it felt strange to play against Ireland. I was pleased that my performances for Celtic had been recognized, but when the band played 'God Save the Queen' I didn't sing. Had the band played 'Scotland the Brave' or 'Flowers of Scotland' I would have joined in, but I couldn't sing 'God Save the Queen' when I loathed what the British royal family stood for. When the Irish national anthem started I sang along. I confused Billy

McNeill and probably a few of the other players standing alongside me.

Four days later Scotland played the Republic at Dalymount Park in Dublin in another World Cup game and again we won comprehensively, 3–0. I always gave my best when I played for Scotland and I was proud to be acknowledged as one of the better players in those games against Ireland, but Irish fans booed me off the pitch after I kicked one of their players. I felt as Irish as them, but they didn't see it the same way.

If I was playing today, I would choose to play for the Republic of Ireland, but you weren't allowed to decide your allegiance in those days. When I used to watch Scotland at Hampden Park as a kid, I'd support Northern Ireland or the Republic of Ireland against Scotland.

A week after the game in Dublin we had another important World Cup qualifier against Czechoslovakia in Bratislava. I usually played in the same half-back line as my Celtic team-mate Billy McNeill and Jim Baxter of Rangers. Many Scots thought that we were so good that we would not only qualify for the 1962 World Cup Finals in Chile, but that we would win the competition. Buoyed by the two convincing wins against the Republic of Ireland, we went to Bratislava in good spirits. Our hosts made us feel welcome and the day before that game we visited a chocolate factory. We came out and gave the chocolate away to kids. The police stopped us and that annoyed me. They were my chocolates and I should have been able to give them to who I wanted. Had I argued with them, they would have probably arrested me.

The game was a nightmare, as the Czechs beat us 4–0 and I was sent off along with their inside-forward, Kvasnak. I found out later that it was his job to deliberately needle me. He was about 6ft 3in and he kicked me, so I chinned him. As I walked off the pitch, I could see that the crowd were going potty and

I was thinking, 'I've got a big problem here because he'll kill me off the field.' I was preparing myself for a fight, but as I neared the tunnel I saw him do a runner, leaving me to stroll gently back to the dressing room. I knew I'd let myself down badly, but I was surprised to get a fine of £200, nearly ten times my weekly wage. No doubt some of the Scottish selectors enjoyed seeing me get that. And if that sounds embittered it's because I was.

We beat the Czechs 3–2 at Hampden Park in October 1961. That result meant that we had to play a one-off game, again against Czechoslovakia, to decide who qualified for the 1962 World Cup finals. The play-off was at the Heysel Stadium in Brussels. We had a lot of players out but we were leading 2–1 with just a few minutes to go when they equalized. After 90 minutes the score remained 2–2 and we gathered around before extra-time. The trainer passed me a sponge and Jim Baxter tried to grab it out of my hand. We finished up on the ground trying to punch each other. We were about to play the most important half hour in Scotland's football history and yet we were fighting with each other over a sponge. We were both pals, but we were so angry because they had equalized so late on that we took it out on each other in the heat of the moment. We lost 4–2 in the end.

I played in an unofficial Scotland game when an Italian league XI came to play the Scottish League XI in November 1961. Denis Law played for the Italian league as he was in Serie A with Torino. Almost 120,000 showed up at Hampden to see us gain a creditable 1–1 draw, before the Italians went to Old Trafford and beat the best of the English league four days later. I remember being in a hotel in Glasgow before the game and seeing Matt Busby for the first time. I admired him, but I didn't have the courage to introduce myself to Matt.

A Grand Old Team to Play For?

Playing alongside my friend Jim Baxter was one of the best things about my international career. Although he was one of the greatest footballers Scotland has ever produced, Jim was also a head banger. Nothing fazed him and he had such a carefree attitude. Coming from Fife, religious bigotry didn't mean a thing to him either. Despite playing for Rangers, he'd join the Celtic players each afternoon in a restaurant called Ferrari's at the top of Buchanan Street. It made the best minestrone soup I've ever had. He came because he was mates with me, Billy McNeill, Mick Jackson, and Jimmy Daly. The Rangers board were not happy and they warned him off coming a few times, but he didn't change. And of course Bob Kelly loved the idea of Rangers' best player eating with the Celtic lads every day.

Even when I didn't see Jim we still kept in frequent contact. My mother got a telephone in her house, which was unusual in the Gorbals, and once Jim got hold of the number he used to ring me all the time, at all hours. He did his National Service stint in the army at Stirling and used to ring me when he should have been on guard duty. The man in charge was a Celtic fan, but he loved Jimmy so much that he let him do what he wanted.

When I got called up to do National Service I didn't want to go. Somebody told me that a good way of getting out of it was to explain that you wet the bed. I said that I was a bed-wetter on my application form and then I had to go for questioning at an office in Buchanan Street, Glasgow. The official asked me how serious my bed-wetting problem was. I told him that it was driving my mother to despair. So I was deemed unfit for National Service.

Jim once stayed up gambling all night before a Rangers v Celtic game and claimed that he had won £3,000. It didn't affect him the next day as they beat us 3–0. When he signed

37

for Raith Rovers, his first professional club, Jim struck a deal where he got a £250 signing on fee – plus a washing machine for his mum.

There were rumours that my sister Bridie was dating Jim. Newspapers ran articles; one even suggested that they were secretly married. There was a silly story that Jim was going to change religion and play for Celtic. People started shouting 'turncoat' at him in the street.

Jimmy was a big drinker and everyone loved him – even Celtic fans. Celtic and Rangers fans loved great footballers. Jim was one of the best natural footballers I have played with or against. When he got possession he hated to pass until he was satisfied that the man he was giving the ball to was in a position to use the opening to advantage. He didn't just dominate matches, he took them over. Jim won ten winner's medals in his five years at Rangers in the first half of the 1960s. I didn't win one at Celtic. When he died in 2001, Celtic fans paid their respects, just as Rangers fans did when Bobby Murdoch died. Glaswegians love football – how else can you explain how 127,000 turned out for the 1960 European Cup Final between Real Madrid and Eintracht Frankfurt at Hampden?

I used to watch Rangers play in European games when I was a Celtic player and they used to look after us. Rangers played Eintracht in the semi-final and I went with Billy McNeill and Jock Stein. Rangers were a tremendous team, but Eintracht won 6–1 in Germany and 6–3 at Ibrox. Rangers were a different class to us, Eintracht were in a different league to them. Then Real Madrid beat Eintracht in the best European Cup final ever. Loads of Rangers fans went to that game. Most supported Eintracht because Real Madrid was perceived to be a Catholic club, given that Spain is a Catholic country.

Jim came from Fife but he was an idol in Glasgow, where Rangers fans worshipped the ground he walked on. Nicknamed 'Slim Jim' because of his tall, slight build, he was the best football-playing half-back to kick a ball. He did not have great defensive powers, but with the ball at his feet you could not hope to see a better player. He had a natural ability which made him the complete master of the ball and he possessed unlimited self-confidence. I remember before one game at Hampden there had been a great deal of talk about how we were going to mark the opposition, but as we ran down the tunnel I heard Jim's voice at my side saying, 'Ah'll no be markin' anybody. Let them mark me!'

Which, of course, was a difficult thing to do. He could beat a man with ease, so the only way was to stop him getting the ball. Once it was at his feet the opposition were bang in trouble because he had a brilliant football brain and a delicate touch which allowed him to slip perfect passes exactly where he wanted to put them. Jim, at his best, could almost guarantee a Scottish victory when he was in a dark blue jersey and his best performance was in our victory over England at Hampden in 1962.

That was a special game because of what had happened the previous year at Wembley when we suffered a humiliating 9–3 defeat. When England came to Hampden a year later there wasn't a Scot in the ground who did not fear a repeat. There was tension in the days before the game, and on the eve of the match I was glad to get to bed and be alone with my thoughts.

As usual when we played for Scotland, Jim and I were sharing a room. We were staying in a hotel in Kilmacolm, which Scottish teams used a lot in those days. The SFA chose it because it was usually quiet, but that night was different as two coach loads of England fans had booked in there. They were in no hurry to go to their beds.

It was getting late when three of them stopped to have a loud conversation outside our bedroom door. Jim didn't like the idea of English people disturbing the Scottish team, and he told me to go and give them a telling off. But I said I would just ignore them as I didn't want to get up again.

Jim waited a few minutes more, then jumped from his bed, threw open the door, and gave the English lady and her two friends a dressing down they wouldn't forget in a hurry. If Jim's words shocked them, then his appearance must have given them a bigger shock. Jim never wore pyjamas and didn't have a stitch on.

Jim had a brilliant game the following afternoon and we beat England 2–0, but I doubt whether the Scottish left-half made as big an impact on those three supporters in the game as he had done the night before. We did a lap of honour after the game as it was the first time Scotland had beaten England in eleven years, but I think it wouldn't have been unfair if Jim had gone around the track on his own.

I wasn't to know that my eleven appearances for Scotland between 1961 and 1963 were to be followed by only five more. Nor that my love affair with Celtic was soon to hit the rocks.

THREE

End of a Dream

My personal life changed in 1961, when I started going out seriously with Noreen Ferry, my only girlfriend. I first saw her waiting outside St John's church before the 12 o'clock mass one Sunday in 1956. That was always busy because it was where all the best looking girls went. She was fifteen and I was sixteen and I thought straightaway that I was going to marry her. I said to her, 'I'm going to come back and get you when I'm a famous footballer.' Daft isn't it?

I carried on going to church, though, and still do, although not as often as I should. I was always taught that everyone is your brother and sister and you look after one another. It seemed to me that Jesus Christ was the first ever communist.

I didn't see Noreen again for three years, then I spotted her at the Ancient Order of Hibernian dance hall on Errol Street in 1959. The boys stood on one side of the hall and the girls on the other. You had to be brave to cross the dance floor and ask a girl to dance. You had to be quick off your mark, too, because the best girls would go quickly.

Noreen used to say no to a lot of lads and I rescued her from one called Tommy Moy. He was the best looking boy in

41

the Gorbals and Noreen had been on a date with him. I could see that he was pestering her to dance. But I could also see that she wasn't getting up to dance with him. To refuse to get up and dance with a boy was a big insult. Everyone noticed it because he was the only boy who had gone over to ask some-one to dance. I was sitting near the stage and looking at Noreen. If I'd gone over there would have been a fight, so I beckoned Noreen over. She later said that she would have never got up to any lad like that, but she wanted to escape from Tommy. And she'll be the first to admit that she thought she was god's gift, because she was the best-looking girl in the Gorbals. She had won beauty prizes.

Noreen walked over and I started talking to her. Tommy Moy turned round to Noreen and said, 'Oh, you're into foot-ballers are you?' Tommy followed Noreen down the street after the evening had finished and I was walking behind. He was bigger than me and had a very high opinion of himself, which in some ways was justified because every girl in the Gorbals fancied him. I told him where to go and to leave Noreen alone. At first he looked me in the eye and I don't think he could believe what I was telling him. I looked straight back at him. I was deadly serious and he backed down and walked off.

We went out a few times and I considered Noreen to be my girlfriend, but I'm not sure that she thought the same about me – as I soon realized. A new dance hall opened in town and Noreen won a competition for being the most beautiful girl in there. She won £50 – a fortune in those days – and her picture was printed in the newspaper the following day. This lad had asked her to dance that night – it turned out to be Bobby Carroll. I saw him in training the next morning and he said, 'I saw that girl you said you were going out with last night at the new dance hall.'

Noreen had told me that she was washing her hair and I believed her so I told him he must be mistaken. Then he showed me the *Daily Record*, which had a picture of Noreen in it. I felt pretty stupid. I was supposed to be going to the cinema with her later that day, so, when we met up, I asked her if she had stayed in and washed her hair the night before. She told me that she had. She must have thought that I was daft.

We walked towards the cinema, the Coliseum on Ellington Street, and there was a big queue. The lads at the front saw me and ushered me straight in, which was a bit embarrassing because a lot of my friends were there. I asked her again what she had done the night before and she still stuck to her story. I used to give her one shilling to buy some chocolates before we went in, but on this occasion I didn't. That set her mind wondering. I then bought one cinema ticket. We were on a platform overlooking the queue and people were looking up at us – it wasn't just that I played for Celtic, but Noreen's picture had been in the newspaper. I gave her the ticket and announced, 'I hope you enjoy the film, because I am going.' She was flustered so I told her that I knew she hadn't stayed in and washed her hair the night before. She panicked. She was mortified at all her friends seeing her left alone and she said to me, 'If you buy another ticket I'll tell you the truth.' I had her good and proper.

Noreen told me, 'I'm not your girlfriend.' She had been seeing other lads, too, so I gave her an ultimatum, saying, 'You're either my girlfriend or you're not.' She chose me. She later told me that her brothers had told her never to say no to any boy from the Gorbals.

When Noreen told her brothers that she was dating me, they said, 'What does he see in you?' But she said that they were happy because I was Catholic and especially because I played for Celtic. Not that they were against Protestants and Noreen had been out with them before. Noreen's mother needed more convincing. She remembered me from when I played for Scotland against Ireland in Dublin in my second international game. It was televised and she had watched it with Noreen's dad. It was a tough game and I was accused of being dirty. When she found out that Noreen was going out with me, she wasn't impressed and told her that I was a hooligan.

I may have been fiery on the football pitch but I was a saint compared to many of the people I'd grown up with. Early in my Celtic career I visited Barlinie jail in Glasgow with Jim Baxter. We were asked to go there by one of the prison officials and we were held up as role models, examples of how you could be a success even if you came from a poor area. I couldn't believe how many of the people I knew in there. We had a football quiz and as I looked at those who stood up to ask questions and the others sitting around them, I realized that I knew most of them by their first names.

They had either been at school with me or lived in the streets nearby in the Gorbals. The only difference between them and me, I decided, was that they hadn't been so lucky to have a mother like mine. I didn't have a father but my mother was a very strong person. She'd give us a belt if we were naughty and told us to face life's problems straight on. You had to look after yourself because nobody else would. It made you a strong character, but too many strong characters went the wrong way. Until I was nine years old I was in bed every night at 6.30 pm. And until I was seventeen I was never allowed out after 9.30 pm. This kind of discipline was the only way to keep a boy from getting into the kind of mischief that, for so many, eventually turned to crime.

Richer people could buy their way out of problems, but poorer people couldn't. Most of the lads were in Bar-L for robbing. They robbed because they didn't have anything. During our visit the idea was for the prisoners to ask Jimmy and me questions, which some of them did. But so many of them hid away because they were embarrassed and didn't want me to see them in there.

Back on the pitch, the biggest fixtures of the season were of course the Old Firm games. There was segregation at these games long before it became the norm in England. At Celtic Park, the fans approached and left the stadium down different roads to keep them apart. There were always incidents, with people fighting at the ground and all over the city. It wasn't nice – decent working class people beating each other up. Being a socialist, it always saddened me.

We were told to play to the whistle before every game and never to get involved in any incident with any other player. This was underlined before Rangers games. I had a great hatred of Rangers as a club – that came with growing up in the Gorbals – but I never agreed with the fighting. Later, I always had the needle with Rangers as a football club because I was never allowed to play for their team. I would never have gone there, but it would have been nice to say no. And yet I got to know a lot of the Rangers players when I played for Scotland and they were smashing lads. Bobby Shearer looked after me and made me feel welcome when I first got in the Scotland team, yet he was the Rangers player that most Celtic fans hated because he used to kick other players. I was a young lad when I first played for Scotland, but Bobby was like a father figure and was someone I could go to if I had a problem. When I was an older player, I treated the younger lads like Bobby had treated me.

We used to get a bonus of £25 for beating Rangers, almost three times our weekly wage. Invariably, we didn't beat them because they were a far better side with players like Jimmy

Baxter, Jimmy Millar, Ralph Brand, Bobby Shearer, Eric Caldow, Harold Davis, and Alec Scott. The best players in Scotland were not confined to Ibrox though. Pat Quinn of Motherwell was probably the toughest opponent I played against because I couldn't get near him. He was an inside-forward, a great passer of the ball with the imagination to beat players in different ways. Several English teams were looking at him.

One of my lowest moments for Celtic was when I missed a penalty in an Old Firm game at Parkhead, which we lost 1–0. Jim Baxter started messing about with the ball on the penalty spot to try and distract me. He succeeded. I had to get back to the Gorbals after the game and it was difficult not to be noticed. I took a tram car and then a bus. I just kept my head down and tried to be inconspicuous, but I was wearing a shirt and tie which made me stand out. I saw my pals on the corner that night and they were not happy. As I approached them, someone shouted: 'Professional footballer and you can't score from 12 yards out.' For once, I didn't reply.

Missing that penalty hit me hard, so much so that I asked to be relieved of the job of penalty taker at Celtic. The decision drew an interested reaction from Matt Busby. Matt had missed a penalty playing for Scotland against England so he knew how I felt. He wrote a consolatory piece in the Scottish *Daily Express* about my predicament. He mentioned United's great penalty takers like Charlie Mitten and Bobby Charlton, saying that they had also missed penalties and asked to have been relieved of their position. 'While footballers remain human,' Busby wrote, 'even the greatest marksmen will miss a penalty. And the penalty for that should certainly be something less than shooting the shooter.'

The way Celtic was run remained a shambles. The disorganization ran from top to bottom and top players continued to leave. There was even more lack of direction at the club, with Bob Kelly, ever the autocrat, picking the team, no question. It was a standing joke which Alex Ferguson and I still talk about now, marvelling at how such a situation was allowed to be. We often speak about life in early 60s Glasgow and the characters from that time. The crisis at the club was a heartbreaker for me because I was a Celtic fan, yet my illusions were being shattered when I saw the reality of the way the club was being run. The community I had been brought up in were mad about Celtic. The club was supposed to light people's lives.

Rangers were winning everything and, seeing the chaos at Parkhead, I knew why. I didn't have the heart to tell people on the streets what a mess the club was in. I'd tell them that we were optimistic about the future and that results would change, but I knew they wouldn't. It was that bad. Had you told me Celtic would be European champions in 1967 I would have laughed out loud.

The problem wasn't the lack of talent, but the bizarre team selections and naïve technical decisions and I blamed Bob Kelly. For example, our team coach edged towards the ground at Airdrie for one game when Kelly spotted Willie Goldie, a former Celtic reserve goalkeeper, walking along to the ground as a fan wearing a green and white scarf. Kelly stopped the coach and invited him to play. The players couldn't believe it, but anyone who stood up to Kelly didn't have a future at Celtic.

On one hand I admired Kelly's idea of bringing youth through, but he made major errors. Bertie Auld was a great footballer, a hard inside-forward and a typical Glaswegian. If he looked in the mirror he'd try and start a fight with his reflection. He wasn't afraid of answering back and that was to be his downfall at Celtic. In one game against Rangers in

1960, Bertie ruffled the hair of the Rangers' player Harold Davis after he had scored an own goal at Parkhead in a Glasgow cup tie. Davis was furious and ran the length of the park to catch up with him. Bertie was just having a laugh and maybe he shouldn't have done it. Bertie would often fly off the handle at the smallest thing – if he couldn't find one of his boots in the dressing room he would start raging – and Bob Kelly didn't like his style. He was transferred at the end of the season. Bertie eventually returned to Celtic and was a key player in the side that won the European Cup in 1967, but in 1960 those in power at Parkhead wanted rid of him.

Jimmy McGrory was a soft manager who used to let anything go. Maybe he should have been stronger with Bertie and told him to be quiet once in a while, but Jimmy didn't do discipline. A balance was needed because players should be allowed to have an opinion otherwise resentments fester, but under Bob Kelly, anybody with an opinion that didn't tally with his was seen as a dissenting voice.

Another example of Kelly's amateurism was how he dealt with Mick Jackson, who wasn't a full-time professional when he should have been. He had a heavy shift as a printer and one day finished work at 3.00 pm so that he could make a 4.30 pm kick-off against Rangers in the semi-final of the Scottish Cup at Hampden Park. Things like that would never have happened at Rangers.

Despite the problems, I loved playing for Celtic. Players like John Colrain and Mick Jackson were real characters. One of my highlights for the club was a friendly game in 1962 against Real Madrid. Over 73,000 filled Celtic Park to see us play a side that included Ferenc Puskas, Paco Gento, and Alfredo Di Stefano. The speed of their passing was incredible, so simple and yet so devastating, and they were 2–0 up after half an hour, three after an hour. We kept battling and pulled a goal back to make it 3–1. We felt that we had been outclassed, but done ourselves justice and even 3–1 was a magnificent result. The crowd agreed. 'We want Celtic, We want Celtic,' they roared until we left the dressing room and returned for an unlikely lap of honour. Most of us only had our socks on, but the fans were going wild. Puskas said that he had never seen anything like it.

By 1962 I was the highest paid Celtic player on £22 a week. I was seen as Bob Kelly's boy and indeed he loved me for a short period of time, probably because I was a good player. I wasn't the quickest runner and I wasn't good in the air, but then I had Billy McNeill alongside me who was great in the air. My qualities were that I passed the ball well and I could tackle.

Kelly was the main reason why I came to leave Celtic. I never wanted to go, but my situation at the club became untenable. We played against Rangers at Ibrox on New Year's Day 1963; the game should never have been played because it was a brick hard pitch. I argued with the coach, Sean Fallon, with whom I normally got on well, about what kind of tactics we should play. Sean was a former Celtic player who had played in the double-winning team in 1954. He had legendary status among fans because after breaking a collarbone in a game against Hearts, he left the pitch for twenty minutes only to return with his arm in a sling. Sean earned the nickname 'the Iron Man' for his part in Celtic's momentous 7–1 League Cup final victory over Rangers in 1957. He retired a year later but remained a major figure at Celtic and eventually became assistant manager when Jock Stein took over in 1965. In truth, Sean and I differed on our football theories that day and I couldn't hide my feelings any longer. We were trailing 1–0 when we trudged back into the dressing room and the lid came off.

'We need to knock long balls forward,' said Sean in a measured and firm manner.

'No, we need to pass the ball to feet,' I replied angrily. 'The long ball won't work.'

'No, we play long balls forward,' replied Sean, clearly agitated. 'And you, Crerand, don't move so far up the park.'

'I'm not going back on the field if we have to play like that,' I said. 'You don't know what you are talking about.' The toys had well and truly been thrown from my cot.

'You're wrong Crerand, you're wrong,' Sean replied. I was, especially as there were no substitutes in those days, and after a few minutes I backed down and walked back angrily onto the pitch. Bob Kelly was in the dressing room and witnessed everything. He didn't say a word though. Nor did ten of my team-mates. It was me against the rest.

We were hammered 4–0 anyway and one of the goals was a deflection off me. I can't take anything away from Rangers because they were a better organized team with better players, but I was distraught and very angry when we returned to the dressing room, where I had another stand up row with just about every Celtic player and Sean. I adore Sean; he's one of the greatest Celts that has ever lived. He was from Sligo in Ireland and when he was given the Freedom of Sligo in 2002 I was honoured to be invited along with him. But that day at Ibrox I was furious with everyone, especially Sean.

The repercussions were serious. Bob Kelly got the needle and dropped me for a game against Aberdeen five days later. Celtic never stayed overnight and we travelled to Aberdeen by train in the third class carriage, with wooden seats and no toilet. When we got to Aberdeen I wasn't named in the team. There was no explanation as to why. I was particularly annoyed because my mum had got a train from Glasgow to watch me play. I met her outside the ground before the match to give her a ticket and told her that I wasn't playing. She didn't say anything, but I could see her disappointment.

It was obvious to me that the club either wanted rid of me or that I was just not good enough to be in the side, despite being a Scottish international. Because of a bad spell of weather – one game between Partick Thistle and Morton was called off ten times – there was no play in the Scottish Leagues for four weeks. Then I was dropped for a game against Falkirk. I decided that enough was enough and asked for a move in a written transfer request. I didn't consult Noreen or my mum, when I should have done. Mum found out when a newspaper journalist went to her front door. 'This has come as a great shock to me. In fact I am stunned,' she told him.

I handed in my transfer request. The news made the front page of the Scottish *Daily Express* at a time when football stories were rare on the front pages. 'Crerand Shock: Transfer Plea,' said the headline.

Noreen, by this time my fiancée, was quoted in this article saying, 'I was surprised when Pat told me that he had asked for a transfer – but I was even more surprised when he was dropped for the game against Falkirk on Monday night. This will make no difference to our wedding plans. If Pat does move, then I will go wherever he wants me to go. I don't see much point in him staying at Parkhead if he is not happy.'

After 120 appearances and five goals, I would never play for Celtic again. Unbeknown to me, Bob Kelly and Matt Busby at Manchester United had an agreement that Matt would have first refusal on me if I ever left Celtic.

I came home from mass on Sunday and found Jim Rodger, a journalist from the *Daily Record*, waiting at the door. He knew everything about Scottish football and was big pals with Matt Busby, and, in later years, Alex Ferguson. He told me that I was going to Manchester United and explained that Matt Busby and a delegation from United had been in Manchester discussing my transfer with Celtic. I didn't play any part in discussions about my future. My mother started crying.

The journalist told me that I was going to Manchester the following day to meet Matt Busby. My initial thought was that Noreen and I had both had family ties in Glasgow and were reluctant to leave. Noreen had never even been to England before.

I went to Celtic Park for training the following morning and trained as normal. Nobody said anything to me and I assumed that Jim Rodger was wrong. Then, after training Jimmy McGrory asked for a word. He told me that there had been talks between Celtic and Manchester United and that a fee had been agreed for me to move to England.

'That's what I've been told to tell you Pat,' he said, as if it was nothing to do with him. Jimmy, despite being manager, wouldn't have had a choice whether I was sold or not as he would have been acting on Bob Kelly's orders. There was no room for negotiation, I was going to Manchester and that was that.

I went for something to eat with Mick Jackson. My head was spinning. He convinced me to go to Old Trafford. He wasn't to know it, but two months later he would be on his way from Parkhead, too, deemed to be 'disruptive' by Bob Kelly. Another good friend, a bookmaker Tony Queen who was also a great pal of Jock Stein, agreed. 'Go to Manchester, Pat. Celtic are going nowhere.' Deep down, I knew he was right.

The Celtic fans were up in arms when they found out I was going. I got loads of letters telling me not to go and the newspapers were full of the same thing but what could I do?

Looking back now I realize that my doubts had set in during 1960/61, another unspectacular season as we could only finish fourth in the league. We did better in the Scottish Cup, reaching the final, only to be beaten in the replay. I left the Hampden pitch that night with tears in my eyes. It was bad enough to be beaten. What made it unbearable was the fact that Jock Stein was the Dunfermline manager and it angered me to think that he had been allowed to leave Parkhead in 1960. He had transformed them into a team good enough to win the Scottish Cup. I don't think that Celtic realized his coaching talents when they let him leave, but the young players who had played under him, players like myself and Billy McNeill, did.

That Dunfermline game brought home to me what a shambles Celtic was. Bertie Peacock was the captain of the team and the most experienced player. After recovering from injury, it was assumed he would go straight back into the team for the final. The inexperienced John Clark was picked instead for both the final and the replay. Bertie was not even considered for the replay and Celtic even gave him permission to turn out for Northern Ireland against Italy the day before. Northern Ireland had asked Jock Stein to release their full-back Willie Cunningham. There was no way Jock would let him go.

The bizarre decisions continued after I left Celtic. The team went on to reach the Scottish Cup final in 1963 against Rangers. After doing well to get a draw, Celtic dropped Jimmy Johnstone, who was the best player in the first game, and replaced him with veteran Bobby Craig, who put in a poor performance. Rangers won 3–0 and I was later told by my former team-mates that they were livid with the constant tinkering by a man who was not even manager.

It was heartbreaking for me to see the state of the club I had supported all my life. The training schedule, for example, was so bad that you were never put in any situations where you were under pressure. Training amounted to a long jog followed by a game of five-a-side. There was never any tactical talk, feedback from previous games or information about our opponents. I maintain to this day that fans should just support their team and their manager rather than trying to find out what is happening behind the scenes, because they won't like what they see.

Celtic would only change when Jock Stein took charge in 1965 when he won nine league titles in succession and took them to become the first British European Cup winners in 1967. I doubt that I would have ever left Celtic if Jock Stein had been in charge, but then I might not have got in the team that won the European Cup with Bobby Murdoch there.

Even though I was disgruntled with Celtic, I still felt that I was pushed out of Parkhead because the club knew that they could get money for me. I had an opinion and usually answered back which didn't go down well with Kelly. Maybe sometimes I had too much of an opinion, but I wanted what was best for Celtic and what I saw was a disorganized rabble.

On the morning of 6 February 1963, myself, Noreen and a journalist called John McPhail flew down to Manchester airport, which was little more than a house. John wrote for the *Daily Record*. He was an ex-Celtic centre forward and a great fella.

Matt Busby was waiting at the airport with Denis Law and his wife Diana. United were cute as anything. I had never met Matt Busby before, but Diana Law took Noreen shopping in Manchester and made sure that she was looked after. Some photographers followed them and there was a picture in the paper the next day of the pair of them looking at shoes.

I went to Old Trafford to negotiate my contract. I was a nervous 23-year-old, completely in awe of Matt Busby. He said that he was building a strong team and that United had been ambitious enough to sign Denis Law who joined from

Torino in 1962. He said that he needed somebody to play the ball up to the forwards and that player would be me. He could have told me anything and I would have agreed. I didn't so much as negotiate as listen to what United were saying. They offered me £45 a week – more than twice what I was on at Celtic – plus crowd bonuses. We would get £1 extra if the crowd was over 35,000, £2 if it was over 40,000 and £3 if it was over 45,000. That was quite a lot of money when you consider that the maximum wage of £20 a week had only been abolished in 1961. United agreed a fee of £43,000 – not the £57,000 often reported – the most ever by an English club for a Scottish player and £3,000 more than Manchester City had paid Kilmarnock for wing-half Bobby Kennedy.

Bad weather meant we couldn't fly back to Glasgow that night and Noreen got the sack from her job at Singer's. She had taken a day off work to travel to Manchester with me and not explained why, but the story of me going to United was plastered all over the papers and her bosses were not impressed.

I signed for Manchester United on 6 February 1963, five years to the day since the Munich air disaster, as part of Busby's plans to build another great side.

FOUR

South of the Border

The winter of 1963 was savage. It was the coldest on record with an average temperature of zero degrees across Britain. All you ever saw on the news were stories about the big freeze, cattle being stranded and pictures of snow being piled up against front doors.

No trophies had been won at Manchester United since the Munich air disaster. Matt Busby was rebuilding, but the fans didn't see it that way. United had finished a very creditable second in 1958/59, the first full season after the disaster, but then slipped to seventh a year later and fifteenth in 1961/62. United may have attracted many new fans across the country who felt a sympathy with the club after the disaster, but many of these didn't come to watch matches at Old Trafford and average gates had fallen away badly. Crowds of 25,000 were not uncommon, a figure well under half the capacity.

I walked into a club where confidence was low and the team hadn't been playing well. And because of the weather, United didn't have a chance to find some form. The team didn't play a league game between Boxing Day and 23 February and the FA Cup third round wasn't staged until 4 March.

I had plenty of time, therefore, to study the little red book given to all players, containing a list of training rules and instructions. Some of these regulations, expressed in the most pompous of tones, were standard. Firstly, this pass book had to be carried with you at all times and it was supposed to be shown so you could gain entry to the ground. Players were expected to 'attend the Ground, or such other place as the directors may appoint, at 10.00 every morning (except Saturday) to undergo such training as the Manager or Trainer appointed by the Directors shall order'. There were two training sessions: 10.00 am to 12.00 pm and 2.30 pm to 4.00 pm. You were expected to turn up forty-five minutes before kick-off for home matches and at the station or coach pick-up fifteen minutes before departure, and you weren't allowed to slope off during a trip without permission. If you had an accident or were ill, then you had to notify the manager and see the club doctor, unless you lived away from the club, when in 'necessitous cases' you could 'consult your practitioner' and send in a doctor's certificate. Not that the club expected to pick up the bill, as they were careful to state. Any player rendering himself unfit to perform his duties through drinking or any other causes would be severely dealt with, and friends or acquaintances were to be kept well away from the ground or the dressing room.

Rule 11 would raise a few eyebrows today. 'Smoking is strictly prohibited during training hours, and players are earnestly requested to reduce smoking to the absolute minimum on the day of a match.' Brilliant isn't it, a request to cut down on smoking on a match day? I didn't smoke, but fellow Scot Denis Law, one of the few lads I knew at United when I arrived, took a sly fag now and then. Denis was one reason Matt bought me. He'd watched us link up well for Scotland and he had a long term plan for United which included us two, with me being Denis's main supply line. Some people told me that another reason why Matt had gone over the border to sign me was that he considered my style of play the closest to the kind of role he himself once had while playing for Manchester City. Matt never said that to me, but others did.

Despite knowing Denis Law, I still felt like an outsider and the whole experience was a bit strange for me because I'd only lived in Glasgow and I was a bit of a mummy's boy. To make matters worse, I was described by the Scottish newspapers as an 'Anglo', a phrase I hated, which was used to describe Scottish players who played in England.

It took a while for me to find my feet at Old Trafford, to adjust to life in a new city and at a new football club where I wasn't used to the players. I had no real friends and even though my team-mates made me feel welcome, they had issues of their own to deal with. There was discontent with the training, despite the two sessions laid down in the pass book, and matters became quite tense, with some players thinking that training could be more challenging. A meeting was sought with Matt Busby and club captain Noel Cantwell but I was new to the club and stayed on the sidelines – the last time I spoke my mind a few months earlier Celtic had transferred me. Players were looking to apportion blame to anyone but themselves, but I just wanted to get back on the pitch so that we could lift the mood.

To make matters worse, there was a thief in the changing room, with valuables frequently going missing. Matt gathered everyone together in the room, about thirty players including the reserves. He said, 'We have a nigger in the woodpile.' Dennis Walker, United's first black player, was sitting there. I was so embarrassed for Dennis and so were the other lads. Matt wasn't a racist – it was an expression which was used by his generation – but we thought Matt had put his foot in it. Dennis was a talented footballer who would have made it if he wasn't so shy. As it happened, he only played one game, filling in for a resting Bobby Charlton before the 1963 FA Cup Final. The thief was eventually found, a reserve player who was bombed out of the club straightaway.

To add to the poor spirit, there were stories of match rigging when I arrived at Old Trafford. Harry Gregg, who I befriended, told me that he took part in a United game which was bent. Harry was straight, but he claimed several matches involving United were thrown during that season. I was new to Old Trafford, but I had seen evidence in Scotland of match fixing, seen that players had received money to lose games, even at the biggest clubs. Me? I have never received money to throw a game.

My first game in a Manchester United shirt was a friendly in Cork against Bolton Wanderers on 13 February 1963. The weather wasn't as harsh in Ireland as it was in Britain, hence the location. We beat Bolton 4–2 and I scored a hilarious goal. I took a shot which deflected off a stone and past the goalkeeper. There was a big crowd, despite the terrible rain and the afternoon kick-off because there were no floodlights. Roy Keane's father Mossy was at the game as a supporter – he took the afternoon off and got the sack for his troubles. Some have said that he's never worked since!

I didn't stay in the team hotel, but at Noel Cantwell's house. Noel was from Cork and we had a great night out at a shebeen called Kitty Barry's. Together with Harry Gregg, Noel was fantastic in helping me settle. He used to stress the importance of what he called 'moral courage' – players not shirking responsibilities on the field. I'd like to think that I didn't.

The three of us were mad about football and would go and watch other teams from the north west play if we did not have a game. Because I didn't drive, one of them would drive to Liverpool and we'd stand on the Kop, despite being Manchester United players. The Scousers would have a word with us, but it was good humoured. United fans might be surprised, but I always had great respect for Liverpool Football Club and Bill Shankly. I still respect the older generation of Liverpool football fans. When I go to Anfield I speak to longstanding Liverpool fans who can't put up with what the rivalry has become – with the hooliganism and the nastiness between the fans. Liverpool and Manchester are both working-class cities that have produced two of the greatest football clubs in the world. People should be proud of that, but they are not.

I became friends with Shankly when I moved to England, a friendship which endured for decades. When I played for Scotland at Wembley in 1965, he came to see me in the dressing room. I was wearing number four, his old number, for Scotland and he touched my shirt and held it up with a real reverence – as though it was the most sacred number that a player could wear for Scotland. He didn't say anything but he was almost crying.

In 1981, the United players put on a testimonial dinner for Sir Matt Busby at the Piccadilly Hotel in Manchester. It was to raise money for Matt because he wasn't flush with cash, although he never liked to say anything. I asked Matt if he wanted anyone to come from Liverpool and he said Bill Shankly. I called Bill to invite him and his wife Nessie. He said he thought it was great that we were doing it for Matt and that nobody had ever done anything like that for him at Liverpool. Bill felt he had been treated badly by Liverpool in his final years. He used the Anfield gym on a daily basis and said to me that he wanted to be the fittest man in the graveyard, but he cut a lonely figure. He asked me the date of the dinner.

'Monday 30 November,' I told him.

'Pat,' he said, 'do you know what date the 30 November is? Have you been in England so long that you have forgotten the feast day of the Patron Saint of Scotland, St Andrew?'

I had. Bill Shankly never made it to the function. He died that September.

Jock Stein, who was at Dunfermline, would travel down to watch United and Liverpool and if I knew he was coming I would ask him to bring some Glasgow rolls, a type of bread roll – in Manchester they have a version called barmcakes – which tasted much nicer than anything in England. You couldn't – and still can't – get the real thing in Manchester. Jock's son-in-law was a baker and Jock used to fill his car with them and Irn Bru, because the Irn Bru in England tasted totally different from what I was used to in Scotland. There were certain sweets that you couldn't get in Manchester so Denis Law and I would fight over them and the Glasgow rolls. I wouldn't mind, but Denis wasn't even from Glasgow. Despite the cultural differences, as I settled in I found Mancunians to be very much like Glaswegians. They were warm and would come and talk to you, it was that working-class thing.

I hadn't been at Old Trafford long when one evening I went along to see a United youth team match. I had heard that our youth team were pretty impressive and I wanted to see for myself. I sat on the trainer's bench with the coach Jack Crompton, but you didn't need to be that close to see who the star of this game was – United's right-winger, a skinny boy with thick black hair. His ball control was a dream. He gave you the impression he could beat his man any way he wanted, although he was inclined to take on too many at a time. I couldn't have been more impressed.

'See that winger,' I said to Jack at half-time, 'you have a great prospect there.'

Jack didn't even turn round. He just nodded his head and said, 'I know.' I thought Jack was being a bit arrogant and that he could have shown a bit more enthusiasm.

'The way he carries the ball, his positioning, his touch, his speed,' I went on, 'he's easily the best player I've seen at this level.' Jack let me talk on for a while then, in a father to son manner, he put me fully in the picture.

'Paddy,' he said, 'you've made no great discovery. Everybody at Old Trafford knows about this boy. He's a wonderful prospect.'

Even though United were going through a difficult period, the lad was about sixteen, so they had to wait until he grew older and developed, and hope that nothing would happen to take the shine off what they thought was a football gem. His name, as if you haven't guessed it, was George Best.

The first place Noreen and I lived in when we moved to Manchester was some digs with a Mrs Scott on Marsland Road, Sale. The rent was £6 a week. Even though I was United's second most expensive signing, there was no star treatment. In fact, the traffic was so noisy outside that it drove me mental. Mrs Scott was a United nut and a lovely person. She wasn't a Catholic, but she used to go to the local church and pray for United every Saturday morning. It was hard living in digs because we'd never lived away from home before, nor under the same roof, albeit in different beds. Noreen used to return to Glasgow once a month, but I couldn't because I had to play.

Bobby and Norma Charlton invited us out to dinner on one of our first weekends in Manchester. I'd always respected and admired him as a player. He was quite shy, so I appreciated him inviting us to a pub in Flixton near where he lived. Bobby asked me what I wanted to drink and I asked for a sherry. I wasn't into alcohol and I didn't even drink sherry, but I thought it would be a sensible choice. He did a double take, thinking that I was such a big Glaswegian drinker that I drank neat sherry instead of beer. We had a smashing night, but I hardly drank anything. The goalkeeper Harry Gregg collared me on Monday morning and asked me how Saturday night had gone.

'Fine.' I said. 'Why?'

'Because Bobby was shitting himself that you would go potty if the waiter spilt something or someone said something to you.'

'Am I that bad?' I asked Harry. I couldn't believe that I had a reputation for being a snapper after just a few weeks living in Manchester. Actually, the reputation stuck. Denis Law once said, 'If Pat starts, the best thing to do is put out the lights and lie on the floor.' Denis also used to tell me that I had two speeds – slow and dead stop. I don't think that I am bad tempered, but if someone did something to me I could be.

When the weather finally began to thaw and United started playing, I wasn't an immediate success. My first competitive game was against Blackpool who had my nemesis Pat Quinn, previously of Motherwell, playing for them. The game was at Old Trafford on 23 February. The crowd was 43,121. Old Trafford was big, but three sides of the ground were predominantly terracing and it was no grander than Ibrox or Celtic Park. In the following months I would play at smarter stadiums like Goodison Park and Highbury. It wasn't until the sweeping cantilever stand went up at Old Trafford for the 1966 World Cup that the stadium began to be considered one of the best in Britain.

New players take time to adjust to their surroundings and I was no different. I over-hit passes and because I didn't know how people played I had to get used to my team-mates. I wasn't the player I knew I could be, but I always felt that Matt respected me, especially as he sought my opinions about other players he was considering signing.

Sir Alex Ferguson does it now, as in the case of Cristiano Ronaldo. He saw for himself how good Ronaldo was when Sporting Lisbon played United in a pre-season friendly in 2003, but when his players came into the dressing room raving about him that made him more certain that he should sign him. He did the same with Eric Cantona in 1992 after Steve Bruce and Gary Pallister told him that the Frenchman was easily the best player they had come up against.

Matt asked Denis about me and he asked him about Jim Baxter, too. He wanted to know about players' backgrounds and what type of person they were. I was told that Denis said that while Jimmy was probably the better player, his lifestyle could lead to problems. Denis said that I had what it took to be a Manchester United player because I looked after myself and wasn't a big drinker or gambler. Matt had an idea of what constituted a Manchester United player and was assessing whether players he liked would be good professionals or trouble makers. His judgement was based on far more than an individual having talent.

It was sensible of Matt to seek opinions from his players because players know which opponents are difficult to play against. I felt honoured that Matt respected my views so soon after joining. He asked me about the Dundee defender Ian Ure. It seems incredible now, but Dundee had a great team and were playing in the semi-final of the European Cup against Milan. I said that Ian was a good player, but that he struggled in the air a little bit. Dundee lost in Milan and three of their goals were from headers. Having seen that game, Matt came to me the next day and thanked me for my thoughts. Ian later came to United, but it wasn't Matt who signed him.

One thing I found refreshing in England was the lack of sectarian abuse during games. Surprisingly, Rangers players were one of the few of our rivals in Scotland who had never given us abuse, but at other grounds it was commonplace. In many grounds we played, opponents and fans would call us Fenian bastards for 90 minutes. I liked the absence of that in England.

The perception was that United were big spenders after my transfer fee and the record £115,000 spent on Denis Law a year earlier. But the club wasn't flush. When Matt had gone for Denis the chairman Harold Hardman was reluctant to spend that much money. He had been at the club long enough to know United were unable to pay high wages and extravagance didn't appeal to him. The Manchester bookmaker Johnny Foy, who was a great friend of Matt's, offered to underwrite the bid for Denis. United never made this public, but in the end I think United gave the impression that they had paid the money themselves, when they had in fact accepted the underwriting from Foy.

Things started to go right for me by the time we played Southampton in the semi-final of the FA Cup at Villa Park on 27 April. It was not a good game on a terrible pitch. Denis Law scored the only goal in front of 65,000 but we went back to the Cromford Club, which was owned by Matt's friend Paddy McGrath, to celebrate after the game. Gigi Peronace was in there. He was a football agent in the days before football agents. He was great friends with Denis, having been responsible for his move to Torino. I must have been doing something right because he asked me if I was interested in joining Roma. Jean Busby, Matt's wife, overheard and said, 'He's going nowhere.' Coming to England was a big enough jump for me.

Matt paid for champagne for the whole team that night. A lot of Manchester people saw us in the Cromford Club, and as the word got passed from mouth to mouth the stories got more colourful. Manchester was like a village when it came to gossip. Apparently we were all plastered and Matt was worse than anyone. Nonsense. We all had a few, but we'd just reached the FA Cup Final so why couldn't we celebrate?

People said that Matt was so close to his top players that he could not bring himself to discipline them. Rubbish. Did people really imagine that United could be successful if there was no discipline? Every great manager has to be a disciplinarian. Matt was like a father figure, but fathers are sometimes required to kick you up the backside and he could sort you out, believe me. Whoever said 'iron fist in a velvet glove' about him was right. He could be a hard taskmaster. There were plenty of blow outs, but people didn't read about them because what happened inside Old Trafford stayed inside Old Trafford. Matt believed that punishment was a private affair and he rarely criticized his players publicly, just like Sir Alex Ferguson now.

If you were suspended for ill-discipline then you didn't get paid. That meant you had to answer to your wife because you weren't bringing a wage home. Matt never swore, but if he raised his voice you were almost disappointed in yourself because you had let him down. Matt could back up his words with a formidable physical presence. He was a former miner and soldier and had it come to a fight, he would have probably got the better of all his players, not that he ever fought with them.

Matt gave Manchester United dignity. Matt Busby and Alex Ferguson are great losers. It kills them to lose, but they maintain their respect for other people. Other managers will show contempt or disregard. Matt had that respect for others and graciousness in defeat in abundance.

Matt probably brought the comments upon himself because he readily socialized with players and he said in many interviews that he allowed his players to 'play it off the cuff'. People took that to mean that we went out to play on a Saturday without any real plan, but that wasn't true. When Matt talked about playing it off the cuff he meant that he laid down no rigid set of rules for the forwards. You couldn't tell players like Denis Law or Bobby Charlton what to do with the ball at their feet … instinct did that.

We played the first fifteen minutes of every game with a calculated defensive plan until we assessed the strength of the opposition. I won't forget my first Manchester derby in May 1963 when we played our final four league games in just eleven days because of the backlog of fixtures caused by the inclement weather. Both United and City were in serious danger of going down and we drew 1–1 at Maine Road. We didn't deserve a point. The City player David Wagstaff had a go at me just before half-time. I didn't like players who had a go on the pitch and said, 'If you've got something to say then do it off the pitch.' Well, he did. He came up to me in the tunnel and shouted, 'You, you c**t …' I turned round and belted him and he went down like a ton of bricks. Then City's trainer came for me and I said, 'You f**k off too or you'll get it.' He took me seriously and retreated.

Matt came in the changing room and he was livid, absolutely furious. I'd never seen him like that before. He walked straight up to me and said, 'Did you hit David Wagstaff?' I said, 'No.' I was afraid of Matt; he was going off his head. The fight made the papers and I didn't come out of it too well, but I got off lightly in comparison to my punishment if it had happened today. Matt knew it was me, but he never mentioned the incident again. I was young, daft and had acted in the heat of the moment. There was nothing personal against Wagstaff – he was a very talented player whom Matt considered signing for United. I got in a few scrapes in the future, but

I never went down. You don't go down when you are from the Gorbals.

We finally left Manchester for London on the Wednesday afternoon. We passed the twin towers of Wembley and the floodlights were on for a rather special occasion – Milan were playing Benfica in the European Cup Final.

Leicester City, our opponents, were favourites to win the cup. They had finished the season fourth behind champions Everton, Tottenham, and Burnley, whereas United only just avoided relegation by finishing in nineteenth place. It was a bleak time in Manchester – City were relegated, not that we were too concerned as we prepared to play Leicester.

The bookmakers were not confident about United, but we were and thought we'd play them at their own game, even though I'm not a gambler. Denis Law knew a bookie in Aberdeen and four players bet £100 each on United to win the Cup – a fortune and over twice my weekly wage. I wasn't usually a gambler, but we stood to win £150 on top of our stake if we won.

Noel Cantwell, our captain, went to Wembley the day before the game to do a television piece with the Leicester captain for the BBC. They wanted Noel to walk up the Wembley steps to lift the cup, but he refused, saying that he didn't want to tempt fate. The team was named on the day of the game and it surprised me. Nobby Stiles was left out – he never did play in an FA Cup Final. Harry Gregg was dropped for David Gaskell and Shay Brennan was omitted. They weren't happy, but what could we say to them? It happens in football. I'd never seen an English Cup Final live in my life and I wanted to savour the moment. The first time I had heard of United was when I listened to the 1948 FA Cup Final on a radio in the Gorbals and here I was fifteen years later about to play in one for the Reds, with United again underdogs.

The Wembley dressing room was roasting, which was no surprise as the game was played on 25 May. Before the match I went for a walk in my kit. I didn't tell anyone where I was going. Having watched the English Cup Final so many times on television, I wanted to see the band on the pitch and that man in the daft white outfit who waved a stick around when they sang 'Abide with Me'. I stood there marvelling and thinking, 'This is magnificent.' I wasn't nervous, just curious.

Apparently Matt was frantic with worry and wondered where I had got to. He wasn't happy when he saw me, but he didn't have time to tell me off as the game was due to start. And he didn't tell me off after the game because the 1963 Cup Final was my best individual game for Manchester United. The whole team played superbly and while Denis and I got the credit, Johnny Giles and Bobby Charlton were outstanding as we beat Leicester 3–1 with two goals from David Herd and one from Denis Law. I sent Denis in for a goal on the half hour and after that Leicester just couldn't shut us down.

Gordon Banks, the Leicester and England goalkeeper, spilled a shot by Bobby Charlton and David Herd nipped in to make it two. Leicester's Ken Keyworth headed a goal back for them, but then Banks made another error and Herd got his second. If we had won the game by six or seven people would have said it was a fair result. More importantly, it was United's finest hour since the tragedy at Munich and the start of a great six years.

The *Daily Telegraph*, not a paper I've ever been in the habit of buying, paid me a glowing tribute. Referring to the European Cup Final between Milan and Benfica at Wembley, played a few days before we beat Leicester, it said: 'Even Rivera and Eusebio, the bright young stars of European soccer, did nothing on Wednesday that Law did not equal on Saturday. No Italian or Portuguese half-back showed greater intelligence or craftsmanship than did Crerand. All the team-work which won Milan the European championship was no sounder than that which earned United the Cup.'

The Queen was waiting to present the trophy. I'm many things, but a royalist is not one of them so I just kept my head down and picked up my medal.

We had a banquet at the Savoy Hotel afterwards. We were allowed to take two guests and I took my wife and my mother. None of us were used to going into flash hotels and I was a bit in awe, more so when I saw a man on our table beckon a waiter over. He handed him a five pound note, a lot of money, and said, 'When I want a drink I shall point my finger and I expect you to be here.' The waiter was round him like a fly round shit all night. The man was Paddy McGrath, a great friend of Sir Matt Busby and a big United fan. Paddy was a successful entrepreneur and bought the first executive box at Old Trafford, right on the halfway line.

Although he was two decades older than me, Paddy would become a great friend of mine, too. He became a father figure to me and whenever I had problems he helped me a lot. I could confide in him and if I wasn't playing well then I could speak to him. I'd not really had a father figure in my life. Charlie Duffy, who married my mum, was a great guy but I saw him as a pal, rather than a father. I'd go back to Glasgow when I could and would walk to High Street train station with Charlie on his way to work as I had done since I was a child. I loved that walk and it didn't bother me when I was recognized by people.

Unfortunately, Paddy was also responsible for introducing me to a vice that I've kept to this day – red wine. I've never smoked or really drank beer, but wine is a weakness. We were allowed to have a few glasses that night, with the ever attentive waiter doing his job.

Paddy McGrath owned the Cromford Club near Market Street. Lots of famous performers went on stage there like Frank Carson and Shirley Bassey. It was *the* place in Manchester and Paddy was a real leftie like me. Paddy was hard, too. He had been based at Heaton Park during the war and never went away to fight. He claims that the Germans never landed in Manchester because of him. One of the visitors at his club one night was Patrick McGoohan, who played 'Dangerman' on television. He was rude to one of the waitresses and Paddy got the right needle with him and went over. 'Call yourself Dangerman?' he said. 'Well you've never been in as much danger as you are now.' Paddy made McGoohan apologize to the waitress.

Paddy had dealings with the Kray twins in Manchester. They wanted to buy the Cromford Club, but Paddy wasn't selling. They had a meeting in the Midland Hotel, where the Krays threatened Paddy. He wasn't fazed. They didn't realize that he was carrying a serious weapon. And Paddy didn't realize that the waiters were actually undercover police officers. The police marched the Krays to the train station and they never came back to Manchester.

I'd first heard the Krays mentioned the night of the 1963 Cup Final. We went to the Astor club in the west end after we'd been at the Savoy and Leicester's Frank McLintock was there with us. A man asked Noreen to dance and she refused him. He kept pestering her and he was at it for a while. His pal asked Diana Law to dance and she accepted. The guy asking Noreen wouldn't take no for an answer. I saw red and approached him. Without saying anything to him or Noreen, I punched him flat out. He was standing by some stairs and he went flying down them, like something from a Wild West film. Denis Law shouted, 'Oh Paddy, you've only gone and done it again.' Unbeknown to me, the man I punched was one of the

Krays' henchmen. Had I known that before I would not have punched him, but he didn't get up for more.

Malcolm Allison was also in our party. He told me straightaway that I'd hit the wrong person and said that the whole group of us could be in trouble. Malcolm was a big-time Londoner who knew everybody. He was very charismatic and great company. When I heard this I wanted out of the club straightaway, I wasn't stupid. I was later told that the Kray twins were there and that they had just said 'let it go' even though I had hit one of their men. They must have been feeling charitable that night because we were footballers.

One of my most vivid early memories of George Best comes from the following morning. We were leaving our hotel with hangovers to go back to Manchester and I looked up to see a small face in one of the windows. The youth players had been treated to a trip to the Cup Final. He was watching us carry the cup onto the bus, completely awestruck.

All the players got £25 each for winning the FA Cup – and that was money from the Football Association. United didn't give us a bonus and that caused a lot of frustration. I had no idea how much the other lads were on, but the word was that United were the lowest payers in the first division. Players who came through the ranks were particularly badly paid. Matt and Bill Shankly had got together when the maximum wage was abolished in 1961 and agreed to pay players similar amounts. In later years Matt admitted that was a mistake, and that players should have earned more. Agents get a bad press, but I agree with them. We were working-class lads who loved football and were lucky enough to get paid to play it, not lads who knew the finer details of contracts or how to negotiate with the businessmen who ran football clubs. We earned more than the average man, but footballers were treated badly and the money from the huge crowds certainly didn't go in our pockets.

The mood around Old Trafford began to be more relaxed with the FA Cup win and, from speaking to people in different areas of the club, I began to realize that there was a quiet obsession with winning the European Cup.

Following the Munich air crash, United enjoyed a close relationship with Real Madrid, a team that had been crowned champions of Europe on several occasions. The Spanish giants had offered to pay for the Munich survivors to have a holiday in Spain and visited Manchester three years in succession to play friendlies against United, travelling to England for less than half their usual price. Madrid had even offered Matt Busby the job of manager, saying, 'We'll make it heaven on earth for you.' Matt replied, 'I'm already in heaven.' In truth he could have won the European Cup several times with Madrid, but his ambitions were firmly at Old Trafford. He wanted to commemorate the lads who had died at Munich by lifting the trophy they would have probably won if it hadn't been for the disaster. The responsibility for winning the biggest prize lay with us players, but in order to qualify for the European Cup, first we had to win the English league. We had just finished nineteenth in Division One and knew that much work was needed, but there was a buzz about the club, a confidence I'd never experienced in my career so far.

FIVE

The Making of Champions

The summer of 1963 was an enjoyable one for me. United increased my wages from £45 to £65 a week for the 1963/64 season. Negotiations amounted to a conversation with Matt Busby where he told you what you would be getting the following season, with contracts working on a year-to-year basis. In later years I'd have a bit of an argument with Matt, but I had so much respect for him that I didn't push it. Players were like serfs though; the power lay with the clubs. They had the right to terminate your contract if they felt that you had done anything wrong.

My wages had increased three-fold in the space of six months so I couldn't complain. I had something to spend it on for Noreen and I got married on 25 June 1963. I had proposed to Noreen one night after we had been for a meal with Jim Kennedy, the Celtic player, and his wife when I was at Parkhead. They were teasing, saying that we should get married.

Afterwards, I said to Noreen, 'If I asked you to marry me, what would you say?'

She replied, 'You'll have to ask me first.'

I was trying to cover myself in case she said no. But I knew she was the one for me and I was pretty sure she felt the same. She said that she liked my steely blue eyes, that they were like the actor Paul Newman's! And she liked the fact I played for Celtic. We tied the knot at St Laurence's R.C. church in Drumchapel, over the road from where Noreen had lived before moving to Manchester. We got married on a Tuesday because we didn't think there would be as many people there, but all the local school kids bunked off school and came along. The comedian Billy Connolly was one of them. I got to know Billy in later years and I asked him to speak at the Catholic Sportsmen's Club in Manchester in the late 1970s. When I enquired about his fee, he said that he would appear for nothing on the condition that he could sit beside Matt Busby. Billy was awestruck. I swear he followed Matt to the toilets a few times just so he could be close to him. We had booked Billy a hotel, but he insisted on coming back to my house for a drink. Before he went to sleep, he took his clothes off and left them all over the house. There was a shoe in the kitchen and his trousers on the stairs. He woke Noreen up the next morning by tapping on the bedroom door to ask her to make him breakfast.

In 1984, I was invited to a televised debate in Manchester to discuss the Miners' Strike. I was supporting the miners when I saw a commotion at the studio door. Billy had been performing in Manchester that night and had watched the debate. He was staying over the road from the Granada television studios and came over to join in and back me up. Security wouldn't let him through which is a shame because it would have made great television.

Back at my wedding, he had to jostle with teenagers waving Celtic scarves and middle aged housewives. Scores of police had to try and keep order and hundreds of people rushed over to us as we left the church. One elderly woman stumbled and fell into a flower bed. She wasn't the only one who suffered discomfort as Noreen had toothache throughout the ceremony.

Billy McNeill got married the week before us – footballers had to get married off season. We married at 9 o'clock in the morning and had a function in a hotel on the Great Western Road. Our honeymoon was in Magaluf, Majorca. There were three hotels there in 1963 – a year later there were thirty. We still love Majorca. Noreen thought it was the island of love, beauty and seduction and was mesmerized by it. She has been there every year since.

Back in Manchester, we moved from our lodgings in Sale to a rented house at 1100 Chester Road, Stretford, while we searched for a home which the club would buy for us – and we'd pay rent. Thousands of United fans pass the house on Chester Road on their way to Old Trafford. It's on one of the main thoroughfares into Manchester and even then the traffic was unbearable and this gave us the impetus to find some-where else quickly. I went to see the house in Erlington Avenue, Chorlton, with team-mates Maurice Setters and Noel Cantwell. There was a little room in there with a bar in it. They both said, 'This is the house for you!'

We took that house and paid rent on it for many years. When we came to buy it the club only charged us what they had paid for it, which was good of them. Denis Law lived nearby in leafy Chortonville. The family next door to us, the Kings, were Irish and absolutely crazy United fans. When United played in Barcelona in 1994 and lost 4–0 I bumped into them. They didn't have tickets for the match and yet I saw them sitting near the press box during the game. Then I saw them get thrown out for being sat in the wrong end. Their identity had been uncovered because they were not best pleased after Barça scored.

Things had started to come together for United in 1963/64. Just a few months after looking like slipping out of the First Division, United were back in Europe as worthy representatives of English football for the first time in five years, after winning the FA Cup.

I looked around at my team-mates and weighed them up. You can have twenty lads in the same dressing room and they are not all going to like each other. That's natural – we are work colleagues after all and not lifelong friends – but the press make too big a deal of it. We were close at United but some people liked me, some didn't, and I was fine with that.

There was one lad who everyone liked at United and that was Shay Brennan. There wasn't a nasty bone in his body and he was as soft as anything, despite coming from Wythenshawe which is next to wealthy Hale. He never actually admitted where he was from and used to say 'Hale East' if asked. There is a difference – Wythenshawe was the largest council estate in Europe, Hale is one of the poshest places to live in the north of England.

Shay was the first player not born in Ireland to play for the Republic of Ireland. He played at right-back, had great pace, was very comfortable on the ball and he was a real boy. He loved drinking, smoking, and gambling. You would go in the toilet before a game and see the smoke from his cigarettes wafting above the door. Smoking wasn't that unusual. In fact Matt would come in the changing rooms and hand out cigarettes after games and people like Denis Law, Bobby Charlton, and Shay would take them. Shay, Nobby, and Bobby were the best of pals. They were always together and always taking the mickey out of each other. They would organize card schools, but rarely for money because Matt disapproved of players gambling for cash. So they would usually gamble for a forfeit. If you saw Bobby lugging three cases on an away trip with

Nobby and Shay walking happily alongside him unencumbered then you knew it was because he'd lost at cards.

He was a bright lad, Shay, which went against many people's preconceptions about footballers' lack of intelligence. It really annoys me when people assume that all footballers are thick. I was at a function a couple of years ago when this successful businessman started slagging David Beckham off for just that.

'Do you know David Beckham?' I said.

He didn't.

'So how do you know he's a thick f***er?'

'Because I read the papers.'

'David Beckham might not be a rocket scientist,' I told him, 'but you get a rocket scientist out on the pitch and ask him to pass the ball like Beckham. Beckham is terrific at his job and his life has been a huge success.'

Tony Dunne was a great full-back, one of the most underrated players in England. He was quick as lightning and strong in the air for a small fella. A quiet Dubliner, all he did when he got the ball was pass it to someone who could do something with it like me or Bobby. He played over 500 games for United – not bad for someone who was initially signed as cover for Shay Brennan or Noel Cantwell.

David Sadler had signed as a professional for United in February 1963, the same month as me. At £750 from Maidstone United, where he had a day job in a bank, he was a lot cheaper. He was only 17, mind. David was a well bred southern lad who wore nice clothes and spoke in a posh accent. So much for the perception that Matt only went for tough, scraggy arse kids from poor areas. We weren't used to cultured and refined individuals like David, but I really liked him. He was very well-mannered and the lads used to rip the piss out of him, but he settled in quickly and could hold his own.

David had played for England at amateur level the year before, aged just 16, and was bought as a striker to replace David Herd. He ended up playing as a central defender. David moved into Mrs Fullaway's house in Chorlton with George Best. She was a trusted club landlady and was very helpful to George throughout his time in Manchester. David and George became pals. They had a lot in common because they were both very quiet. David met a girl, Christine, who kept him on the straight and narrow. He could have easily finished up like George and gone out far too often. David would have been a top quality player if he could have been a bit nastier, but that was just not his nature. He was so easy going – and still is – that it would drive me potty sometimes. No matter how much you goaded him he would never lose his temper. He was a skilful, elegant footballer who was good in the air and could use both feet. He did a great job at United and made the England team, winning four caps. I see a lot of him now because we're both on the committee of United's former players' association.

Another player I see quite a lot of is Bill Foulkes. He wasn't the most well-liked player at the club and his nickname 'Mr Popular' was ironic. He could be a selfish player who marked the number nine and saw it as a success if the nine didn't score, regardless of the result. Bill could be a bit arrogant, but forwards hated playing against him because he was a great tackler and would usually win everything in the air.

Another good tackler was Nobby Stiles. He later told me that he felt threatened by my arrival because we played in similar positions and that he thought he was on the road out when I came. He disliked me because of this, but that wasn't my fault. It happens in football. When he got to know me he liked me. Nobby was a bad tempered, cantankerous, moody so and so. And that was with his own team-mates. Nobby never, ever, stopped moaning at me, calling me a bastard for this or that, especially if I made a mistake. Roy Keane was an amateur compared with Nobby. But I loved Nobby devotedly. He was a hard nut on the pitch but off it he was as quiet as a mouse. He was a United fanatic too. We played at Maine Road one year and Nobby wasn't happy that we'd only got a draw so he went mad in the dressing room and started punching the wall. Nobby was a great reader of the game, a really intelligent player. His job was to stop the other team playing and he did that well, protecting Bill Foulkes behind him. I think Bill played for a couple more years than he might have done because Nobby was in front of him.

Football ability apart, Nobby had nothing going for him – he was tiny and couldn't see the other side of a room without contact lenses. We called him Clouseau after the bungling detective played by Peter Sellers in the *Pink Panther* films, because like Inspector Clouseau, Nobby made all the mistakes you could ever make because of his poor eyesight. I once saw him tuck a tablecloth into his trousers rather than a napkin in a posh London hotel. And when he got up to go to the toilet he took half the table with him. The lenses he used were not like the ones we have now. Nobby's looked like gob stoppers and he used to make me feel sick when he put them in before a game.

Following an England v Scotland game in 1965, a banquet was held for both teams at the Savoy hotel. I sat with Nobby because we were United team-mates. Nobby went to the toilet and didn't return for ages so I went to find him. I couldn't see him anywhere and found him back at the table when I returned to my seat.

'Where the f**k have you been?' I asked him.

'Don't tell anybody because I'm so embarrassed,' he said, 'but I've just walked into a wedding reception and sat at the end of the table. I knew it wasn't right because I didn't recognize anybody. Then a man came up and asked me if I was with the bride or the groom.'

When we went to the cinema, we would often toss a coin to decide who paid for the lads to get in. Because Nobby couldn't see, we'd often tell him that head was tails and he'd have to pay us all in.

Nobby ended up winning a European Cup Winner's medal and a World Cup winner's medal. I was delighted by the success that Nobby eventually achieved. I would never support England in any sport, but I wanted the United lads – and especially Nobby – to do well for England. Nobby turned out to be a very important player for his club and country.

I had a great relationship with George Best, who made his United debut in the same year as me. He was very shy and I always thought that he took a drink to give him some confidence. I have spoken earlier about how I realized his incredible ability when I saw him in a youth team match. There was nothing of him and he was really slight, but he went past players easily. He was brave and would fight anybody for the ball. It was difficult to tell what his natural foot was, so accomplished was he with both.

I wouldn't often socialize with George because there was a big age gap. In 1964 I was 25 and married, while George was 18 and single. Our lives were different, but on the Saturday evening after a game, most of the players would eat in an Italian restaurant called Arturo's in Faulkner Street, Manchester. George would pop in with Mike Summerbee, who played for City, for fifteen minutes and then bugger off into town. It was about showing his face with his team-mates. He was a lovely fella who had been brought up well and his drinking was not a problem early on in his career.

A few of the lads fancied themselves as ladies' men, but George was in a different league. If he had been born ugly then he would have played until he was fifty because nobody would have hounded him. Malcolm Wagner was his best pal. He had a hairdressing salon in town but he wasn't a football fan. People criticized George for having a lot of hangers on, but he didn't. He wasn't daft and knocked about with the same people for years. Other people tried to influence George in later years and because he was sensitive, he would run away from his troubles if the press got on his back, rather than face them.

For instance, Phil Hughes, George's agent, came to shake my hand outside Manchester cathedral before a memorial service for George after he had passed away in November 2005. I told him that I wasn't going to shake his hand, and I called him a few names. He looked at me and didn't know what to say. The comedian Stan Boardman was standing close by and said, 'Paddy, how to win friends and influence people.' George was a very simple, straightforward lad and he was easy to take advantage of.

George opened a shop selling clothes near my house and I went along on the first day. It was unbelievable; I had never seen so many young girls in my life. It was as if the Beatles were inside. These were girls who had little interest in football.

There were scenes of hysteria around George whenever we played in London. We would catch a train to Euston and then a coach to a hotel, usually The Russell in Russell Square. In early 1964, Matt decided to change to the Imperial for one game and the Beatles were staying there. Cilla Black was with them. Beatlemania was just kicking in, but Matt didn't have a clue who they were and thought they were Freddie and the Dreamers, a Manchester band whose act was based around the comic antics of the 5ft 3in tall Freddie Garrity, a United fan who was famous for bouncing around the stage with arms

Man and Bhoy. Me in a Celtic training top, August 1961.

Above Street lights for goalposts. Surrounded by kids and with my cousin Charlie Gallagher, another Gorbals lad who also played for Celtic, 1960.

Left A luxury we didn't have at home, Celtic Park, 1962.

Right My Celtic team, 1959. L-R: Fallon, Peacock, Evans (hidden), Crerand, Auld, Tully (in hat), Mackay, Mochan, Smith and McVittie. We were welcoming Italian triallist Santessori (No 3) to Celtic Park.

Left The vanquished heroes. Doing a lap of honour after being thoroughly outclassed by Real Madrid in Glasgow, September 1962.

Above Pitch invader. I'm not sure what I'm doing, but it looks like I'm a specialist dog trainer during Celtic v Aberdeen, 1963.

Left These shoes weren't made for walking. The beautiful Noreen and I on our wedding day, Glasgow, summer 1963.

Left Bobby Charlton and I, 1968.

Below Buenos Aires, 1968, with Bobby standing, Denis Law suffering a practical joke and a callow Brain Kidd sitting at the front.

Above Walking with the boys on the streets of Buenos Aires, 1968. And that's our minder, not Peter Sellers, in the glasses.

Right My first big trophy, the 1963 FA Cup, in which we beat Leicester City in the final. L-R: Dunne, Charlton, Cantwell, me, Quixall, Herd and Giles.

Above Champions, this time in 1967. We parade the trophy after the final game of the season against Stoke City.

Left Even in the 1960s George was thinking about squad rotation.

Left Following the 1958 Munich air disaster, we always flew scheduled, even if it meant eighteen hours travelling and two flight changes…

Above …until we played Gornik Zabrze in Poland in 1968, when a plane was chartered.

Left The wives and girlfriends of the 1960s. L-R: Noreen, Teresa Foulkes, Norma Charlton, Kay Stiles and her sister, Pam Stepney.

Noreen and I in Russell Square, London, the morning after United won the European Cup. I'm feeling a little better...

Right Doctors look at my injury, sustained after the bad-tempered Estudiantes match in 1968. Our daughter Lorraine looks on.

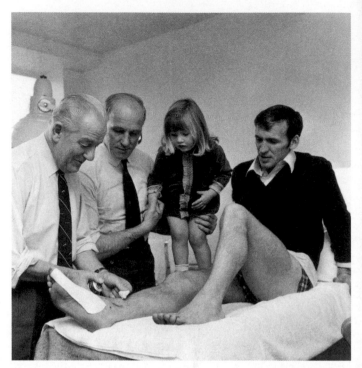

Above Jock Stein, Billy McNeill and I in Scotland blazers before we depart for Warsaw.

and legs flying. Paul McCartney said, very politely: 'Mr Busby, we're The Beatles, we're not Freddie and the Dreamers.' Like most of the players, I was introduced to The Beatles and shook their hands and wished them well. A few years later, it would have been impossible for The Beatles and George Best to have been in the same place, such would have been the hysteria.

George never really brought girls along to see games at Old Trafford. There wasn't a players' lounge at the ground until I had a word with Matt Busby and said that the wives and girl-friends should have somewhere to go. It made no difference to me as Noreen had no interest in football, save for a semi-final or final, but it was equally important for the players to be able to go somewhere after the game while the fans cleared away. An old gym was converted into the players' lounge in 1964.

A free bar was put in there and both teams would use it after the game. One minute we'd be kicking lumps out of the opposition on the field, the next we'd be having a drink with them. The players' bar was an informal arrangement for friends and family, but it became a place to be seen in Mancunian social circles. Because there wasn't really anyone keeping control of who went in, entry went unchecked until Martin Buchan became United captain in the 1970s. He took his role very seriously – too seriously for some – and started to watch carefully who went in the players' lounge. He arranged for tickets to be printed, which he started collecting on the door, sometimes wearing his kit. The other players laughed about this and, to confuse him, Lou Macari printed about 400 counterfeit tickets. He gave them to the type of hangers on whom Martin was trying to exclude. Martin gave up collecting tickets soon after.

One of my team-mates that I ranked very highly was Denis Law. He was a brilliant, brilliant footballer and Matt Busby thought so too. I was in a restaurant with Sir Matt long after he had retired.

'Would you like a scotch, boss?' I said, as he liked Black Label whisky.

'The doctors have told me that I shouldn't drink Black Label,' Matt replied.

'You're eighty, what difference does it make?'

He looked at me with a little glint and said, 'Well, I suppose it doesn't … I'll have one then.'

We sat down and talked football. I asked him who was the best player he ever had at Manchester United. He said: 'I don't like ranking players because I don't like hurting feelings.' Then he paused before saying, 'Denis Law.'

I agreed with him. If you needed a goal Denis would get it for you. He's certainly the best player I ever played with, partly because he was so selfless. If Denis Law was in front of goal with a 95 per cent chance of scoring, and someone was stood in a better position with a 99 per cent chance of scoring he'd pass the ball. He always did the right thing. People didn't realize that he was a dirty, vicious, nasty bastard on the pitch. He had to be because the only way you could stop great players playing was to kick them. He'd kick a player back. He was great in the air, fantastically brave and had a sharp football brain and quick feet.

Denis was great fun as a person. He could be strange at times; a little introverted and was probably the shyest member of the team. He pretended to be outgoing, but I think that was only to hide his shyness in social situations. I hadn't always had such a glowing opinion of Denis. The first time I saw him play I thought he was the most arrogant person I had ever seen on a football field. He didn't just act as if it was his ball; he acted as if it was his stadium. When somebody took the ball from him he glared at them as if they had a cheek. And even when he scored a goal he made you wonder if anyone had ever scored a goal before.

Then, when we were both chosen for a Scottish Under-23 international, I met him for the first time. We got on well and became friends. By the time I joined United he often used to pop round mine for a cup of tea. Drinking my tea meant that he had to buy less of his own.

Maurice Setters always thought that he was Alfredo Di Stefano. When I first came to the club he was a central defender alongside Bill Foulkes and he was great at it – but he always thought he could come into the midfield and play like Di Stefano. He couldn't. Matt and I used to have arguments with him all the time and ask him what he was doing. He was very good to me when I first came to Manchester. He was best man at Bobby Charlton's wedding and became big pals with Jackie Charlton, that's why he became assistant manager of Ireland under Jackie. He was a rum character Maurice, a George Best type figure before George's off the field profile became famous. Maurice was into wine, women, and song – three attributes that don't necessarily go with being a top level professional. You would never describe him as good-looking, but he was full of charm. He would occasionally call me on a Sunday afternoon after he had finished playing, drunk and keen to reminisce.

Fans or the press don't know who the characters are. One of the best characters in football, for example, is Kenny Dalglish. His sense of humour is fantastic. He goes on television and takes the rise out of people and they don't realize he is doing it.

Harry Gregg was a serious character, but I loved him devotedly. He was a tremendous goalkeeper, especially when you consider that he played for years with a damaged right shoulder. Time and time again he dislocated his shoulder until the surgeons decided the only way they could fix it properly would be to put steel pins through the bone. The operation was a success, but for years Harry was unable to raise his arm much above his head. People saw him as indestructible, but he often played in tremendous pain. He lived around the corner from me and used to bring his family round. They were like the Von Trapps from the *Sound of Music*, forever playing various musical instruments. He wasn't a big drinker, but he loved to sing. I've never heard anyone play the guitar and sing 'Danny Boy' like Harry Gregg. He is a Protestant, but his favourite goalkeeper was John Thompson at Celtic, who died after receiving a kick on the head after a collision with Rangers' Sam English in 1931. We spoke about the situation in the north of Ireland all the time. I would take the side of the republicans because, in my eyes, they were the ones suffering the most abuse from the British in their own country. Despite the sensitive nature of the topic, it would always be a sensible discussion and George Best, who was bright as a pin, would join in. We couldn't afford to fall out over politics, but we found common cause because not just the Catholic, but also the Protestant working classes were suffering at the hands of the British government and our conversations went on for hours. We talked about the prospect of a United Ireland team and then worked out which players would be in it.

Harry got called up to play for Northern Ireland in the 1958 World Cup finals in Sweden a few months after Munich. It wasn't just his fitness and amazing reflexes which made Harry a great keeper, however. He read the game so well he could anticipate what most players were going to do with the ball, and when it came to tactics his views were always worth listening to. This made him unusual as the goalkeepers I had come across before had very little idea about the tactical side of the game.

Bobby Charlton was great to play with. We were completely different characters. He was quiet, I wasn't. People did and still do consider him dour. He could be, but the public image of Bobby is not the real him. He's not an outgoing man, but he's a nice fella who loves United as much as any fan. He's great for the club and an accomplished ambassador.

Bobby is only comfortable with certain people. When you saw him with his mates like Shay and Nobby he was a totally different person: funny and happy go lucky. He was a practical joker who used to come into training and start raving about a film he had seen the night before. He would build it up so much that you couldn't wait to get to the cinema quick enough. So I'd take Noreen along and before long she would tell me that she was unimpressed. And soon you realized that it was one of the worst films that you had ever seen. The next morning, Bobby would be grinning from ear to ear. He knew that the film was awful, but wanted to rope others into seeing it to share his punishment. Bobby was easy to get back – all you had to do was deprive him of a cream cake. Other players wouldn't eat them in case they put on weight, but Bobby loved them.

Bobby was an honest player and football was his life. We used to meet on a Saturday morning and he was like a cat with two tails looking forward to the match. When he had the ball in the pre-match warm up he was like a kid with a new toy. He was a great player, but he never got over the thrill of having the ball at his feet.

Bobby and I had a good understanding in midfield which came naturally. He was an easy player to play with. When I had the ball, I hardly needed to look up to see where he was because if I held it long enough for him to take up position I knew where he would be. Bobby was an artist of a player and looked like a ballerina compared with a clogger like me. Other players could do the same things with a ball as Bobby, but he always looked twice as good when he did them.

We did have problems because we played close to each other and we both wanted the ball all the time. Such was our desire to get the ball, we almost fought. We never did and two team-mates fighting would have looked ridiculous, but we'd scowl and have our own little battle for midfield domination. Matt knew what was going on but didn't say anything; he liked the ultra competitive edge that came from having two players like Bobby and I in the centre of his team. When I first came to the club, I would give the ball to Bobby rather than make a pass myself, maybe because he was a stronger personality than me. Other players tried to hide if things were not going well, but Bobby always shouldered responsibility. Harry Gregg said that Bobby changed a lot after the Munich air crash, that his game wasn't quite the same. When eight of your pals die like that, I'm sure it would change you.

Noel Cantwell was our captain. A big handsome Irishman, he could charm the birds out of the trees. He was from Cork and I think he nicked the Blarney stone before he came over to Manchester. Ladies loved Noel. A neighbour of mine once held a party and Noel was invited with his wife Maggie. Miss Great Britain for 1967, Jennifer Lowe, was there too. She was absolutely stunning and both George Best and Manchester City's Mike Summerbee were admiring her. It was Noel who she was dancing with though, which would have been fine if he wasn't married and his wife wasn't in the next room. Maggie was not pleased at what she saw and picked up an ice bucket. She charged into the room where her husband was dancing with Miss UK and threw the ice and water over him.

'I think you had better cool down,' she said calmly, before walking back into the kitchen. Noel stood there drenched not knowing what to do, while Jennifer realized it wasn't a good idea to be dancing with someone else's husband.

Men liked Noel because he was a very intelligent fella, who was seen as being a successor to Matt by some.

One player who wouldn't be featuring much was Albert Quixall. He was a great player at Sheffield Wednesday, the golden boy of football who was capped by England at twenty. He was Matt's first big signing after Munich for a record £45,000 fee. He'd scored in almost every round of the cup in 1963, but was dropped more and more the following season. The papers said that he was too nervous, but we didn't realize that he had a mental breakdown at Old Trafford. He used to come out in big red blotches before games and was very agitated. Some players handled the pressure of being a Manchester United player better than others. New signings could come to Old Trafford and wither under the pressure of the media spotlight, which was intense even in the 1960s. Sadly Albert was one of them who didn't handle it well.

Another player that didn't feature for long was Johnny Giles. After we were well-beaten in the 1963 Charity Shield by Everton, four of the FA Cup winning team – David Herd, David Gaskell, Quixall, and Giles were dropped for the first away game of the season against Sheffield Wednesday. I was surprised. Johnny Giles wouldn't play for United again.

There were issues between him and Matt before I joined the club, with Johnny always one to speak his mind. That grated on Matt, but I still don't think he should have sold him because he was a tremendous player. When it became clear that Giles might be leaving, Don Revie called me from Leeds and asked me what I thought about his ability. I said he was a very intelligent footballer and a great passer of the ball. Giles moved to Leeds, where he got better and better and was a key man in their successful sides. I think he learned a few things about attitude and competitiveness from Bobby Collins who had been one of Celtic's best midfielders for a decade before I arrived at Parkhead. Matt later said that selling Johnny Giles was his greatest mistake. I agree with him.

Such was the quality of players at United, we did well in 1963/64 without Johnny. Scoring goals was not a problem for us: as well as Denis, Bobby and an emerging George Best, we had David Herd, who got 27 in 1963/64. I'd played with him for Scotland and he was a nice lad. David was one of Sir Matt Busby's most accomplished signings. A centre-forward who was born close to Matt in Lanarkshire, and a proven goal-scorer at Arsenal, David joined us in 1961 for £37,000. In seven seasons at Old Trafford, Herd scored 144 goals in 263 games, including two in the 1963 FA Cup Final victory over Leicester. He also scored on his United debuts in the FA Cup, League Cup, and all three European competitions.

Before he went to Arsenal, Herd played for Stockport County where he became the first player in league history to play in the same team as his dad. Father Alec had starred for Manchester City. Whilst still at United, Herd bought a garage in Davyhulme, five miles from Old Trafford. Can you imagine Wayne Rooney buying a garage now?

Phil Chisnall was a local lad from Stretford who played almost thirty games in 1963/64. He had played in United's youth team with Nobby Stiles, before breaking into the first team at aged nineteen. Then he lost his place in the side and Bill Shankly made an offer for him to go to Liverpool, just in time for them to win the league. He remains the last player to be transferred between the two clubs.

When the season started, we scored five against Everton in August and seven away at Ipswich three days later. We had a few heavy defeats that season, though. Everton took revenge and beat us 4–0 away and Burnley put six past us a week later.

I got sent off in that game. I couldn't get a player called Ian Towers off my back, so I swung at him and was deservedly dismissed. I was in the players' room at the end of the game when this girl came up to me and starting calling the referee every name under the sun. Then the referee walked in and she shouted, 'You bastard for sending him off!' The referee was stunned. I found out later it was his girlfriend. He didn't include my sending off in his report and I got away with it.

Just to confuse our fans even more, we played Burnley two days later in the league at Old Trafford and beat them 5–1. The difference? George Best, who had not really figured since making his first team debut in September. He had been allowed home to Belfast for Christmas, but was recalled and came over on the next plane. George was like a matchstick and we wanted to protect him, but he was sensational against Burnley, who were a good side. They had won the league three years earlier and finished third the season before. George absolutely blitzed John Angus, who was a good player. That's when people really started to take notice of him. George stayed in the side on the right or left wing for the rest of the season. I wasn't surprised how good he was because I'd seen him taking the mickey out of proven internationals in training.

George introduced shampoo into the dressing room. I used to wash my hair with red carbolic soap like everyone else. Suddenly we had this lad with a hair dryer and I was thinking, 'What is all that about?' He dressed well too – before his dress sense turned loud and outrageous.

Reuben Kaye was a Manchester accountant whose family was – and still are – mad United fans. I met him on a train back from Ipswich after we had played there in 1963. He was severely wounded in Monte Cassino in Italy during the war, but while he was physically handicapped, his brain was very sharp. He became an accountant for me and many of the first team players. If it wasn't for his advice most of us would have ended up completely skint. We all owed him a lot.

United did well in the European Cup Winners' Cup in 1963/64, beating Dutch side Willem II Tilberg 7–2 over two legs. Willem II were only a second division side in Holland and we could only draw 1–1 in the first leg. It could have been worse as David Herd was sent off for a foul and they nearly grabbed a late winner. Rusty, that's what we were in Europe. We were determined to get it right in the second leg. We knew that we were far better players than them and we destroyed them 6–1 at Old Trafford, including three goals in four minutes in the second half.

We drew Tottenham in the next round and we knew that wasn't going to be easy. They were in the competition as holders. Our first and second choice goalkeepers were injured so we travelled to White Hart Lane with our third choice keeper, a big ginger haired Ulsterman called Ronnie Briggs. He had let in six in his first United game at Leicester. He was never really good enough to play for Manchester United and I think he knew it because he was shaking in the dressing room before the game, absolutely terrified. He was visibly falling apart. The kick-off was 7.30 pm. We went onto the pitch at 7.20 pm and it was a beautiful night. Within five minutes you couldn't see your hand in front of you for fog and the game was abandoned. David Gaskell, our second choice keeper, made it back for the re-arranged game. We held out for sixty-seven minutes until Spurs scored through Dave Mackay. With four minutes to go they got another after Tony Dunne made a rare error by passing weakly towards Gaskell. Terry Dyson picked up the ball and Spurs won 2–0. Spurs thought they were going through, especially when they found out that we would be without Nobby Stiles and Denis Law for the second leg, but we were up for it at home again.

Herd put us one up straightaway but then Spurs got unlucky. They lost Mackay after eight minutes when he was stretchered off after colliding with Noel Cantwell and that meant they had to play with ten men. They played well and we didn't get a second goal until ten minutes into the second half, again from Herd. Yet Spurs came back at us, with Greaves making it 2–1 on the night. They were playing superbly but they couldn't deal with Bobby Charlton scoring two belters in the last fifteen minutes. His second, the one which won the tie, came three minutes from time.

Sporting Lisbon were our opponents in the quarter-finals. We beat them 4–1 in the first leg, with Denis Law scoring two penalties to record a hat-trick. We really fancied our chances of reaching the semi-finals as confidence was so high on the field.

We were pushing Liverpool for the league and doing well in both cup competitions, yet off the field there were problems. We were going for a treble, but all wasn't well and there were grumblings about money. We would get crowd bonuses, a certain amount for a crowd over 30,000, 40,000 and so on. But the players never really trusted the crowd figures given by the club and felt that the club reported lower numbers to avoid paying out. Gates were sometimes given out at thirty-odd thousand when the ground looked full. I was the union man at Old Trafford having taken over from Noel Cantwell and I used to argue and argue with the players' union about television money. Some players didn't want to get involved and that was fine, but I felt aggrieved. Manchester United would invariably be on *Match of the Day* and the players received next to nothing for it. We didn't get any bonuses for winning cup matches and a group of us went to complain to Matt. He saw our point and a new system was agreed where wins in cup matches were taken into account. It would kick in for the two big cup games that were approaching: West Ham in the semi-final of the FA Cup on 14 March and Sporting Lisbon in the second leg of the European Cup Winners' Cup quarter-final.

I passed my driving test in 1964 – the day that we drew West Ham in the cup. It had been hard reaching that stage. We needed three games to get past Sunderland in the quarter-finals, finally winning easily enough in the second replay at Huddersfield when Denis Law got a hat-trick. After that game we thought we had as good as retained the FA Cup. The three other teams left in the competition were Swansea, Preston, and West Ham. West Ham, with players like Bobby Moore, were the strongest, but not many people fancied them to beat us.

With the new win bonus in place, we travelled to Hillsborough to face West Ham in the semi-final with considerable optimism, as the week before we'd beaten them in the league away 2–0, a game which saw me play as United captain for the one and only time. I was a good talker, but I wasn't captain material. Noel Cantwell or Bobby Charlton led by example and unlike me, they weren't bad tempered.

The pitch was poor in that semi-final tie because of heavy rain. I offered my opinion to the referee before the game and he said, 'It's the same for both teams.' I told him that was nonsense and said, 'If there was a cart horse and a race horse and they had a race, the cart horse would win because of the surface.' Traditionally, referees test a ground by bouncing a ball to find out if the pitch is 'dead'. That afternoon when the referee dropped the ball down it didn't come up again but stuck in the mud. Yet he still claimed that the ground was playable. So we went out and played in the worst conditions I have experienced. I'm convinced that we would have beaten West Ham any other day, but on a mud heap like that the great players in our team had no chance to use their ability. We lost 3–1 and I was sick after that defeat, but it gave West Ham a real breakthrough. They went on to beat Preston 3–2 in the final at Wembley, which earned them a place in the Cup Winners' Cup. They won that trophy the following year, beating TSV Munich at Wembley.

Although out of the FA Cup, we still had a huge game against Sporting Lisbon in the Cup Winners' Cup. But they beat us 5–0. Even though we had won the first leg 4–1 at Old Trafford, we went out of Europe 6–4 on aggregate. A scoreline of 14–4 would have been fairer. Matt's philosophy away in Europe was usually to keep it tight at the back for the first twenty minutes until the crowd had gone quiet. Yet our goalkeeper David Gaskell had a nightmare; Silva and Geo in the Sporting attack were fine, fine players and Nobby and me just couldn't get hold of them.

Matt was furious after that match. As I've said before, he was renowned for his dignity and keeping a cool head. He was usually graceful in defeat, no matter how disappointed he was. He always seemed to keep his temper, but after the defeat in Lisbon he ranted and raged at us after throwing away a lead which should have been big enough to have seen us through to the semi-finals. I can't say that I blamed him. Success in Europe was special to Matt after what happened at Munich and we'd just been beaten 5–0. He said that our performance was an insult to the people of Manchester and that we had let ourselves and him down badly. To make matters worse a few of us went out after the defeat, probably thinking that we could drown our sorrows. About five or six came back to the hotel late and we were told that we would be fined for missing our curfew.

United were a little naïve in Europe that season. We didn't fully appreciate the way continental teams varied their tactics and style over two legs. When they travelled away they sometimes didn't offer much resistance and simply concentrated on keeping the score down. Sporting Lisbon were like that. We had so many chances at Old Trafford we could have scored eight, so we had a real surprise in Portugal when they went for all out attack. We were two down before we knew what had hit us and we never looked liked pulling anything back.

We still had the championship to play for and flew from Lisbon to London for a game against Tottenham. We played really well and beat Spurs 3–2. That night we went to the House of Commons for a meal. We were the first British football team to be invited there, by a Manchester MP. I loved that because of my interest in politics, being at the seat of power where people make decisions about your life.

Matt enjoyed the night and told us that he would forget about the fines he had been threatening in Lisbon. He actually apologized for losing his temper, which says a great deal about Matt Busby's character and his stature. But there was no need to apologize because we deserved every word of his criticism. After the performance in Lisbon we deserved to be shouted at.

Beating Spurs kept us in contention for the title but then we drew three games in succession. Liverpool edged in front of us and, after they beat us 3–0 at Anfield in April, all but confirmed themselves as league winners. We finished runners-up, four points behind them at the end. One moment we were chasing glory in three competitions and the next we were out of the lot.

Finishing 1963/64 without a trophy was a shattering experience, but after getting over the initial disappointment, we knew deep down that something was stirring at Old Trafford, that we were getting better season after season. Bill Foulkes and I made fifty-four appearances after missing just one game each, more than anyone else at the club, but Denis Law was the main man. He scored an incredible forty-six goals. There was an increasing consistency to United, but that meant nothing if we weren't winning trophies.

Noreen and I did have reason to be happy though, because our first child, Patrick, was born on 15 April 1964. I was amazed when I first saw him. I just looked down and there was this little fella with a big nose. Everyone who has a baby thinks that their baby is beautiful, but every new baby is ugly and I told Noreen that. She went off her head, which I can understand given what she had just been through. Having a kid quietened me down. Well, a bit.

Noreen and I spent a lot of time in Glasgow during the close season of 1964 so that the family could see Patrick. I can remember one day vividly. I had been at the Odeon cinema and when I came out I spotted a newspaper bill with the words, 'John White Sensation.' I bought the paper thinking that it was some transfer or other. Then I read how John, the great Tottenham and Scotland striker, had been killed after being struck by lightning on Crews Hill golf course near his north London home in Enfield, aged just twenty-four.

I don't think any newspaper headline has ever stunned me so much. The lightning missed his golf trolley but struck a ring on his finger as he was sheltering under a tree. John was a key player in the great Spurs side that won the double in 1960/61. What made it harder for me to take was that not long before he died, Noreen and I had spent a wonderful holiday with John and his wife in Jersey. I really liked him, he was a great joker and marvellous fun.

Back in Manchester, finishing runners-up in the league meant that we stayed in Europe for the 1964/65 season with a place in the Inter Cities Fairs' Cup, the forerunner to the UEFA Cup. Matt signed John Connelly, a winger from Burnley, who had won the league at Turf Moor. He made a difference to us and was absolutely fantastic throughout, a great player who scored fifteen league goals in that first season. It was sad that John's career didn't continue as it should have done. He was good enough to play the first game for England in the 1966 World Cup, and he was a great, great player for Manchester United in 1964/65.

John Aston made his debut in the 1964/65 season. A Manchester lad whose father had played in the 1948 FA Cup Final for United, John Junior became probably the most underrated player in my time at Old Trafford. He was great company, and had a dry sense of humour. It was difficult for him because he was an attacker playing in a team with Law, Best, and Charlton – and fans expected him to be as good as those three. Invariably, supporters barracked him when he wasn't. They should have been kinder to him, especially as he had come through the ranks like his father. John would have been the first to admit that he wasn't as good as those players, but few were, and he ran himself into the ground for Manchester United.

We also had a new goalkeeper in Pat Dunne and he did well that season, with the defence tighter than in the previous year and the attack scoring plenty. Denis Law scored twenty-eight in the league, David Herd got another twenty while George Best and Bobby Charlton got ten each.

Our first opponents in Europe were Djurgaarden of Stockholm. We were about to lose that game 1–0 until David Herd equalized three minutes from time. We battered the Swedes 6–1 at Old Trafford in the second leg, with Denis Law getting yet another hat-trick and United scoring four in ten minutes in the second half.

We also won our next game in Europe 6–1, beating Borussia Dortmund in Germany. The Germans were no pushover – they had reached the semi-final of the European Cup the previous season. We played so well that night that the Dortmund fans ran onto the pitch to applaud us. Bobby scored three – I think he wanted to prove a point to Alf Ramsey who had dropped him from the England team – but George Best was man of the match. We beat them 4–0 at home in the second leg making it 10–1 on aggregate, before drawing Everton in the next round. We drew 1–1 in the first leg in Manchester and they probably fancied their chances against us at Goodison. Their European ambitions were to end though as United won 2–1. That game was played at the start of February, yet the next round, against Racing Strasbourg of France, was not due to be played until mid-May! And that was only the quarter-finals. So attention switched to the league and the FA Cup semi-final.

The 1964/65 season saw some interesting off the field events. We met the Duke of Edinburgh at an official function in the Midland hotel in Manchester. The other lads were asking him about polo and horses and stuff. But I said to him, 'I believe you were in Derry during the war?'

'As a matter of fact I was,' he replied.

'Aye, I thought so,' I said. 'I believe you used to go into Donegal. I know a couple of people you knocked around with.'

He just laughed it off. Kitty Kelly, the American author of exhaustive and highly unflattering biographies of Frank Sinatra, Jackie Onassis, and the British royal family, once rang me about that story. She was hugely famous and I didn't believe that it was her on the phone so I told her where to go. She convinced me that it really was Kitty Kelley and I started to believe her and answered her questions. She promised to send me the book she was writing but never did.

The cross-Pennine rivalry with Leeds really exploded in the spring of 1965, when United reached their fourth consecutive FA Cup semi-final. Leeds, now in Real Madrid-inspired all white, were, like ourselves, battling for success in the League and Cup. Don Revie's side had come up from the Second Division and were really starting to make a name for themselves. In front of 65,000 at Hillsborough, Jack Charlton and Denis Law wrestled like two schoolboys in a playground as players swapped punches and did neither side credit. I was in the middle as usual, scrapping with Billy Bremner or any other Leeds player who wanted a fight. Bremner was a great player, but you often find that someone who is small with red hair and from Scotland has a point to prove in life and are usually aggressive. Billy was and did. I got on great with him off the field and he was a fanatical Celtic supporter which people didn't know, but we often lost our heads with each other on the pitch.

The game finished 0–0, with the referee, both managers and players all being criticized for their conduct. I always felt that there was a great deal of jealousy from Leeds players towards Manchester United. They had a great side that often beat us so there was no need to be jealous, but I believe they felt that they were playing for the inferior club. Leeds were a dirty, cheating side when they didn't need to be because they had the talent to win trophies without stooping to rolling about all over the pitch.

The replay was in Nottingham four days later, and there were fists raised on the pitch again. Rival fans followed suit, with one running on the pitch and knocking the referee to the ground, and there were disturbances on the terraces. The police later confirmed that fans were thrown into the River Trent. Leeds won the tie 1–0 with a last minute goal, a header from Billy Bremner which was set up by Johnny Giles.

We were to get revenge, big time. Our league form in 1964/65 was the best since I had arrived at the club. I had been dropped for the first two games of the season, which we drew and lost, but Matt quickly recalled me and United were soon motoring, winning thirteen, drawing one, and not losing a game between mid-September and the end of November.

We hammered Aston Villa 7–0 at Old Trafford and beat Tottenham 4–1, a game I'll remember because I scored twice. The run only came to an end when league leaders Leeds beat us 1–0 at Old Trafford.

By late April 1965, and the return game at Elland Road, we were on a run of seven straight league wins and only three points behind Leeds – it was two points for a win then. Elland Road was packed with over 52,000 an hour before the game. Such a game would be designated all-ticket today, but fans could pay at the gate and thousands were locked out. Just before kick-off, I was told that someone wanted to see me at the front door. I went down and an old friend from Glasgow called Eddie Duffy was there. He didn't have a penny in his pocket so God alone knows how he'd got down from Glasgow. I smuggled him into the ground and he watched the match sitting on the bench next to the United trainer Jack Crompton.

It was a windy day and a tough match, with tackles flying that would have left only six men on the pitch if it had been played these days. We beat them 1–0 with a goal from Connelly. Bobby Collins was playing for Leeds and he was a dirty little sod. He went over the top to tackle Connelly but John went higher. Bobby got carried off.

We played at Birmingham on the Monday and beat them 4–2. Leeds played Sheffield Wednesday and lost, so we were a point ahead. We beat Liverpool 3–0 the following week and Arsenal 3–1 two days later on a Monday night. Denis Law scored twice, but he should never have played because he had a terrible gash on his leg.

Leeds could only draw at relegated Birmingham so we were champions – unless Leeds could win their last game 20–0. There wasn't much happening in Manchester on a Monday night, so all the players came back to mine in Chorlton for a party after the game.

United finished the season on the same points as Leeds because Aston Villa beat us 2–1 in the final game of the season. We might have lost, but Bobby Charlton scored one of the greatest goals I've seen in my life after beating five players. We'd won the league on goal difference – that really annoyed Leeds.

We were also still in Europe, in the quarter-finals. We travelled to Strasbourg in France and beat them 5–0. The 0–0 at home in the second leg was disappointing, but we were feeling the effects of a long season – Nobby Stiles played sixty-six games in 1964/65.

I enjoyed the European trips but I never really grasped the fact that people could speak English outside of Britain and Ireland. We would be having breakfast at a posh hotel in a cosmopolitan city and I would ask for butter by getting the waiter over and pretending to spread butter with a non-existent knife on an imaginary piece of bread. Invariably, the waiter would look at me as if I had no brain and say, in perfect English. 'Would you like some butter, Sir?'

United were drawn with the Hungarian side Ferencvaros in the semi-final. We played them at home in the first leg and they were easily the best team we'd played in Europe that season. Florian Albert was their forward and he had a real battle with Bill Foulkes. Yet despite winning the league we had produced some of our best football in Europe – and we played well against Ferencvaros. We were winning 3–1 and doing fine until Pat Dunne misjudged a long lob and it bounced over his head into the net. With a 3–2 lead, we knew it would be difficult in Budapest.

We had a nightmare getting over there, delayed in London by a strike and then another hold-up in Brussels. I wasn't in the best of moods then, but I can't blame that for me being sent off for fighting with their player Orosz, who was sent off, too.

They beat us 1–0 but with away goals not counting double then, we had to play a third game with the venue being decided by the toss of a coin. The Hungarians won and we had to fly back to Manchester before returning to Budapest ten days later. It was now 16 June, well past the usual end of season for us. The Hungarians were well up for it and 75,000 watched the game. We didn't disgrace ourselves, but couldn't score. They could and went 2–0 up, before we started to create chances of our own and got a goal from John Connelly, which wasn't enough to stop us going out. Ferencvaros played Juventus in the final in Turin, a special one-legged game because the season had overrun. They probably played that in mid-August.

By then, as champions of England for the first time since Munich, we'd be thinking about our next challenge – to win the greatest trophy of all, the European Cup.

SIX

Best Team in England

The Manchester United of 1965 was the best team I've ever played in. Matt and his assistant Jimmy Murphy had bought very well when they signed the quick winger John Connelly from Burnley for £60,000 in April 1964. In doing so, Matt effectively completed his third great United side following the 1948 FA Cup winners and the Busby Babes who were decimated at Munich. While Connelly was expensive, United had benefited from nurturing young talent, too. We had won the FA Youth Cup for the first time since the Busby Babes in 1964 with a promising team that included youngsters like goalkeeper Jimmy Rimmer, defenders David Sadler and Bobby Noble, plus attackers Willie Anderson, and George Best, who, like Ryan Giggs twenty-eight years later, was a first-teamer inspiring his peers to success. Of the United team that would draw 2–2 with Liverpool in December 1966, six were home-grown talents under the age of 20. In fact only four players had cost United anything: myself, Tony Dunne, David Herd, and Alex Stepney.

At the start of the 1965/66 season we considered Liverpool our greatest domestic rivals. We drew with them in the

104

Charity Shield at Old Trafford in a game that saw the new cantilever stand opened ahead of the World Cup finals. That stand provided the template for the development of Old Trafford over the next four decades and that was down to the vision of the chairman Louis Edwards. While clubs like Manchester City, Leeds, and Liverpool built stands which looked completely different to the ones next to them or bolted benches onto old terraces, United had sleek cantilever stands which joined up and this was Edwards' idea. Each of the stands had standing paddocks by the side of the pitch, so we had our noisiest fans right by us. Edwards' vision took almost thirty years to complete, finished when the Stretford End was finally rebuilt and the stadium became virtually all-seater in 1993, but long before then Old Trafford was the finest stadium in Britain.

Matt and Bill Shankly, the Liverpool manager, had a great mutual respect. They came from the same environment, from mining stock in the west of Scotland, and had triumphed in England at the biggest clubs. We knew all the Liverpool players very well and Ian St John, a superb footballer, was a great friend of mine. He frequently travelled over from Liverpool to stay at ours in Manchester and we'd socialize together.

Bill Shankly was such an interesting man to talk to. I got to know him because he would drive me mad before games, talking about football. Manchester United would be about to play Liverpool and he would collar you close to the dressing rooms at Anfield or Old Trafford to pick your brain. Can you imagine Jose Mourinho having a word with Gary Neville before a game now? Bill would never ask about the game ahead – that would be off limits – but about other aspects of football, such as which players would move clubs in the close season. He was always wanting to increase his knowledge of football, that's all we spoke about. There were no airs or graces about him. He was obsessed by detail and used to ring me at 9 o'clock on a Sunday morning, without fail, throughout the 1960s. I would be about to go to Mass, but I couldn't get him off the phone. He would grill me about the team we had played the day before, wanting information about formations and how well each man had performed.

He rang one morning when I had already left for church, so he spoke to Noreen instead. She knows nothing about football, so I was surprised a few weeks later when he said that my wife knew football inside out. She told me that she said two words in the entire conversation – 'yes' and 'no'. She must have said them at the right time because he was impressed.

Match day at Old Trafford in the mid-1960s followed a set pattern. Before the game, players would drive to Old Trafford around 11.30 am, from where a coach would take us to Davyhulme golf course, about five miles away. We'd have our pre-match meal there – I'd have poached egg on toast, followed by a cup of tea. George would have Welsh rarebit with fried eggs. Most others would have a steak, which would take about five hours to digest. We'd been brought up during the war and thought that a steak was just about the best thing you could eat to make you big and strong, so eat them we did. There were no dieticians at United like there are now to tell us what we should be eating.

This was before the members of Davyhulme got the needle with us and stopped United using their club in this way. Golf clubs would pay for the association with United these days and free memberships would be thrown in for the players, but Davyhulme's members decided that they didn't want the United players in their clubhouse before matches. It was a shame, because I had become used to the pattern of a home match day. After eating at Davyhulme, we'd drive through

Trafford Park on the coach back to Old Trafford at about 1.30 pm. The fans recognized the bus and would clap us along the way, which helped us get up for the game.

Matt would be sensible in his pre-match talks. He'd say, 'Don't give the ball away.' It might surprise people, but he was very defensive minded. We could win 4–0 and he would be happier with the fact that we'd not conceded a goal rather than that we had scored four. He didn't like fancy defenders, he just wanted the ball to be cleared and for the football to be played well away from the 18-yard line.

Matt encouraged me to try passes which hurt the opposition, ones which troubled defenders and led to a goal. There was a greater risk in making them and the crowd could get on my back if they didn't come off, but Matt always wanted me to try adventurous passes, rather than just playing a short ball which didn't trouble anybody.

He was a great believer in 4–4–2, with central midfielders who could pass the ball and with the two wingers being the first line of defence. George Best and John Aston played on the wings for United throughout much of the second half of the 1960s. It must have been heaven for the United full-backs to have had those two playing in front of them, because they worked their backsides off defensively, much like Beckham and Giggs in later years. It's an exciting way to play – the minute you break, you have two wingers flying down the line and two strikers ahead of them.

Assistant manager Jimmy Murphy was a more aggressive foil for Matt. He would say, 'F***ing sort so and so out, Pat.' He would scout a lot and give us detailed information about the opposition, but the focus was always more on United's strengths. Jimmy was a nightmare on post-season tours, which were looked on as a holiday by the players. We'd go away for as long as six weeks at a time and saw the world.

Jimmy loved a drink, a sing-song, and to play the piano. Everybody adored him, but nobody wanted to be in a room either side of Jimmy because he'd pull you in late at night for a last drink. 'Come and have a chat,' he'd say, before talking about his life and football until three or four in the morning. He was an interesting man who would tell us about what he'd done in the war, where he'd met Matt. He loved United and was great with the younger players.

Before kick-off, a few players would take a nip of whisky to help with their breathing. It was considered medicinal. The whisky was kept in the hamper which contained the strips. I couldn't stomach the stuff, but other players drank it through routine. Bobby Charlton swore by it. Harry Gregg, who wasn't a drinker, always took a sip. We'd do a few stretches in the dressing room and walk out on the pitch five minutes before the game. There was no warm up on the pitch.

The Old Trafford atmosphere was loud. It was a pure buzz that cocaine or Marilyn Monroe couldn't compete with – not that I've experienced either. It was the noise that hit you. It invaded your senses and gave you a huge lift. You would run out and the whole ground would be making a din. The Stretford End was the noisiest, maybe because it was predominantly standing and covered, but there was standing on all four sides of Old Trafford and you wouldn't even notice away fans. Songs would usually radiate out of the centre of the Stretford End, either side of the tunnel. The fans would sing songs to lift each of the players. For me, they sang: *'Paddy, Paddy Crerand, Paddy Crerand in midfield.'* When I'd finished playing, they later adapted it for Willie Morgan, changing the words to 'Willie Morgan on the wing.' I didn't really watch the crowd during the game, but for a minute or two before it I would glance up and see the densely packed Stretford End swaying from side to side from the sheer weight of people.

I can understand why seats were introduced to football grounds after the Hillsborough disaster, but they affected the atmosphere badly. The ground would be full, the turnstiles locked an hour before kick-off. I'm surprised that there weren't accidents on the terraces, but as a player the noise inspired you. I didn't even realize that there were 2,000 seats at the back of the Stretford End until after I had finished playing.

George Best was the most popular player with the fans, but Denis Law was the King of the Stretford End. George and Denis would applaud the crowd who sang their names and we'd offer each other encouragement. We were always confident and most teams went away from Old Trafford defeated.

Once the game got under way, it was always important for me to have a good first touch. If I had a good first touch then I'd have a good game. There was no logic to that, but it was psychological and my first pass would always be a simple one rather than a daring cross field ball.

Matt would never discuss a game immediately afterwards. He'd wait until the Monday until everyone had cooled down, so that he didn't say things in the heat of the moment.

Players were different. Nobby and I could swear at each other in the changing room, but our words would be forgotten as soon as we left. Others players were more sensitive and wouldn't speak to you for weeks if you had a go. People react differently to criticism. Bobby Charlton could go quiet for long periods if you had a go. I didn't take Bobby's actions personally, that was Bobby's way. Denis Law would get angry if you slated him, but he'd use that to motivate himself to do better and prove you wrong. David Herd would take criticism so personally that I never gave him any.

Denis Law could be very hard on David Herd. Denis was a world class player and he thought that every pass should be perfect. I told him that he had to be a bit lenient and Denis couldn't fathom it. But when David was out of the side for a few games, Denis began to miss him and he realized the truth of what I had said. David Herd wasn't in Denis's class, but he consistently scored twenty goals a season for Manchester United and was well worth his place in a great team.

Yet despite the quality in our side and despite us being champions, we started poorly, in 1965/66 winning just one of our first five league games. Burnley gave us the run-around and beat us 3–0 at Turf Moor in September. That day also saw the first signs of hooliganism, with rival fans fighting inside and outside the ground. Burnley was only thirty miles from Manchester. It was a tough East Lancashire mill town and despite having a population of just 90,000, consistently produced good teams. Burnley had been champions in 1960, but their fans didn't take too kindly to Manchester United buying their best players like John Connelly. I'd seen trouble following Celtic v Rangers games, with rival fans throwing bottles at each other. Segregation was introduced in Glasgow long before it became the norm in England in the 1970s. Some United fans were proud of the reputation they were earning as being the most active hooligans, but the behaviour of some United fans really embarrassed Matt, and I too felt that these supporters were letting the club down. Matt was quite old fashioned. He once appealed for fans to not use bad language in his programme notes. Fans responded by singing, 'It makes you want to swear,' when we played badly a few weeks later.

Matt felt that there needed to be a dialogue with supporters, because problems could be overcome by communication, but it took until 1968 for an official United supporters' club to be formed. The club were slow to act because directors feared the power such clubs might gain. One fan, David Smith, started out as a committee member of the supporters' club but within seven years was the chairman and travel organizer, working from an office within Old Trafford. There was a lot of unwillingness to give David this office, but that reluctance came from Louis Edwards, never Matt Busby. Matt felt that if the fans were onside then the club could have more influence on their behaviour.

Unfortunately, it was never quite as simple as that, and hooliganism plagued United for long periods in the 1970s. United had the biggest support and I always felt that the club attracted more of every type of fan, from executive fans to fans who looked to cause problems. When United's hooligan following began to attract national headlines as they ransacked towns throughout England, that probably attracted a load of new nutters who got a buzz from the trouble. They felt part of a group who were in the news every week and got their identity from that.

Back on the pitch, and with only eight goals from eight games, we were the second lowest scorers in the league. Drastic measures were taken. George Best was dropped and replaced by 18-year-old winger John Aston for a game against Chelsea. The change worked as United won 4–1 and Aston was one of our best players. That was one of my finest United performances as Bobby Charlton and I tore players out of position all over the field.

I felt like I was at the top of my game. I'm not a vain man, and don't like to big myself up, but I was honoured when the godfather of football journalism Geoffrey Green, who started writing for *The Times* in the 1930s when football was not afforded much respectability by the paper's superior readership, wrote the following about me.

'Crerand at that time was regarded by many sound judges as one of the ablest wing halves in Britain if not even in all Europe. In acquiring him for a creative role in midfield

Busby's judgement again hit the jackpot. The part he played in feeding the overflowing skills of the Manchester United attack in those days can not be over-estimated. A one-paced player of steady, measured stride, he glided smoothly over the ground rather than ran. His perception and reading of the game took him to the right places at the right time so that interception and creative distribution were his strong points, just as they had been Busby's in his own playing days.

'Perhaps even Busby found an artistic echo of himself in this fellow Scot, though Crerand proved to be a quite different, a more fiery, quick-tempered player, apt to retaliate at the slightest provocation with unhappy results.' Who was I to disagree with that comment?

Green, a classic English gent of formidable intelligence, was often seen around at United and he was a dear friend of Matt's. Unlike now, the players had a good relationship with the press. They were mainly interested in football stories, not what was going on in people's private lives. We'd often have a drink with the press lads after matches, especially in Europe. We didn't always agree with what they wrote, but there was a respect. The demands are higher these days and there is a lack of trust between the media and the players. Editors want stories about players for the news pages as well as the sports pages. Private lives are written about and that destroys any working relationship. We knew the journalists by name. Privately, we thought that half of them knew nothing about football, but that was just footballers thinking we knew more because we played the game for a living. Journalists could and would ring us at home for a quote or interview. I had a huge amount of respect for writers like Green and Hugh McIlvanney. I loved the quality of their writing, more like literature than journalism. David Meek from the *Manchester Evening News* used to travel on the team coach to matches. He was a similar age to most of the players and we got on. He only stopped travelling with the team when he wrote a story in the early 1970s which the board disagreed with. Today, the only contact United players get with the national newspapers is when they walk through a mixed zone and stop to answer questions for a few minutes. The official club media have better access and I'm now part of that, but as the demands of the media have increased, the co-operation between players and elements of the media has decreased.

The football of the 1960s suited my style. It was more free-flowing than now, with wingers on both flanks. The best I saw were Tom Finney and George Best, who were both even greater than Stanley Matthews because he never scored like those two. Best often scored more than twenty a season, while Finney got as many as twenty-eight one year for Preston. But there were other fine players around then such as Jimmy Greaves who, like Denis Law, could conjure a goal out of nothing. John White, Dave Mackay, and Danny Blanchflower at Spurs and big John Charles at Leeds were the top, top players of the time. John Charles was a big pal of mine and was United daft. He used to tell me that whenever Law and Best got the ball he used to find himself on the edge of his seat.

The win against Chelsea set us up nicely for our opening game in the European Cup which was in Finland against Helsinki HJK in the first leg of the preliminary round. They were amateurs – one of their players was the leader in a band which regularly appeared on Finnish television – and we beat them 3–2 in the Olympic Stadium. The crowd was only 14,000, and many of them were locals supporting Manchester United. I probably shouldn't have played in that game because I had picked up a bad gash on my shin in training which needed four stitches. Matt didn't want to play me, but the doctor examined the stitching before the game and I was declared fit. Matt had a column in the *Daily Express* at the time and made a point of the incident.

'It was touching,' he wrote, 'the insistence of this splendid athlete that he was fit to play. What could I do? I had to say, "All right, Pat, we'll give it a go." And give it a go he did. Padded though he was, Pat was absolutely magnificent. Seldom in my time in football have I seen a better example of courage, resilience, stoicism and devotion to the club.'

He was exaggerating, it was only a gash. That scoreline in Helsinki flattered the Finns and we crushed them 6–0 at Old Trafford in the second leg.

In the league, we were back to our best when we beat Liverpool 2–0 at Old Trafford.

Then, one week later we played Tottenham at White Hart Lane. It was Matt's twentieth anniversary as United manager and the players chipped in to buy him a glass vase. Matt was so touched that he stepped outside the room to compose himself when we presented it to him. We were anything but composed in the game – Tottenham beat us 5–1 – and, having lost as many games as we had won, our chances of retaining the title began to look more distant. Deep down, the European Cup was the trophy we were aiming for and I thought we were good enough to win it.

We were drawn against the East German army side ASK Vorwaerts of East Berlin in the next round. Matt had been to watch them a few weeks earlier and was reasonably impressed. He stressed that we had the quality to beat them and didn't seem all that concerned as we flew into West Berlin. He was a few hours later though – and all because of me. As we crossed through Checkpoint Charlie into communist East Berlin we were given forms to fill in. Matt got all serious and said, 'Don't muck about. These people have no sense of humour.' All the boys thought that they had made it through the checkpoint until a loudspeaker blared, in broken English, 'Herr Crerand, report back to the office.' I had been unable to resist filling in my immigration card thus: Name – Bond, James; Destination – Moscow; Purpose of visit – Espionage.

Matt was raging. The East Germans knew that I was joking, but their serious expressions did not change. Matt carried on going at me, saying that it wasn't even a funny thing to do.

The contrast between West and East Berlin was stark. In the west we'd seen people, shops, and busy bars. It was dreadful in the east and the street lights were so dimly lit that there seemed no point them being on. We took our own food with us because the food was terrible there, so bad that you couldn't eat it.

Sleet was falling in the huge, stark bowl of the ground and the pitch was frozen. We weren't able to train on it the day before the game. The surface was slightly better on match day and we played the game on a Wednesday afternoon because there were no floodlights. We won 2–0 – we just had too much quality for them and were able to snuff out any of their moves early on. The Germans were gracious in defeat and went out of their way to be hospitable after the game, taking us out to a working men's style club late into the night.

I was very impressed at how hospitable they were, and not just because they were plying us with brandy and I was one of the few players who didn't touch it. If it had been red wine it would have been different. We were happy to relax because we had been apprehensive before travelling behind the Iron Curtain, because the media had portrayed communism as evil and communists as cold, humourless, monsters. Given my socialist sympathies, I suspected that to be nonsense and I found out it was in East Berlin. Our translator mounted an articulate and passionate defence of what was happening in

East Germany. She said that she was really proud of what the country was achieving, with people being equal. She opined that the Berlin Wall was a good thing because it stopped all the professionals from East Germany fleeing to the West. She had a point.

Some of the players were carried away with the heady atmosphere of the evening. Bobby, uncharacteristically for him, probably drank one more brandy than he should and the journalist David Meek was very inebriated. We'd done our work on the pitch, but he had to telephone his match report through the following morning. He had to excuse himself three times while on the phone to his copy editor as he went out to vomit in the bathroom.

In the second leg at Old Trafford we beat the Germans 3–1, and found that for our pains we had drawn Benfica in the quarter-finals. The champions of Portugal had reached the final of the European Cup four times in the previous five seasons, winning twice, in 1961 and 1962. They had lost in the final to Milan in 1963 and Internazionale in 1965. Unbeaten on their own ground, the Stadium of Light, in European competition, no team had been as consistent as them in world football in the 1960s. Their side, which provided the majority of the Portuguese national team, remained practically unchanged for years.

We knew that we had to make the most of home advantage in the first leg, yet Eusebio, their greatest player, crossed for Augusto to head in and give them an early lead. We showed our spirit by coming back with goals from Herd and Law to lead 2–1 at half-time. Old Trafford was packed with 64,000 inside and they were watching European football at its finest, so much so that the fans separately applauded both sets of teams back onto the pitch for the second half. Bill Foulkes made it 3–1 with a header with half an hour to go, but Benfica pulled another goal back through Torres. The headline in *The Times* the following day summed it up. 'Precarious lead plucked from a magnificent match.' The report went on: 'One goal in the bank may not be good enough for Manchester United. But at least this night cannot be taken away. It was something to remember.'

Most of the newspapers said the same thing, but they didn't know how disappointed we'd been two years earlier in Lisbon when we lost 5–0. We wanted revenge and while it wasn't to be against Sporting, a victory over Benfica – their better supported, more successful rivals – would be even sweeter. We were Manchester United, we had pride in that name and we were well up for it. We were going to attack and not defend.

Benfica held up the kick-off of the second leg by fifteen minutes so that Eusebio could be presented with the 1965 European Player of the Year award. They knew they'd have a game on their hands against United and they delayed the kick-off because they wanted to get the crowd at it. The same crowd had been holding five fingers up at our coach and beating on the windows as we edged towards the stadium. They thought they were going to beat us 5–0. That wound me up even more. 'Not a chance in hell,' I thought.

The game was kicking off late enough as it was at 10pm and they knew we weren't used to such late starts and wanted to make us even more nervous. It worked. Most of the lads in our dressing room were a bag of nerves. Me? I wasn't bothered at all and kicked a football around the room as we waited. There was a mirror running the full length of the dressing room and I accidentally hit the ball against it, spreading shattered glass everywhere. Everyone went quiet, then Denis Law shouted, 'You crazy bastard. That's it; we don't stand a chance now.' Many of the other lads agreed. But I wasn't superstitious.

I don't think Matt approved of my actions, but he was too focused on the game to deliver a reprimand. He kept telling us to keep the game tight, keep possession until the crowd had quietened down. Fortunately for Matt, George Best chose to completely ignore this advice. He ran amok from start to finish and absolutely slaughtered Benfica. Pulverized them. He scored his first in the sixth minute, his second in the twelfth. Two minutes later he set up John Connelly to make it three. We were so dominant that we had two further efforts disallowed in the first half. George was nineteen and he had just stunned 75,000 fans. They expected to beat United and who could blame them when they had a European home record that read: Played 19, Won 18, Drawn 1, Lost 0?

Benfica got a goal back from an own goal early in the second half, but we'd done them and they knew it. I got United's fourth ten minutes from time, after Denis Law had played a pass which put me through on goal. Bobby made it 5–1 after creeping past several Portuguese defenders and planting a shot into the bottom corner. Cushions rained down from the stands as the fans showed their displeasure. A couple of them ran on the pitch at the end and tried to jostle us. I've been more scared sitting at home in my slippers with a cup of tea.

Benfica 1 Manchester United 5 – largely thanks to George Best. It was the greatest Manchester United performance I have ever been part of. I should have smashed a mirror at every game thereafter.

Matt's mood contrasted sharply with our last visit to the Portuguese capital. He described it as his finest hour. They didn't need to do it, but the Benfica lads took us out that night and showed us round some tavernas in Lisbon. A few of them could speak English and I thought they were great lads. One of them, the brilliant winger Augusto, wasn't there. He'd lost his best friend from childhood the night before. I don't know how he managed to play in that game against us.

The following morning George was dubbed 'El Beatle' in the Portuguese press, the headlines accompanied by a photograph of him wearing an enormous sombrero. He bought it as a joke because that's what people did when they went to then exotic destinations like Spain and Portugal. I used to come home with all kinds of nonsense like inflatable bulls.

Everyone had been impressed with our performance in Lisbon. We played Chelsea at Stamford Bridge on the Saturday after the game and 60,269 were inside the ground, with another 10,000 locked out on Fulham Broadway. But, unfortunately, we were completely drained and turned in a poor performance, losing 2–0, a result which realistically ended any hopes of retaining the title.

Partizan Belgrade were our opponents in the European Cup semi-final. That meant a poignant return to the Yugoslav capital, with the game played at the Yugoslavs' People's Army stadium, the same place where United had drawn with Red Star Belgrade on 5 February 1958.

The home team were offered a bonus of one-third of the match takings if they beat United. There was little chance of something like that happening at Old Trafford. On their home turf, in front of 55,000, Partizan were physical and skilful, and defeated us 2–0. Denis Law missed an open goal from two yards out, but we defended poorly. We also picked up crucial injuries during the match, with George Best aggravating a knee problem before the end. That meant he would play no further part in our season.

Coming back from a two-goal deficit was a big ask, especially as we expected them to defend. Unfortunately, I got sent off, for what I considered a nothing incident. Nobby had punched one of their players and I went over to take Nobby

119

away from further trouble. Their outside-left, Ljubomir Mihaj-lovic, grabbed hold of me and I pushed him away. The Swiss referee Dienst, who went on to referee the World Cup Final at Wembley, said that I kicked the Yugoslav. I didn't. Both of us were sent off, but Nobby stayed on the pitch, despite punching the guy. There were twenty minutes left and it was 0–0.

We didn't need to be down to ten men and I realized that even if we did win then I would miss the final. I was raging, absolutely furious, and started to cry. Nobby scored – although it was credited as an own goal – for United with seventeen minutes left, but Partizan held out. They lost 2–1 to Real Madrid in the final.

Matt considered retiring after that game. He said to me, 'We'll never win the European Cup now.' He looked beaten, distraught. I felt the same. I'd been sent off and I'd been crying in the dressing room, but nobody knew that. I felt that I had to reassure Matt and replied, 'We're going to win the league next year and the European Cup the year after.' I was saying it to lift myself as much as Matt, but he looked so crushed, so tired. I think Matt seriously considered calling it a day. I think Lady Jean persuaded him to stay on, saying that those who died at Munich would have insisted that Matt tried again. She was right and deep down Matt knew that. If he had quit then he would have spent the rest of his life regretting it, but I could understand why he felt so low. We'd get close to the top of the mountain but we could never reach the top before someone kicked us off it and we had to start climbing from the bottom all over again.

There was a banquet for both teams in the Midland Hotel after the game. I was still fuming. Mihajlovic, the lad who had got me sent off, was on a table nearby. I looked at him with my eyes blazing and shouted to him that I was going to kill him. He got up to go to the toilet and I followed him. He went in the cubicle and locked the door. I started kicking the cubicle to try and get him out of the toilet. I was shouting, 'Come out, you bastard'. He was frightened and shitting himself in more ways than one. I was off my head. The racket I was making could be heard outside and people came in and dragged me away. I ended up leaving and going to the Brown Bull pub in Salford with the journalist Hugh McIlvanney. The place was heaving and a few City lads were in there too. Malcolm Allison, City's assistant manager, was there with his cigar. He was pleased that United had been beaten and was smiling with his mates. That really wound McIlvanney up, so much so that he squared up to him. He was going to punch him one, but for once I played the role of peacemaker.

Our wives loved those post match banquets, but for most of the players it meant getting home in the early hours of Thursday morning. So we needed a long lie in and were excused from training. It's not wise to train hard on the Friday before a game. Club captain Noel Cantwell and I reckoned that we were never quite at our best on the Saturday. The team's results on the Saturdays backed up our suspicion that the banquets were doing our football no good, despite the benefits to our marriages. After that Partizan game we lost 1–0 to Everton in the semi-final of the FA Cup at Bolton. It was our fourth semi-final in succession, but we lost for the third time in a row. The reason was simple. By the time the game came around we were absolutely shattered. We'd played six games in fifteen days, including a European Cup semi-final. Everton went on to win the FA Cup, but they didn't meet us at our best.

That's when we went to speak to Matt about the banquets. Matt heard us out and then completely agreed with us. The banquets were stopped thereafter. The wives were not happy but Matt appreciated the move because to him, the most important thing was the team's performance. He told me on more than one occasion, 'The press may write about what I do for the club, or Bobby or Denis, but the team is always more important than any individual. The team is what matters to the public. They want a successful side.'

Banquets were also the custom for away games in Europe, so we couldn't control them, but I still didn't like them. Some suit would get up and say something in English then another suit would repeat what he'd said in the language of whatever country we were playing in. It still goes on today, but only at director level.

United fell apart in April 1966. We played too many games in a short period of time, important ones too. And clubs didn't have the squad of players that they have today. As well as going out of the European and FA Cup, we played six league games of which we only won one match, drawing two and losing three. Just 23,039 saw our penultimate home game of the season against Aston Villa. The stay away fans missed a treat as we won 6–1, but a season that had promised so much ended with us finishing fourth in the league, behind Burnley, Leeds, and ten points behind champions Liverpool. They had a really strong and fit side with Yeats, their massive centre-half and captain leading the line. Ian Callaghan and Ian St John were the stand out players. We only lost two more games than Liverpool and we scored more goals than them, but we drew fifteen matches that season, more than any other team in the league. Clearly, we'd have to improve.

I couldn't focus on the disappointment too much because Noreen gave birth to our second child, a daughter we called Lorraine, who was born on 10 May 1966.

The summer of 1966 was dominated by the World Cup Finals. I watched some of them, but not being involved I had a bitter-sweet feeling about them. I was a midfielder for what I considered to be the best team in Europe, but as Ryan Giggs will tell you, not every top-level player gets to play in the World Cup Finals.

On the day of the final, Denis Law was playing golf at Chorlton Golf Club. He arranged the tee-off to coincide with the match. It was raining heavily that day. I knew that he was playing and went along to Chorlton after the game. Denis was coming up the eighteenth fairway when I got to him; his long blond hair was soaking. He asked me what I was doing and who had won the final. I said that England had won after extra-time. He took his glove off and snapped his club. He was raving mad, even though Bobby and Nobby were playing in the final. It brought them at least a happy end to a barren season. We had earned honour for our performances, but no honours. That had to change.

I had an unwelcome start to the new season. After playing practically every game in 1965/66, I was surprised to be dropped for the opening match against West Brom. Under the headline 'Crerand Axed', one newspaper wrote, 'Manchester United will drop Pat Crerand today. Matt Busby starts the new season at Old Trafford by fielding John Fitzpatrick and Nobby Stiles against West Bromwich tomorrow.

'United's £56,000 Scottish international right half becomes the latest victim in one of Busby's swift purges. Busby is obviously warning his team that even a winning side will be changed in the interests of greater efficiency.

'Just before last season [it was actually two seasons previous] he dropped three internationals – Johnny Giles (now with Leeds), Albert Quixall and David Herd. But that followed a 4–0 defeat by Everton in the Charity Shield match. Manager Busby refused to name his team last night, but said Denis Law was expected to be passed fit this morning.'

Could you imagine Alex Ferguson's team news coming out in a newspaper the day before a game?

The truth was that I tended to be something of a slow starter. I don't know why, it just took me time to get into my rhythm. I'll admit I was disappointed to be dropped, nobody is ever happy to be left out. Matt wasn't a respecter of reputations and he could be ruthless, but it was for the good of the team. I was angry and wanted to prove him wrong as soon as possible and I didn't have to wait long for my chance.

The pre-season had been difficult for the team too. Celtic beat us 4–1 in a friendly at Parkhead. In fact they slaughtered us. My former club were quicker and fitter, but then they were at a more advanced stage of pre-season than us. And United were without Bobby Charlton and Nobby Stiles, our two World Cup winners, who were given a few weeks off after beating Germany at Wembley.

Bayern Munich also subjected us to a 4–1 drubbing and, just a week before the season started, Austrian side Rapid Vienna put five past us, and we could only manage two goals in reply.

Given the high number of goals we were leaking, it was no surprise to hear the Blackburn Rovers defender Mike England being linked with a move to United, but the asking price was apparently too high. There was a new addition in Alex Stepney who joined us from Chelsea for £55,000 in September 1966, a record fee for a goalkeeper. We needed a new keeper because Harry Gregg was thirty-four and Pat Dunne, who played throughout the 1964/65 season, was a touch quiet and didn't come off his line enough. David Gaskell was still at the club, but I don't think he had a future at Old Trafford in Matt's eyes.

Alex was a top class goalkeeper and he did it without being flash. He never over elaborated nor made a save look spectacular if he didn't need to. He was mad, which is typical for a goalie, but terrific company and a very funny lad. I roomed with Alex for a long time and he used to drive me mental. He would get up at 7.30 am and make a cup of tea, stirring it just loudly enough to wind me up.

Alex was great for me on the field because I would just go to the side line and knew instinctively that he would throw out there, but while his signing was a welcome addition to the squad, there were once again problems with other players at Old Trafford, and it was down to money.

Despite United being one of the best supported teams in the country, no United player, five years after the minimum wage was abolished, earned more than £100 a week. The team was comprised of proven internationals who drew sell-out crowds wherever we played. We knew that a lot of money was involved, but we weren't seeing much of it.

Denis Law came out and said that he wanted a pay increase. Matt wasn't happy and said that he was going to put Denis on the transfer list. Denis heard about this when he was away in Scotland and came back to Old Trafford for a meeting with Matt. I saw the manager that morning and said, 'Boss, you can't let Denis go. He's too important for us.'

Matt replied, 'Well, he'll have to do as he's told.' I knew then that despite Matt appearing to be adamant, that he was going to negotiate a solution with Denis. I knew that Matt rated Denis higher than any other player so he was never going to cut off his nose to spite his face, but in his mind he had to show who was boss. They met and did a deal where Denis had to apologize publicly, but he also got some of the rise for which he had asked. We didn't know what each other was earning, but we did have gripes with bonuses.

Bobby Noble was another player who became a regular in 1966/67. Had it not been for a horrific car accident which almost took his life, I think Bobby would have made 100 England caps at full-back. He was that good – tough, two-footed and quick. Bobby was only twenty-one at the time of his car crash. He was driving through Sale, where a lot of the players went to live in the 1960s, when a car came through red lights and hit his. He never played again. Bobby's crash brought it home to me how easily our great football careers could be taken away.

We only had the domestic trophies – the League, League Cup and the FA Cup – to focus on in 1966/67. In the League Cup, we went out to Blackpool (they beat us 5–1) but I don't think Matt was too concerned about that competition – United hadn't entered it for the previous five seasons. I can remember turning up at Bloomfield Road for that match and Bill Shankly was there. He considered United as Liverpool's main rivals for the league and came to watch us. He collared me and Denis Law before the game to tell us how bad Blackpool were. He was telling us what a bad player their big centre-forward was and he ended up scoring a hat-trick.

Noel Cantwell left the club in 1967. He'd been offered a coaching job at Manchester City but told me that he wanted to be a manager. I told him that he'd have to travel if that was his ambition and, funnily enough, Matt called him into his office an hour later to say that Coventry City wanted him to be their manager.

In the league, we tended to win at home and draw away. George Best recovered fully from the injury picked up in Belgrade at the end of the previous season and was our most consistent performer, with forty-five appearances. Bobby Charlton played only one game fewer.

We were neck and neck with reigning champions Liverpool up to Christmas, although Nottingham Forest, who eventually finished second that season, were the best team we met. They had a very good side and beat us 4–1 at the City Ground after we'd arrived only about twenty minutes before kick-off. Joe

Baker was up front and John Barnwell, who is now in charge of the League Managers' Association, was a great player for them that day.

We drew 2–2 with Liverpool in December, then Sheffield United unexpectedly beat us 2–1 away on Boxing Day. Although this made headlines, we wouldn't lose another game all season. The next day, we played Sheffield United at Old Trafford, back to back Christmas matches being the custom then. Before the game, it was announced that Bobby Charlton had been crowned European Footballer of the Year for 1966, ahead of Eusebio and Franz Beckenbauer. We beat the Blades 2–0, with one of the goals being a rare 30 yard screamer from me. That result put us two points clear of Liverpool at the top.

The biggest crowd of that season came in the FA Cup third round when we played Stoke City at Old Trafford. Almost 64,000, including 21,000 from the Potteries, saw us win 2–0. That was one of my best games of the year, but we were knocked out in the fourth round after losing 2–1 to Norwich at Old Trafford, having murdered them. That was the only game we lost at home.

Liverpool's form dipped after Christmas and our home match against Forest was seen as a title decider, even though it was in February. It was a tight game and with a minute to go, there was no score. Then we got a corner and up went Denis Law to make a fantastic header. It looked a certain goal, but the Forest keeper Peter Grummitt was as sharp as Denis and brought off a fabulous save, turning the ball away for a corner. There was time for the corner to be taken, but I felt it didn't matter. It seemed to me if we were meant to get a goal then that header would have been it. I thought that Denis could do no more, but I was wrong. With his back to goal, Denis spectacularly scissor-kicked the ball into the net for the winner. 1–0. After that we knew that we were on to win the title.

Another huge crowd of almost 64,000 watched us draw against Arsenal away the following month. That number was supplemented by another 28,423 who watched the game on a big screen at Old Trafford – the first time a league game had been shown this way.

After one game at Sunderland in April, we returned to Manchester and went in the Brown Bull pub, a favourite of the players. A thick fog descended on Manchester and you could barely see in front of you, it was a real pea souper. That was the night that Bobby Noble had his car crash. Noreen was supposed to be meeting me in town and we were going to go for a meal, but the public transport was closed down. I stayed in the Brown Bull because it was unsafe for cars. I stopped there until five o'clock in the morning with Denis, George, and Malcolm Allison, until the fog lifted. We weren't out by choice. I knew I was going to get my ears chewed off by Noreen, though. I got a lift home off a friend, Mick Goodwin, and I told him to open the front door because I was scared about Noreen's reaction. As he put the keys into the lock and pushed it open, Noreen threw a large pan of water over him. I burst out laughing while Noreen was mortified and had to apologize. She had waited up all night for me.

The Brown Bull was the place to be in Manchester in 1967. An American guy owned the pub and he made a fortune. He used to give us lock-ins and the pub would be packed with a whole range of Mancunian characters – solicitors, rogues, actors, and footballers. The company was great. George set the trend. Nobody went there until George started going in. He went because he wanted peace and quiet, but then everyone followed him. Matt could never get the name of the pub right.

He used to say to me, 'You were in the Brown Cow at the weekend.'

I'd assure him, hand on heart, 'No I wasn't.'

'No, you were in the Black Bull.'

'No, Boss, I wasn't.'

We were playing so well that Matt wasn't inclined to dig too deeply. We won the league for the second time in three years, scoring eighty-four league goals, more than any other team. The vast majority came from Law, Best, Charlton, and Herd, but I scored three goals that season – a career best.

One of those goals was during the penultimate match against West Ham at the Boleyn ground. Strangely, the East Londoners were the team with the second highest number of goals, despite being in sixteenth place. We needed two points to win the championship and we had Stoke at home the following Saturday. I got a header to make it 3–0 in a 6–1 victory. We scored with virtually the first kick of the ball. Matt had just climbed into his seat to see West Ham taking a centre. He hadn't realized that we had already taken the lead. At half-time he thought it was 2–0 when it was actually 3–0.

He said, 'Well done, lads. Just keep it tight at 2–0.'

We looked at him and said, 'What the *hell* are you going on about? It's 3–0.'

He smiled and changed his whole attitude in a split second, telling us to go out and attack West Ham.

We were champions and our fans came onto the pitch. It took an age before we were on the coach to Euston station for the train back to Manchester. The traffic was very heavy and about a mile from Euston, Matt asked me to run ahead and tell the station master that the Manchester United team were running five minutes late. He wanted him to hold the train. He had fast runners in the team like George and Bobby but he chose me. I ran to Euston and explained the situation to the station master. He wasn't prepared to hold it for us and we missed it. So we got the next train to Stoke and Matt arranged for a coach to come and pick us up there. Stoke City, our opponents the following week, were on the train. We mixed with them. Their manager Tony Waddington was an ex-United player and he was trying to tap a load of us up. 'Come and play for Stoke, Pat,' he urged. He offered me more than I was on at Old Trafford, but there was no way I was going.

Unfortunately for me, the game against Stoke did not pass without incident. The day started badly when I was late for the coach from Old Trafford. I was a terrible timekeeper. I always made an excuse, but I never really improved. That day, I climbed on board rather sheepishly. Matt was raging as we pulled up at Davyhulme for our pre-match meal. He looked at me and said: 'You must be a very important person if you can keep the directors and players waiting.' He said it in front of everyone and I was humiliated. I looked at Matt and replied, 'I am very sorry boss, but this is the earliest I have ever been late.' He stared at me and didn't know what to say.

During the game, I spat at the Stoke inside-forward Tony Allen. I wasn't sent off or booked for the incident, but I was condemned by millions who saw it on television. I had been having a bit of a feud with another Stoke player, Peter Dobing. There was nothing vicious about it because Peter and I were good pals, but we weren't holding back. After one hard tackle, we both went to ground, but we started laughing as we got to our feet. Tony Allen wasn't in on the joke and started calling me 'a Scotch bastard'. He was saying that I should be sent off and my instinct was to crack him one, but I knew that the referee would have ordered me off. Bill Foulkes was holding me back, so, in disgust, I spat at Allen. I was sorry seconds after I had done it. I knew it was wrong, yet I was so angry I had to do something. The referee, who had heard everything, must have known how I felt. He didn't even book me.

That was the final game of the season and the next day we left for a post-season tour. Unbeknown to me, the incident with Allen blew up in the media and I wasn't going to be allowed to forget it. Supporters at every away ground made it clear to me what they thought. I was hammered in the press too, especially by people who saw me spitting on television. All this made me realize one of the great dangers of television: people can see exactly what happens in a game, but they cannot hear what led up to it.

My clash with Allen was another case of retaliation. All my on-field lapses have come after provocation. Is that an excuse? I think so. People will disagree and say how it's unthinkable to punch an opponent. I would like to agree with them. I wish that we all lived in a pure world where everyone had a Public School education and we all learned how to be good sports and that there was no nastiness or prejudice, and if anyone broke the rules in any game they immediately said, 'Sorry, old chap' and patted you on the back. Maybe there are some people who actually did have a childhood like that. If nobody ever hit them they would never need to hit back. But it wasn't like that in the Gorbals, nor in Manchester.

SEVEN

Champions of Europe

I watched Celtic's progress to the final of the European Cup in 1967 with divided loyalties. As a Celtic fan, and friend of Jock Stein and many of the players, I hoped the Scots would triumph. But, if I am honest, I was a little bit jealous that the Celts might lift the trophy before United.

During the summer, we went on a seven-week post-season tour of Australia, New Zealand, and the United States. There was no chance of me watching Celtic becoming the first British team to play in the European Cup Final either in person or on television, because we were in the air between Honolulu and Auckland when they took on Internazionale in Lisbon. My mother and my step-father both travelled for the final and I didn't sleep for a minute on that flight as my mind was on Portugal's national stadium in the hills outside Lisbon.

United arrived in Auckland at seven in the morning and I was on the phone as soon as I got to the airport. I rang the local newspaper, the *Auckland Star*, and asked to be put through to the sports desk. This guy came on the phone and I asked him the score of the European Cup Final. He didn't have a clue what I was on about. An English girl was listening into the conversation. She said, 'Excuse me, I was just listening to your accent because I thought it was lovely. I know nothing about football, but whatever happened last night, I heard that it was the first time that a British team had done it.' That's how I found out that Celtic were European champions. I sent a telegram to Jock Stein at Celtic Park to congratulate them. I'm not sure if the telegram ever arrived though because I met Jock many times afterwards and he never mentioned it.

We left for the States, where we played a series of exhibition games, soon after the domestic season had finished. United were billed as 'the champions of England' and it was our job to advertise the English game and all its virtues to the world. Over 250,000 paid to see us play over the dozen matches and Brian Kidd used it as a chance to show what he could do. Just seventeen when we left Manchester, he was the best player on the tour in which we scored fifty-five goals and let in just eleven. Brian became a first team regular the season after.

Brian got plenty of chances because a lot of us were shattered after a long season, but I had known Brian for some time as he was the apprentice responsible for cleaning my boots. I used to give him half a crown a week, so long as he did my shoes too. Nobby had told me that Brian was a Collyhurst lad, so I knew that our backgrounds were of similar working-class Catholic stock. He was also a regular churchgoer and a big United fan who had paid to watch his team as a kid, so I kept an eye out for him and made him feel comfortable when he joined up with the first team. For instance, I was over to help out in a flash when he got sent off against Tottenham in 1967/68. Brian was still young and I didn't want to see any United player get bullied by older professionals.

As I've said before, we viewed those huge post-season tours like an end of season holiday and we visited amazing places to which I've never returned since, such as San Francisco, but we were away for so long our wives hated it.

While in Sydney on tour, I booked a phone call to Noreen at 1.30 am – the middle of the day back home. We were staying in the Coogee Bay Hotel overlooking the Pacific just to the south of the city centre and beaches like Bondi. It wasn't a luxury hotel, but a busy and rowdy place which had the biggest beer garden in Australia and live music every night. Our rooms were above a giant pub on a busy street corner with all kinds of characters walking around and half of them drinking in the hotel.

Alex Stepney was sharing a room with me so I warned him about the call and suggested that he would be better to shift somewhere else for the night if he didn't want his sleep disturbed. This was arranged, as John Fitzpatrick and our reserve keeper Jimmy Rimmer had a big room with three beds just along the corridor.

After I had chatted to Noreen I felt pretty thirsty. As there was nothing to drink and no room service at the time I decided to nip to the room where Stepney and Co. were located and see if there was a bottle of Coke or something lying about. When I got there the door was half open. Quick as a flash, I thought, 'That's funny.' I crept in on tip-toe and prepared to rouse them good and proper. Just as I was drawing breath a man leapt out from behind the door. It gave me the fright of my life, but before I could work out what was going on, he brushed past me and rushed down the corridor. It was dark, but as soon as he got into the dimly lit corridor I could see that he wasn't one of the boys.

'Thief!' I shouted, waking everyone up. 'He's a f***ing robber!'

I was shocked, but began to chase after the intruder barefooted and in my pyjamas. He had already gone past me so it was impossible to grab him. He made for the stairs and because it was me chasing him and not one of the other players, he was soon running down them.

I knew that I had to keep on his tail because it would take the others time to get up, discuss whether I was playing a practical joke or not, and then decide what to do about it. They would be no use. But this was no joke. I was gaining on him and when I turned the last corner, which led to the foyer, he was only a few yards away.

'Come here, you bastard!' I shouted. 'And I'll f***ing kill you!' Given my reputation, that would have frightened rivals on a football field, but here it had a different effect as the robber suddenly stopped and turned. He looked at me. Rather than jump on him, I stopped too, because he was holding a little revolver by his waist. And he was pointing it at me. I looked at his gaunt features. He was a man in his thirties, with menacing dark eyes. And it was him, not me, who was in control of the situation.

'If you come any closer I'm going to kill you,' he said. It wasn't so much the words as the way he said them. He didn't shout. He simply made a matter-of-fact statement. And I didn't doubt that he meant it.

I didn't back off, but turned and sprinted. Had Matt been awake he would have had a go at me for not running that quickly in a match, but I didn't want to be shot before I'd won the European Cup and I ran straight back to the lads' room where the burglar had sprung from. They were awake because of the commotion, but were still lying in bed. I explained what had happened and slammed the door shut behind me, half thinking that the thief was still chasing me and that he was going to kill me. I told the lads to check their belongings. 'Fitz' had been robbed of a few dollars, but nothing else was missing. The police arrived soon after because the receptionist had called them after seeing a man run out of the door with a gun. The officers took me down to the foyer and asked me to make a statement and give a description, but there wasn't much I could say once I had told them about his eyes and his thin face. They kept me there until four o'clock in the morning.

The next day we found that one of the Australian officials accompanying us had been robbed of $200. They never caught the thief.

Australia was a bit of a let-down. We had images of sun and sea, but it rained almost all the time – as it can do in winter in Sydney. Nevertheless, I have a lot of happy memories about that trip and most of them concerned the assistant manager Jimmy Murphy. I got an injury and only played in one game on the whole tour so I spent a lot of time with Jimmy. Jimmy liked a pint of beer. He wasn't one for luxury lounges and preferred working men's bars. I'd often accompany him each morning when the other lads were training. We'd be in a bar in Sydney and he'd be having a few pints, the assistant manager of Manchester United, while I would have a Coke. Jimmy liked to chat to strangers and there were some pretty strange characters in the bars he frequented, usually drunks, waifs and strays.

The tour was sponsored by a tobacco firm and most days one of their representatives would arrive with new supplies of cigarettes for the entire United party. They were always delivered to Jimmy's room and soon they were piled up high against the walls because hardly any of the players smoked. Before we went to the bars, I used to see Jimmy shuffling about the hotel with cartons of cigarettes under his arms – offering them to anyone who wanted them.

Jimmy was a man of tradition. He joined Manchester United when Old Trafford was a bombed out wreck after the Second World War and turned out to be the club's greatest ever coach, the perfect foil for Matt.

He missed the Munich air crash because of his other commitment managing the Welsh national team, who had a World Cup play-off against Israel. Jimmy was worried about Matt because the boss had just undergone an operation on his legs. Jimmy asked Matt if he was strong enough to go to Belgrade and suggested that he should go instead, but Matt wouldn't hear of it and told him to concentrate on his Welsh duties. So Bert Whalley, the trainer, accompanied Matt while Jimmy stayed behind.

Munich didn't just destroy Jimmy's life's work in seconds, he lost his great friends including Whalley. He virtually ran the club during Matt's recovery in hospital, re-arranging fixtures and signing players. A proud Welshman from a little village in the Rhondda Valley, he still took Wales to the quarter-finals of the World Cup in the summer of 1958. He stayed loyal to United despite lucrative offers from Arsenal, Juventus, and the Brazilian national team. High profile jobs were never for Jimmy, he was far happier teaching youngsters and making sure that they were dedicated to practising and improving their game.

Although he was very sociable, Jimmy liked his breakfast in his room when we were away. He opened his door as usual one morning in Sydney and let in a waiter with a huge tray held out in front of him. But it wasn't quite Jimmy's usual breakfast. There were loads of rolls and toast, butter, jam, pots of tea and coffee, fruit juice, cereals, and anything else that could be crammed onto a tray. Jimmy was more surprised when he saw another waiter standing behind with plates of cod, sausage, bacon and eggs, and yet more pots of coffee. Jimmy was perplexed and complained that he hadn't ordered all that food. All the waiters kept saying was, 'That was the order, Sir.' Then another waiter came with another tray full of food and Jimmy twigged that it was a set up. Rather than tell the waiters this, he just started laughing. He had a loud laugh, and we could all hear it. We were about to go to training when Denis Law came in our room.

'What's Jimmy laughing about?' I asked him. Then Denis explained. Having breakfast cards where you tick your order for the following morning on the back of your hotel door was not commonplace in Europe as it is now, but it was in Australia. Denis saw great potential in this and ordered as much food as he could on his own card, before hanging it outside Jimmy's door. He had ticked every single box and the hotel didn't question the order. They knew Manchester United were staying there and probably thought it was a meal for all of us.

There was a big surprise for me on that trip. Someone claiming to be my brother turned up at our game in Sydney. He managed to get to the corridor near the United changing room, where he spoke to Matt Busby. He was suspicious because he knew that I didn't have a brother – Matt knew nothing about my brother John who had died. I went to see who it was and saw Noreen's brother Jack. He had left Glasgow six years earlier and not kept in touch with his family. How do you go away from home and not get in touch for six years? Someone had even told Noreen's mum that he was dead, but she didn't believe that. Noreen had asked me to find him in Australia, by which she hoped that I would see him at a United game.

Jack was a good lad, someone I knew from Glasgow as a kid, but I wasn't happy with him.

'You're out of order,' I said when I saw him. 'Your mother is not getting any younger and you've not been in touch once to let her know how you are.'

'It never crossed my mind,' he said, and I don't think he was joking. He made contact with his family again soon after that.

When we returned to England we made the most of what little there was left of the summer. We drew 3–3 against Tottenham in the Charity Shield at Old Trafford, a game famous for the Spurs goalkeeper Pat Jennings scoring direct from a kick-out.

Everton stunned us in the first game of the season with a 3–1 win, but league concerns would be secondary to winning the European Cup. That was still Matt's big aim, more than ever his big dream, and it became ours too. It started to become an obsession; partly because we knew that time was running out as players got older.

There was some fresh blood. Francis Burns, from Coatbridge near Glasgow, started to play on a regular basis in 1967/68. He was good enough to keep Shay Brennan out of the team at left-back and looked very classy, especially considering he was just nineteen.

Our first European Cup match was against Hibernians of Malta in September 1968. We beat them 4–0 at Old Trafford, before travelling to Valletta for the second leg. It was like Beatlemania over there, with a cavalcade escorting the team from the airport to our hotel. It was chaos at the hotel – if you went to the toilet twenty people followed you. All the players had noticed a big increase in fan mail over the previous two seasons. It wasn't only because we'd been champions twice, but because George Best's high profile had made people view footballers as personalities. Maybe some people thought that they wouldn't get a reply if they wrote to George, so they wrote to the likes of me instead, usually requesting autographs. I found it to be a pain in the backside, having to sit down one afternoon a week to reply to fans' letters, but I kept on top of it because it was the height of bad manners if you didn't reply. I only replied once, which probably frustrated fans who wrote back to my letters hoping that I would be their pen-pal or something. United still forward me letters that are sent to Old Trafford. They are still usually just a request for an autograph, but a lad from Africa wrote to me recently asking for £3,900 to buy his village or something. That went straight in the bin.

The pitch in Valletta was dry and hard like a desert and the ball bounced twice as high as it should do. Hibernians were managed by a Catholic priest, one Father Hilary Taglia-ferro, who seemed in awe of United. He was proud that his team held us to a 0–0 draw, but we never did master the conditions.

We had a few drinks in the hotel bar after the game. There was a great selection of wines; the cheapest, by some distance, was called Farmer's Red. It tasted awful but me and Alex Step-ney drank loads and finished up in Chairman Louis Edwards' room singing to him at three in the morning. I would have gone mad if someone had done it to me, but he just sat there laughing.

Sarajevo were our opponents in the next round in Novem-ber but rather than fly there direct for the match, we flew to Vienna. Matt refused to travel by charter airlines after the Munich air crash, so we always went the circuitous route on scheduled airlines. It would take us forever to get to places and so we'd leave Manchester on a Monday, usually for a flight to London or Amsterdam to change.

It took us seven hours to drive from Vienna to Sarajevo, most of it after we'd crossed the border and driven through Yugoslavia. There were always complications when we went to the Eastern European countries, always hold ups because of problems with visas.

Sarajevo is a beautiful city steeped in history. We went to the spot where the assassin Gavrilo Prinzip shot the Austrian Archduke Ferdinand, which led to the start of the First World

War. There was a plaster model of the assassin and the Archduke at the time of the killing. Jokingly, I asked the lads why the killer had hidden behind a plaster cast of himself before shooting. Some of the lads believed me.

Sarajevo were tough opponents, but we drew 0–0 there before winning the second leg 2–1 at Old Trafford.

Polish side Gornik Zabrze, who played their big games in Chorzow, awaited us in the quarter-finals. We knew it was going to be hard, because the Poles were a well-balanced team who had been strong enough to knock out Dynamo Kiev, the conquerors of holders Celtic. Matt was concerned about their star striker Lubanski, but it was a Brian Kidd goal and an own goal which gave us a 2–0 lead from the first leg, before we travelled east for the return tie.

I played golf the day before we set off for Poland. It took a little longer than I thought and by the time I got home Noreen was raging at me. She had family down from Glasgow and told me how rude I had been. I had missed my dinner, which was waiting for me in the oven. Noreen wouldn't let up and in the end I snapped and said something that I shouldn't have. Noreen picked up a plate and threw it at my head. It caught me above my eye and the blood startied pouring out. I had to call the club doctor and he came round to my house to give me stitches. He wasn't very happy and asked how I had come to get a cut on my head in my own kitchen. I gave him a look which suggested that sometimes, when there's women involved, these things happen. He thought it was very funny.

Katowice, where we stayed, was a bleak, rough place. Poland was a very Catholic country and its population were not happy with the communism that had been imposed on it by the USSR.

Manchester, especially the areas around Old Trafford, has had a strong Polish community since the 1950s. A Polish friend of a friend asked me if I would take some Bibles and rosary beads to Poland. I said yes thinking that they wanted me to take a Bible or two, but then six were dropped at my house and they took up most of the space in my suitcase. If a normal person had been caught smuggling in this banned material, they wouldn't have been let back out, but customs officers used to treat us differently. They had all heard of Manchester United and rather than search you, would ask for autographs. I decided to take the risk and if I was caught I was just going to pretend that the Bibles were for the team as we all read them every night before going to bed.

Soon after getting to the hotel, I received a phone call about the Bibles.

'Mr Crerand,' said a voice in a stilted English accent. 'I will pick up the special books in one hour from you. I will meet you in the hotel reception. I will be wearing a blue hat. Then I will collect the books from your room.'

'F**k off! I'm not having that,' I said. I put the phone down.

I'd previously told the lads what I was doing and I was convinced that one of them was messing about and had made the phone call. I even thought that they said blue because that was the colour Rangers wore. There was no way I was going down to reception to meet someone in a blue hat.

Two minutes later, it rang again. I think the person was a bit startled that I'd just told them where to go, but he was persistent.

'Mr Crerand I am very serious,' stated the caller. 'We have an arrangement for you to bring the books from Manchester, England. Do you have the books here with you in Poland?'

I began to think it wasn't a joke and apologized. If it was the lads then they well and truly had me now. But I couldn't think of any of them who was capable of such a good Polish accent and arranged a meeting with my blue-hatted friend an hour later in reception. I left my room half expecting one of my team-mates to jump out at me, but when I got into reception there was indeed a man in his fifties wearing a blue hat. I shook his hand but it was clear that he didn't want to be seen hanging around and he followed me back to my room. I gave him the Bibles and the rosary beads then he offered me money. There was no way I was taking any money off someone so poor, which he appreciated.

Bibles were not the only thing I took to Poland. I had played there before with Scotland and couldn't find any food over there worth eating so when I knew I was going back with United, I had a chat with Alex Stepney, my room mate. Alex decided to take a primus stove with him and was soon appointed official tea maker. Room 405 of the Hotel Katowice became the tea room for the rest of the players and management. We had also brought some of our own supplies, such as tins of soup, in our bags. We used the outside window ledge of our hotel as a fridge, although it was more like a freezer.

The accountant Reuben Kaye was on that trip to Poland. He travelled with us all the time and the players liked him. He was asleep in his room at three in the morning one night when the phone rang. He picked up the receiver and a voice said, 'Comrade No 10?' Reuben quickly explained that he wasn't Comrade No 10 and that it must be a wrong number. The voice repeated, 'Comrade No 10?' Like most of us, Reuben had read stories about people being accused of spying in countries behind the Iron Curtain. He got a little bit paranoid and tried to explain who he was, but the voice kept repeating in a thick foreign accent 'Comrade No 10'. Trying not to panic he began to wonder if it might not be better to say he was No 10 and hope that it was a lucky number.

Finally, his caller hung up. And Reuben lay there in that dark Polish hotel room waiting for the secret police to burst in at any moment. First thing in the morning he came into my room asking what he should do. He was seriously worried, but I didn't really know what to say.

Hours later, he found out the truth. The caller had been a Polish George Best fan who spoke no English. Since George had played inside-left, the Pole had tried to contact him by asking for Comrade No 10.

On match day there must have been six inches of snow on the ground. Some people were of the opinion that we should postpone the game, and I could see that the boss was worried about the conditions. Personally, I thought that kind of ground was more of a handicap to the team trying to attack whereas we were going to defend. Matt was afraid, however, that a slippery pitch could lead to freak goals.

The referee decided that the game should go ahead and despite the temperature dropping as low as minus four, 105,000 fans turned up to the Slaski Stadium, a socialist built, giant super bowl. Most of them were in their places by half past four in the afternoon for an evening kick-off. Their fans were enthusiastic and passed vodka to ours. Most of them seemed to have horns and they blew them like mad during the game.

We had a lot of injuries but got away with a 1–0 defeat – a goal late on from Lubanski, but we were through. After the game I went for a walk with Matt around the vast empty stadium.

'Surely this must be the year,' he said. His hands were still shaking from the cold. His main concern was the injured Denis Law. 'I've got to get him on the field again. He is the key to it all happening up front. At the back we are wonderful right now. Look at us tonight. But up front nobody can do

Denis's job.' Everyone in football knew that Matt had money – a lot of it – to buy a forward. The brilliant football at Old Trafford meant that, for the first time, United were consistently the best supported team in the country with average attendances well above 50,000. As United were not the best payers when it came to players' wages, there was serious money available for a top class signing. The problem was that the players Matt wanted were not for sale, just as Liverpool wouldn't sell Steve Gerrard or Chelsea John Terry these days.

We visited the former concentration camp at Auschwitz the day after the game. Only a few of us went, as it was a fair journey through the bleak coal fields of Silesia. There was a small museum there and it made me very angry to see what had happened there during the holocaust. I'll never forget the lampshades made of human skin.

It made me realize how insignificant football is when compared with the atrocities of which men are capable. It was hard to understand what would make a human being do that to a fellow human. I couldn't understand why someone would get into a situation where they would want to take such actions. It seemed surreal, looking at gas chambers which had been used to massacre thousands of people. I asked some difficult questions of our guide. The Germans are a sensible and intelligent race of people and I wondered how they could have been fooled by this idiot Hitler. At least the kids of today know who Hitler is – every time I put the television on there is a programme about him.

Critics say that the players of today are out of touch with reality, but I'm not so sure. I travelled to South Africa with the United squad in the summer of 2006 on a pre-season tour and we went to a school in a Johannesburg township where most of the children were HIV positive. The poverty was staggering and much as I felt for children, I really admired the seventeen-

and eighteen-year-olds from richer countries that had given up their time to work as volunteers to help these African kids. I talked to one girl from Kilmarnock, Scotland, who was an unpaid helper.

'Why did you come here?' I asked, as two little kids who'd lost both their parents to AIDS hung off her.

'I just wanted to come to help,' she replied.

'But what do your parents think about you coming to such a dangerous place?'

'It doesn't matter what they think, what matters is that I'm here.'

The young United players heard this and saw the sacrifices someone their own age was making. They saw kids clinging onto them for dear life when they were about to go back to our luxury hotel. We went to meet Nelson Mandela, which was a great honour for me, and a few of the younger players were asking me who he was because they'd never heard of him. One even said: 'Was Nelson Mandela just like Bobby Sands?' I explained who Mandela was and put it in context. Players might lead very fortunate lives, but I think what they saw that day left a deep impact on them.

After the Gornik game in Poland, I made a big decision. I resolved not to play for Scotland again. My priority was winning the European Cup with United and I hadn't been enjoying playing for my country. Despite having a career which spanned over 500 matches playing for Celtic and Manchester United, I played just sixteen times for Scotland.

I always felt that the whole Scotland scene was pro-Rangers and anti-Celtic. The team was chosen not by the manager, but by small time, small minded selectors who thought they were the most important people in the world just because they held an administrative post at somewhere like Montrose. Because they knew nothing about football, they had to be guided by a press which was definitely pro-Rangers. Rangers players would get picked when there were better players in the same positions at Celtic, but when the players got together there was not a 'them and us' mentality. Rangers and Celtic players mixed well, but we didn't speak about the selection system which was akin to apartheid. The Scotland managers must have been driven to distraction by the choices made and in all the time I played for Scotland I don't think the best team possible ever represented the nation.

There were other issues. Celtic players used to get booed playing for Scotland – I did. Hence great Celtic players received scandalously few caps. Bobby Murdoch got about thirteen, Billy McNeill just twenty-nine.

I always felt that I was a reluctant selection. They had to pick me because my performances warranted it, but they would mess me about where they could. I would get picked and then be left on the bench, for instance, in the days when a squad of twelve, not twenty-two, was named for a game. On several occasions I was the one player left out of the starting eleven.

There was another barrier to my international selection. Eleven of my sixteen caps came when I was at Celtic. The number of call-ups mysteriously dried up after I moved south of the border and became an 'Anglo'. The selectors made sure that the bulk of the team were Scottish based. It was almost as if they held a grudge against players like myself and Denis for having the audacity to leave Scotland. You could guarantee the lads who played in England would be singled out for a much rougher ride by the media if Scotland didn't play well. It used to drive Denis Law mad because he would get more criticism than me. At least Denis got picked. Dave Mackay was one of the best players in Britain. He left Hearts for Tottenham in 1959 and won just twenty-two Scotland caps.

Denis and I were always irked by the journalists responsible for comments against players based in England, and we gave them both barrels when our paths crossed. Many a time I saw Denis have an argument in an airport with a journalist that he didn't like. Denis had challenged their small minds by not just moving to English clubs, but also relocating for a time to Italy. He was one of the best players in the world, so why shouldn't he have played for the best clubs in the world?

Although I didn't play in the final game of Scotland's 1966 World Cup qualifying campaign – a 3–0 defeat to Italy in Naples which eliminated Scotland from playing in England – I did take part in other important games of the qualifying stages, and that was because Jock Stein had been installed as caretaker manager. My last outing for Scotland was in a 2–1 victory against Poland in that campaign.

The bias against players who earned their living in England virtually disappeared in the 1970s because so many Scots were the mainstays of English teams – virtually every side had its quota of big Scottish stars. Today, the number of Scottish players at the big English clubs is a tiny fraction of what it once was. The market for players has become a global one for teams like United, and Scotland, with a population of just five million, is a small part of that market. Scotland doesn't produce many great footballers any more which saddens me. Poor coaching, a lack of investment and children playing computer games rather than football in the streets are the explanations. At least now the Scotland manager gets to pick which players he wants in his squad, free from interfering selectors and religious bigotry.

Once I had made my decision I felt relieved and able to concentrate on climbing the next enormous hurdle in United's pursuit of the European Cup. The greatest team of all, Real Madrid, stood between us and a place in the final, but we had

Denis back from injury. There was a buzz about United fans and a lot of them made plans to go to Spain for the second leg of the semi-final. I had a huge amount of respect for Madrid as I'd grown up knowing them as the best team in the world. Alfredo Di Stefano, Paco Gento, and Ferenc Puskas were by common consent the world's three greatest footballers – and they all played in the same team. Di Stefano was the best because his game was so complete. He had skill, a quick brain, and stamina. Gento was the best crosser of the ball. I loved watching him play and so did General Franco – he was Franco's favourite player. If I had known that at the time then I wouldn't have liked him so much. Puskas – 'the Galloping Major' – made up the triumvirate. Puskas had a deadly accurate left-foot and scored virtually a goal a game over 500 matches for Kispest Honved and then Real Madrid. It was a rate he kept up at international level, scoring eighty-four goals in eighty-five games for Hungary, including two in the famous 6–3 victory over England at Wembley in 1953 – England's first home defeat by a continental side.

Jim Baxter told me a story of how he took Puskas out in Glasgow after Real Madrid had beaten Rangers 1–0 at Ibrox in a 1963/64 European Cup match. Puskas loved whisky and wanted to taste the finest Scotland had to offer. He ended up having a skinful in a house on a Glasgow council estate with Jim, but he'd recovered by the time of the second leg as Real Madrid beat Rangers 6–0.

The first leg of our match was at Old Trafford and we knew that we would have to build up a decent lead to defend in Madrid. The Spanish played five across the back, determined not to let us do that.

After just three minutes, Denis cut a cross back for me and I smashed a shot towards goal, but it hit the post. George Best put us in front ten minutes before half-time. We attacked and attacked, but they defended superbly. They were experienced and knew how to soak up pressure and how to remain unfazed in big away matches. The Old Trafford support lifted us, but after ninety minutes all we had was a slender 1–0 lead. It was a game of the highest level played by two of the best teams in Europe.

United didn't pay for the wives to travel to Madrid, so the Irish club in Manchester chartered a plane for fans and wives, costing £22 for a return ticket – about the same as some budget airline fares to Spain forty years later – but then a small fortune.

Most of the Irish in Manchester supported United, partly because the club were seen as the Catholic club with Matt, a devout Catholic, at the helm, and partly because of great Irish United players like Johnny Carey, captain of the 1948 FA Cup winners. He was followed by Shay Brennan, Noel Cantwell, Tony Dunne, Johnny Giles, Paul McGrath, Kevin Moran, Frank Stapleton, Denis Irwin, and Roy Keane. Irish Protestants supported United because of players like George Best and Harry Gregg, Sammy McIlroy and Norman Whiteside. It's not just about religion, though, as United's support has always transcended the political divide in the north of Ireland. Even in the darkest hours of The Troubles you could see kids wearing United shirts in both the predominately Catholic Falls Road and the mainly Protestant Shankill Road.

Paddy McGrath organized the flight, but they had problems when an elderly United fan died in Madrid after collapsing the night before the game. Match tickets were that scarce that the Irish lads on the trip argued about who was to have the dead man's. The body had to stay in Spain for an autopsy, but nobody told the rest of the fans that on the way home. There was some turbulence mid-flight and Paddy told people that it was the coffin moving about in the hold. That really unnerved them.

The bell boy in the wives' hotel tried it on with Noreen and Pam Stepney, Alex's wife. He followed them into their room with their cases and made a move. Spanish lads did that at the time, even if girls were with their boyfriends. He was only a young guy but he fancied his chances, probably because they were giggling after having a few Bacardis. Noreen locked herself in the bathroom and started screaming. That wasn't her style – I would have expected her to stick a punch on him. Pam was knocking on the bathroom door trying to get in, but Noreen wouldn't open it because she was too scared. Pam was screaming her head off and was furious with Noreen. The lad decided to leave and they considered reporting him but decided against it because of his youth and because he would have lost his job.

The wives were chatted up wherever they went in the Spanish capital. The night before the game they went on an organized trip called 'Madrid by night'. They boarded the coach and it literally went round the corner to a nightclub and they saw nothing of the city. Men were all over them because they looked so different from Spanish girls. Spain had started to receive tourists from northern Europe, but hardly any of them went to Madrid.

The Real Madrid president Santiago Bernabéu was more respectful. 'I want Manchester United greeted and treated and respected as the greatest club in the world,' he said. 'And as our friends for many years nothing must go wrong. If we are beaten in the European Cup by Manchester United on Wednesday then we shall have lost to a great team. We have met them on many occasions and it is about time their luck changed.'

About 125,000 people filled the Bernabéu, twice as many as a full Old Trafford could hold. There were two or three thousand United fans – it was probably the club's first significant following for a European away game – and we could hear them because they were behind the goals. The wives sat in the main stand.

Matt had stressed that the first twenty minutes were important. We held out for thirty-two minutes, and nearly went ahead when I curved a free-kick just wide of the post. In truth, Madrid battered us in the first half, with Zoco and Amancio, who had been suspended for the first leg, superb. They played the ball around so quickly that we couldn't get close to them. Pirri headed Amancio's cross to put them 1–0 up and, two minutes before half-time, Paco Gento made it 2–0. A minute later, Zocco put through his own goal when he failed to deal with a Tony Dunne cross, but Madrid made it 3–1 just seconds before the break when that man Amancio hit a half volley which swerved around several United defenders into Stepney's top corner.

As I've said, as a club, the Spaniards had been good to Manchester United in the years after the Munich air crash. They had played friendly games and relations between the two clubs were tight, but that meant nothing to their fans at half-time as we left the field. They were 3–1 up, they were going to the European Cup Final and were soon to retain a trophy they as good as considered their own.

We walked off the field bewildered. There was no escape. The stadium was so big that everywhere we looked we saw happy smiling faces who were revelling in our suffering. In the main stand, the home fans were being friendly and trying to get off with our wives. They were loving life and could afford to be cocksure because their team was so dominant.

I looked around the dressing room and saw only frustration, desperation, anger, and disappointment. Few teams had the quality to take us apart, but Madrid had just done that. And some. It was Matt who brought us to our senses. He stressed the fact that we were only losing 3–2 on aggregate and that we needed to score just one goal to get us back in it. He felt that if we scored one goal then the huge crowd, still the second biggest to watch United in the club's entire history, would become nervous and that would be transmitted to the players.

'Well, lads,' he began calmly, 'We've been playing a defensive game … and we don't play it very well, do we? So let's go out and attack and we should be all right. If we are going to lose then it might as well be by six goals.'

I could hardly believe my ears. Here was a man asking us to attack when we had been struggling to get a kick of the ball. He was so clever, because he had realized that defending wasn't our natural game. As Matt continued his tone became steadily more emotional.

'Now come on boys, believe in yourselves. We're Manchester United; let's have a go at them.' He kept saying it, 'We're Manchester United, let's have a go at them.' If he was desperate – and I think he must have been – then he hid it. Matt probably thought that he would never lift the European Cup. He knew that his side were getting older, as he was, and he also knew this was his last chance. He desperately wanted to lift that trophy for the boys who had died in Munich. I could feel his pain at half-time, but he succeeded in spreading belief and calm.

But we needed more than encouragement and urges to attack at half-time. We needed tactical nous. People sometimes questioned Matt's tactical ability. I never did. He wasn't one for drawing boards. He once told me that football wasn't played on a drawing board with a piece of chalk, but we had to change our game radically otherwise Madrid were going to destroy us.

We waited for more words from Matt. He paced around as we took glugs of water. It was hot in the changing rooms, but there was a feeling of defiance. Maybe Madrid's performance had shocked us into a response. Matt walked back into the centre of the dressing room so that he had everyone's attention. We remained seated, hanging on his every word.

Amancio had tortured us and whacked Nobby Stiles on the thigh.

'Nobby, let Amancio know you are there,' he said sternly. He was hinting, but the message was clear – hit him early in the second half. Nobby nodded, as Deep Heat was rubbed into his leg. He wasn't even sure if he could carry on. David Sadler was told to push up and Matt switched us to 4–3–3. That became 4–2–4 at times.

As we took to the pitch for the second half, our heads were lifted. Matt had made us think we could do it. That second half was one of the greatest forty-five minutes of my life. Real Madrid sat back and relaxed a little. They thought the match was already won and you could see it in their faces. They probably couldn't believe our impudence. Not many teams had made us look fools, so it was time to try and do the same to Madrid. I doubt the home fans had ever seen a team play four attackers in the Bernabéu, but Matt's words kept ringing in our heads: 'We're Manchester United; let's have a go at them.'

And boy, did we have a go.

Nobby went in hard against Amancio as he went to win a goal kick. You couldn't get away with it now, but you could then. As the Spanish fans went mad, I shouted, 'F***ing hell, Nob!!' because I thought he was going to get sent off, but neither the referee or the linesman saw the incident. Nobby then went up to the ref and, pointing at Amancio, said, 'He's injured ref.' Nobby omitted to explain he was responsible. For the rest of the game Nobby snapped away at Amancio who was a diminished force, and barely got a touch of the ball.

We were by far the better side in the second half. Our temperament was more controlled, our desire to win greater. But with fifteen minutes to play we still hadn't scored and were losing the tie. Then we were awarded a free-kick. I looked up and hit a ball into the penalty area, knowing that we had big players like Bill Foulkes and David Sadler who could win the ball. Bill did just that, heading on a free-kick for Dave, who slipped in behind the defenders and knocked the ball in. We were level on aggregate, but there was a surge inside us.

Never mind that a replay in Lisbon had been pencilled in, we had the beating of them and they knew it. The goal gave us a huge lift, a feeling that we were invincible. We didn't need to say anything as we jogged back to re-start the game. There was clarity in our thinking. We'd been too silly too often, losing to Partizan in 1966 and being our own worst enemies. We'd blamed referees and pitches, but deep down we knew we had to do better. And here we were, in front of 125,000, taking Real Madrid apart.

Real Madrid died. Three minutes later I took a long throw for George down the line. George beat both Sanchis and Zocco. They watched bewildered as he ran towards the byline and pulled the ball back for Bill Foulkes. Can you believe it? Our centre-half was playing like a centre-forward. My first reaction was, 'What's that idiot doing there?' But Bill knew best this time. Sixteen years a United player and a Munich survivor, he struck the ball brilliantly into the goal. It was 3–3 on the night, and 4–3 to United on aggregate.

We went mad, absolutely mad, but we also kept our discipline. We made the decision to defend our lead. If we had attacked we would have won the game perhaps by a greater margin, but we sat back a little. We'd done enough for one match.

Some United fans ran on the pitch at the final whistle from behind the goal. The trainer Jack Crompton came from the side and hugged the players. We went back to the Hotel Fenix and hundreds of fans surrounded it and started applauding. They were singing – to the tune of 'Michael, Row the Boat Ashore' – 'We got rid of Real Madrid, Hallelujah! We got rid of Real Madrid, Hallelujah!' Matt's son, Sandy Busby, was absolutely steaming drunk back at the hotel. He was delighted for his dad and tried to get his key off the concierge. If we hadn't helped him he would still be trying to get his key.

As is the norm in Spain, the game had finished very late and we struggled to get something to eat with our wives and girl-friends. Myself, George Best, Alex Stepney, and United fan Freddie Garrity – the tiny lead singer of the chart topping band Freddie and the Dreamers – couldn't find anywhere to eat and ended up in a seedy café. All the café had left was a platter with bits of chicken on it so we ordered it and a couple of bottles of wine, which tasted like petrol.

I was starving and tucked straight into the chicken, and left the bones on the side of the plate. George's then girlfriend, Jackie Glass, was above her station and loved herself. She was very pretty, as George's girls tended to be, but while some of them were down to earth, she seemed posh and I thought that she looked down her nose at people like me because I'd come from a poor background. Jackie told me that it was the height of bad manners to leave the chicken bones by the side of the plate. I said, 'Excuse me, what do you want me to do, throw the chicken bones on the floor, because that would be even worse manners?' She started having a go at me, saying how appalled she was, while Noreen listened. My wife then stood up and whacked her from across the table, knocking Jackie straight off her seat and on to the floor. Noreen then

156

announced, 'Now *that's* bad manners.' I'd never seen anything like it. George burst out laughing. The girls were supposed to then get taxis back to the hotel, but Noreen wouldn't let Jackie in hers. So the girl was stuck in Madrid. George wasn't bothered, he knew that she'd made a fool of herself. That's how we celebrated after reaching the final of the European Cup, where we would play Benfica.

We flew to London the next day for the Professional Footballers' Association annual dinner. We walked in to a standing ovation from the players from all the other clubs. George was named Footballer of the Year for 1968 that night. He collected his statuette and posed for photos, but being crowned Footballer of the Year meant nothing to George. It's sad, but true. He even lost his statuette that night after meeting a girl and going back to her room. That didn't surprise us either. I don't think he ever did find it again so someone, somewhere, has the 1968 Footballer of the Year statuette.

We got the train back to Manchester the following day and not once did he speak about the honour he'd just received. It wasn't that he was being modest, he just didn't care. It would have meant a lot to me, recognition from people in the game, but George's life was spinning too fast, a whirl of success, nights out, media attention and girls, for him to spend any time contemplating it.

Another story about George still staggers me. The distinguished Salfordian artist Harold Riley has always been a United fan. He was friends with L.S. Lowry and has painted portraits of Nelson Mandela and Pope John Paul II. He painted Matt Busby and George, making twenty prints, ten of which he gave to George. He did this because he knew that George was in trouble with the tax man. He presented them to George and said, 'I know an art dealer who will wait for you at Euston Station in London tomorrow. He will pay you

£5,000 for each of your ten prints. Use the money to pay off your tax bill.'

The art dealer called Harold the next day.

'I've met George at Euston,' he said, 'and he's got no prints.' I suspect that George had used them to pay off gambling debts in the casino the night before.

We knew we were going to win the European Cup. I felt that we were absolutely certain to beat Benfica because we'd played them a few times. They had beaten us on a pre-season game in America nine months earlier, but we had been the better team and we knew that we had better players than them.

We'd stayed in the same Los Angeles hotel on that trip to America and I chatted to Eusebio one day in the lift. He got out and I stayed in the lift. As soon as he was out of earshot, the lift attendant said, 'I can't understand why you talk to niggers like him.' I wanted to strangle him. Had I been in Glasgow and not representing Manchester United on tour I would have done. Instead, I abused him verbally and told him that he should be ashamed to use such language. I was right in his face because I was so angry. The lift attendant wasn't expecting my reaction and he looked frightened. Good. I abhor racism, because I suffered it as a Catholic in Glasgow. Someone might describe someone as being 'coloured' and I say, 'What colour are they, pink, yellow, orange? He's a black man, just as we're white.' Although, like most people, I go on holiday every year to try and get a tan to become black.

Our exploits in Europe had made the headlines, but for most of the 1967/68 season our league form was that of champions. Following that opening league day defeat to Everton, we went eleven games unbeaten, before Nottingham Forest beat us 3–1 at the City Ground on 28 October. We lost to title contenders Leeds a couple of weeks later, but then we beat fellow rivals Liverpool and inflicted the same 3–1 score line on Everton at Old Trafford as they had done to us at Goodison Park. Five wins in succession after Christmas meant that by the time we beat Tottenham away 2–1 on 3 February, we were clear favourites to retain the league. I'm not a gambling man, but a lot of the lads went to watch the racing at Kempton Park the day before the game and were offered odds of 1/6 on United winning the league. The next day we beat Tottenham so those odds would have been shortened even more.

Then it started to go wrong. We lost at Burnley the following week, despite them being reduced to ten men for much of the game. Chelsea and Coventry beat us a couple of weeks later, the 2–0 defeat at Highfield Road no real surprise as the game came just two days after we'd returned from the gruelling trip to Poland. Then we played Manchester City on 27 March. Before the game we were first in the table on forty-five points, City second on forty-three.

It remains probably the most important Manchester derby ever played and we started brightly by taking the lead after just thirty-eight seconds through George. City came back brilliantly and scored three times through Colin Bell, Francis Lee and George Heslop. For once, City fans looked forward to going to work the morning after a derby. And it was a feeling to which they would become accustomed as United won just one of the next thirteen encounters. After the game, the league table saw United, City, and Leeds all level on forty-five points, with Liverpool just two points behind.

City's rise had surprised us. We had beaten them 2–1 at Maine Road earlier in the season and I left that game thinking that we were the superior side, with more quality players. But then City manager Joe Mercer had bought Francis Lee from Bolton earlier in the season and he turned their fortunes around. Colin Bell was probably City's best player. He was a

159

great passer with superior vision who could run forever. I thought he was going to transfer to United at one point, but it didn't happen.

Mike Summerbee was also a top class player, brave with good control and a strong will to win. I'm still good friends with him today. He and George Best were very close, though – George was the best man at Mike's wedding – and at one point George and Mike bought a flat together. When he moved in George asked me if we could lend him some sheets for the beds so Noreen gave him a beautiful set of bedding which we'd been given as a wedding present. We never saw the sheets again. When Noreen told him later that she was annoyed because he'd never returned them, George replied, 'I'm sorry, but they've been well used.' Noreen suddenly lost all interest in those sheets.

Mercer's best decision in transforming City was appointing Malcolm Allison as his assistant in 1965. Allison gave players such a lift and told them that they were capable of anything; he was a great motivator of people and a fascinating man. He would charm the birds out of the trees, especially if they were female. He fancied every girl he ever spoke to, but he was respectful and didn't try to crack on to them all. Women loved him; they felt that when he spoke to them that they were the only ones that mattered. There was a lot of talk about Malcolm coming to Old Trafford in later years, but it came to nothing.

Our form didn't improve after the derby defeat, but the league was not to be decided until the final game of the season. We lost at home 2–1 to Sunderland in an Old Trafford that was filled to its then 63,000 capacity. Meanwhile, up at Newcastle, City won 4–3 in a stunning game. That meant we finished the league as runners-up on fifty-six points, with City two points ahead and champions. Matt was gracious in defeat and went straight to the television studios after the game to offer his congratulations to Joe Mercer in a live television link-up. We were a better team than City, but they won the league and all credit to them.

City had a great team and they should have won the league championship more than once. We were friends with City players; they were nice lads, although Nobby Stiles hated City because he was a Mancunian and United through and through. The rivalry with the London clubs was not at the same level. We always wanted to beat them because they thought that they were better than us and that northern teams were from the sticks and all lived in cobbled streets, with outside toilets, but the real rivalry was with City, Leeds, and Liverpool.

After the Sunderland defeat, I said to the lads in the changing room, 'Well, that's it. City have won the title. Now we've got to win the European Cup. It's the biggest prize of the lot ... and anyway, it's all that is left.'

Our preparation for the European Cup Final, held that year at Wembley, was very relaxed. We stayed in a medieval looking hotel in Egham in Surrey. Matt didn't want to tempt fate by booking a hotel for the final so after we beat Real Madrid the trainer Jack Crompton was sent to London to try and find us something suitable. He spent the whole day in the centre of London without success, then a BBC contact told him about Egham and we were fixed up.

We travelled south on the Monday ahead of the game. We were in for a shock when we arrived at the hotel – it was four hundred years old and looked like it hadn't changed its furniture since the day it opened. There were huge fireside chairs with drapes and all sorts of antiques and we kept expecting to see blokes with swords fighting their way across the lounge carpet. Jimmy Murphy came in for a lot of stick because his room had a huge four poster bed. We told him that Richard the Lionheart had once slept in it.

Jimmy, like Matt, was very religious, and he arranged for a private mass. All the players went, regardless of their religion. We felt under no pressure, partly because we were excluded from the hype surrounding the game.

Billy Gillis, a friend of mine from Glasgow, came down to see me in the hotel with his wife. Another lad, Jimmy O'Donnell, who was a mad Celtic fan who owned some nightclubs in Glasgow, came down with three gangster mates, all of them with scars on their faces. They were saying things like, 'That's our European Cup you are trying to win.' I've no idea how they found the hotel, but they attended the mass and Matt didn't mind. No journalists were around, but, as I've said, journalists were viewed differently then to now.

The day before the game, I saw Brian Kidd looking into a small pool in one of the gardens. He was messing around with frogs like a kid would do. As a frog sat on a lily-pad Brian reached out to lift him. But he stretched too far and went into the pool head first. He came out covered in slime and it was a very embarrassing situation for him. We found it hilarious.

Brian's innocence used to make me laugh. When we travelled to London to play games, Matt would take two of the promising younger lads down for the experience of being with the team. Brian Kidd and Francis Burns came down with us for one game at West Ham. We were eating and I said to Brian, 'Do you fancy a prawn cocktail?' He got a bit irate and said, 'Pat, I don't drink.'

Brian's mother-in-law came from the village my family is from in Donegal and they are distantly related to us. I thought he was fantastic when he came onto the scene at Manchester United. He had everything: height, speed, strength. Brian had a great career in football and went on to play for Arsenal,

Everton, Manchester City, and Bolton Wanderers, but his career could have been better – that's how good he was. Maybe that wasn't his fault. Brian was unfortunate with the timing in that he came into a team that started to deteriorate after 1969. If Brian had joined us when we were all around twenty-four or twenty-five, then I think he would have been a big, big star.

Brian excelled as a coach, too, in later years and forged a hugely successful double act when he was assistant to Sir Alex Ferguson between 1991 and 1998. Players like Ryan Giggs and Paul Scholes adored Kiddo because he played such an important part in their development. In the case of Scholes, Kiddo had spotted him playing five-a-side as a kid in Middleton, north Manchester.

Brian was better cut out as an assistant because he enjoyed working with the players on the training ground rather than having to deal with the media and other areas of management. Sir Alex Ferguson rated him very highly and I remember seeing him in the corridor at White Hart Lane in December 1998 trying to persuade Brian to stay at Old Trafford and not join Blackburn Rovers, who had offered him the manager's job. I could understand why, but I could also see why Brian accepted the challenge of management, and not just because he was offered far more than what he was on at Old Trafford. United lost a great servant when Brian Kidd left the club.

With Denis Law in a Manchester hospital recovering from a knee injury that would rule him out of the final, this would be Brian's biggest game. The BBC thought it would be a good idea to put cameras in Denis's hospital room. They wanted to show his reaction and perhaps get his comments after the game. Matt raised no objections to this idea and the hospital authorities were quite willing to allow a camera crew at his bedside. The only person who didn't like the idea was Denis. He said 'No' and that was that.

Denis made few public appearances and preferred his privacy to the fees he could have picked up. He avoided public places where he would be quickly recognized and in many ways was a lone wolf. He even had his own gimmick for not getting involved. If, after training, some of the boys asked him what he was doing in the afternoon, he would always answer 'gardening' with a straight face. He wouldn't know one end of a weed from the other, but it gave him an excuse to go off on his own and earned him the nickname, 'the gardener'.

Denis chose his company very carefully. He would have rather had a beer in a quiet pub with ordinary blokes than mix with celebrities at a cocktail party. If he liked you then Denis could be great company, but there was no middle road with him. If he didn't like someone he wouldn't talk to them.

We trained at Wembley under the floodlights the night before the game. I'd not been there for a few years, but I wasn't in awe of the place. The following day we caught our team coach from the hotel to the ground. The journey took about an hour, but Londoners were clapping us all the way and cars were beeping us. The whole country wanted us to win and there was little evidence of the jealousy which now surrounds Manchester United.

As the bus drove up Wembley Way before the game, I spotted a bloke in the crowd wearing a fez. I could hardly believe my eyes when I saw a bunch of people close to him wearing fezzes too. The comedian Tommy Cooper was popular at the time so I didn't know whether they were mimicking him or not. Then two of them held up a banner and in red letters I read 'Cairo Branch – Manchester United supporters'. I couldn't stop thinking about them. I thought how miserable they would be if we lost and they had to go all the way home with nothing but unhappy memories.

Having said that, it didn't enter my head that we wouldn't win the game for one minute. People were pointing out that Benfica had knocked five past Real Madrid a couple of years earlier, but I was having none of it. When I saw the crowd I became even more certain – 90,000 of the 100,000 there were United fans. They sang 'Happy Birthday' to Brian Kidd before the game as it was his nineteenth birthday. The band played the national anthem but that meant nothing to me. I don't believe in the Royal Family and just stood there. I couldn't believe that we bowed down to people who hadn't done a proper day's work in their lives and I still can't. Other countries have national anthems about their countries, not about their rulers.

The first half was dull. The Italian referee was busy blowing his whistle because the Benfica players tried to hurt George whenever they could. The Benfica manager Otto Gloria was a good man, who had said very complimentary things about Matt and George before the game, but his players had other ideas. Six or seven of that Benfica team had played in the Portugal side which reached the semi-final of the World Cup in 1966, so they were wily as anything. We were most worried about the height of their attacker Torres beforehand.

United were the better team over ninety minutes. Bobby gave us the lead with a rare header from a David Sadler cross, while David himself should have had a hat-trick. Benfica's equalizer, ten minutes from time, knocked the heart out of us and we nearly lost it in the last few minutes of normal time when Eusebio had a great chance to win the game – and Benfica's third European Cup of the 1960s. Alex Stepney kept us alive with a tremendous save. And so the game went to extra-time. While we were having our leg muscles massaged out on the pitch, Matt came among us and was particularly angry with us for giving the ball away too much in the middle. 'Use the ball properly, get hold of the middle of the park again, and you'll find yourselves not nearly as tired as the others. Now go to it and play football.'

We did. From somewhere, we just found heart. Alex Stepney kicked the ball into the Benfica area, where George mesmerized their defenders before rounding the goalkeeper Henrique and flicked the ball nonchalantly into the goal. George took ages to put the ball in and I wondered what he was doing. He had told me in the hotel before the game that he wanted to take on five or six players before getting down on his hands and knees and heading the ball into the net. I'd laughed when he'd revealed his plan, but I wasn't laughing with the game at 1–1 and me thinking that George was going to attempt his daft idea. The ball took an age to cross the line, but when it did I ran up to George and shouted, 'I thought you were never going to put it in.' He just smiled.

Of all the players, I was delighted for John Aston. It was his best game for United and he tormented Adolfo down Benfica's right flank by running at him and getting him on the back foot. Brian Kidd headed United's third. It hadn't been Brian's best game but he headed brilliantly. It was 3–1 and I saw Brian wipe away the tears as he returned to the centre circle. A few minutes later he centred for Bobby who hit a gem of a shot. Manchester United 4, Benfica 1.

The final whistle brought scenes of elation. All the players looked for Matt. We didn't have to go far as he came towards us doing a half jog, half dance of joy from the bench. I was knackered, absolutely exhausted after extra-time on a scorching hot summer night, but buoyed by adrenalin. I made sure that I shook hands with as many Benfica players as possible, such was the respect I had for them, but I just wanted to hug

Matt – we all did. I got close to him and put my arms around him and held him tightly. He was wearing a suit and I noticed how rigid his neck was in his shirt collar. I said, 'I told you we'd do it, I told you.' Matt just grinned, his mouth slack and open, his eyes moist, almost closed. A bespectacled commissioner with 'Wembley Stadium' sewn into the front of his cap was trying to guard Matt, but he didn't want protection from his boys, and especially Bobby who was on the other side of the commissioner. We were in the company of a man who would never be happier and I felt honoured we had helped Matt realize his one ambition – to win the European Cup.

After parading the cup I returned to the dressing room. Matt, who had gathered his thoughts enough to speak, said he was the proudest man in England after the game. He told me that he remembered the words I had said to him two years previously, when I told him we would win the European Cup after the defeat to Partizan Belgrade. I looked at him and he said, 'This has been the greatest moment of my life.' He was truly happy, truly satisfied that he had done everyone justice, especially the boys who died in Munich a decade before. I was happy – of course I was – but I felt really tired and emotionally drained, far more than usual. This sounds strange, but I was more elated seeing United win the European Cup in Barcelona in 1999 than I was after playing in the match which saw us win it in 1968. In Barcelona I was with my two sons and lots of close friends, people I'd known for decades, and we celebrated together.

At Wembley, the trainer Jack Crompton told me my exhaustion was just the after effects of playing in such a demanding game but I wasn't convinced. I told myself that I would feel a lot better after a hot bath, but I didn't. David Coleman, the TV presenter, was a United fan. He had been an athlete who trained with the team pre-Munich. He came to

167

the dressing room at Wembley after the game with a bottle of champagne. It was hot in the dressing room and the cold champagne gave me a chill in my stomach. It made me feel worse straightaway and I wasn't the only one, judging by Bobby's face. Jack suggested that both of us get some fresh air so we loosened our ties and staggered out onto the dog track and across Wembley towards the main stand. The stadium was empty, silent. Even in my awful state I remember thinking how hard it was to believe that a hundred thousand people had been there little more than half-an-hour before. It was then that I vomited and soon after Bobby was doing the same. Jack Crompton was running in between us panicking because he didn't know what was wrong.

We told Jack that we couldn't go to the victory reception but would have to go straight back to the hotel. Jack was marvellous. He had been itching to join in the celebrations, but instead told us to wait where we were while he found us a taxi. We were under the main stand, me clinging to one pillar and Bobby to another. European champions? We looked like two Glaswegian drunks on Argyle Street on a Saturday night.

I hadn't had anything to eat since before the game and this made my illness all the more worrying. A taxi soon took the three of us to our post-match hotel, The Russell. An American lady was checking us in. Bobby and I both threw up again in the lobby. She had no idea who we were and was disgusted. I felt terrible, but I had to go to the post-match reception. I went up to the room where Noreen was dressing. She took one look at me and knew that I wasn't well. Still, I made it back down to the official reception where 'What a Wonderful World' by Louis Armstrong was playing. Matt loved that song. He always fancied himself as a crooner and sang along. Everyone was on such a high.

Except me. I went to back to bed. I put the television on and watched the scenes of celebration, with United fans jumping in the fountains of Trafalgar Square.

After a while my Uncle Hughie and Johnny Speight, who wrote the TV series *'Til Death us do Part*, came up to the room and persuaded me to come down to the banquet. I had got them both tickets for the game together with Warren Mitchell, who starred as Alf Garnett in the show. A Scouser, Johnny was a big Liverpool fan, but he was a pal to all the United players. He took one look at my face and wandered off.

It was about three in the morning when Noreen looked in to see how I was. The party was still in full swing and since I felt a little better I decided to try and go downstairs.

The barmen were working like beavers and Johnny Speight bought me a Coca-Cola so that I didn't look out of place. I tried to make an effort and everyone crowded around me, clapping and congratulating me. John Colerain, the ex-Celt who made a name for himself as a coach in Irish football, was delighted at our win for my sake and kept slapping me on the back. He didn't know that he nearly knocked me out each time. I think he realized when I told him that I was going to the toilets to be sick again.

It should have been the best night of my life but I felt awful. Bobby was also absent from the party but with him, I think it was different. There was more emotion. He'd played with the lads who'd died in 1958 and was in the mood for reflection, not celebration.

A lot of the players and their wives went on to Danny La Rue's club. When they walked in Danny announced, 'Welcome to the great Manchester United, the champions of Europe.' The whole place erupted with applause.

I stayed at the hotel. I intended to go back to my room, but just before I did I met a lady who made me forget my illness for a while. She was the mother of Duncan Edwards, who'd died at Munich. She was there because one of the least publicized gestures which Manchester United made before the European Cup Final was to invite the near relatives of the victims of the Munich air crash to the game. That was Matt's idea and he also invited two representatives from each of the clubs that we had beaten on the way to the final. United had class, no doubt. We all wore a shirt, tie, and club blazer wherever we travelled. Other clubs didn't. Matt would always say, 'You are representing Manchester.' Not Manchester United, but the city of Manchester.

Meeting Duncan's mother was very moving. She was an ordinary working class girl from Dudley and told me that I'd reminded her of Duncan in the style that I played. That was a huge compliment and I didn't know what to say. I'd admired her son so much and had he not died at Munich it is unlikely that I would have ever joined United. I told Mrs Edwards what I great player I reckoned her son was in the half a dozen times I had seen him before the crash. I then slipped away to bed feeling very humble.

I woke very late the next morning. I didn't know the full medical explanation of what happened the previous night. Jack Crompton reckoned it could have been a nervous reaction to the strain of the final. The fact that Bobby was ill, too, suggests that as two older members of the team we may have felt a greater responsibility than the rest. Maybe we realized more how important it was to win. Maybe we were more afraid of losing.

We caught the train back to Manchester at lunchtime. Two fans came up to me at Euston and told me what a great night it had been at Wembley. They explained that they were Scots like myself who lived in Manchester and that they were big United fans. They seemed like a couple of nice blokes enjoying the moment. There were lots of trains leaving London for Manchester that day but ours was a 'special' for the players, families, and officials. The club had arranged it and everything on board was free. If you wanted a bottle from the bar you simply asked for it.

Some of the boys and I were playing cards to pass the time when I suddenly felt a hand on my shoulder and a voice saying, 'Hullo Pat, how's it going? This is a great train isn't it?' I looked up and it was the same two Scots who had talked to me at the station. They looked the same except they each carried a full bottle of whisky under their arm. When they had gone the boys naturally asked who they were and I said that I had no idea. The two chancers probably told people for years what a generous club Manchester United were.

The European Cup had its own compartment on the train and two security guards watched over it. There was a special open-topped bus waiting to take us from Piccadilly Station to the Town Hall. It was led by five white police horses. The idea was that the players would be on the top deck showing off the cup. I climbed the steps of the bus and nearly fell down again in shock when I got upstairs. My two Scottish 'friends' were only sitting up there waiting for the team to join them. I admired their ingenuity but their blagging was going a bit too far and I pointed them out to the club secretary Les Olive. They left cheerily, still clutching their free bottles of whisky. I stood at the front of the bus clasping the European Cup with my right hand and resting my left hand on the shoulder of Matt. I felt proud to stand alongside him.

Mancunians don't need reminding what a special night it was in Manchester. Newspapers estimated that 250,000 packed into the streets around Albert Square. There was a specially erected platform there and we all crowded on to hear speeches from the mayor and Matt.

In Lisbon, a few hundred Benfica fans waited to meet their team at the airport. Mario Coluna, the Benfica captain, said, 'In the first ninety minutes Benfica deserved victory. Unfortunately, in extra-time, we were taken by surprise by the speed of the English.'

The Manchester city police band struck up with 'When the Saints go Marching In' – but the crowd chanted 'United! United!' to drown them out. They drowned out words from the mayor and Matt as they urged us to hold up the European Cup. Over 400 fans were treated for fainting. Matt held the trophy up and the place went wild. 'Champions! Champions!' they sang and we joined in.

All the England internationals – Nobby Stiles, Bobby Charlton, Alex Stepney, and Brian Kidd – couldn't be there as they had travelled to West Germany for a game. Bill Foulkes wasn't there either as he was playing in a qualifying round of the Cheshire County golf championship – that's how seriously Bill took his golf. It was left to me, being the senior pro, to make a speech. I said that the success wasn't just down to the lads who had played at Wembley against Benfica, but all the seventeen or eighteen who had played in all the games – Denis Law being the main example as he missed the final. Like Roy Keane in 1999, Denis felt that he didn't deserve a winner's medal. He got one and he deserved it. The crowd went wild, but I could have said that black was blue and they would have cheered.

As I turned to edge off the platform I heard a voice behind me saying: 'What a night, Pat … what a night, eh?' I thought, 'It can't be. Nobody could talk their way onto that platform.' But they had done. Right behind me were the same two smiling United fans still clutching their bottles. In a way, I was secretly pleased that they had succeeded. Because it proves that if two Scots set out to achieve something then no amount of Englishmen will stop them.

EIGHT

Cheated

Matt had achieved everything he wanted. His desire and
hunger had been sated. He'd reached his goal. A few months
after winning the European Cup I went to see him in the
Cromford Club. He was having a drink with Paddy McGrath
and I joined them. Matt mentioned retiring. It was nothing
much, just what his thoughts were, and he didn't give me
much chance to reply, but when I looked back I thought it was
significant because that was the first time I heard him mention
retirement after the trophy was finally in his hands. We knew
he couldn't go on forever, but we didn't like to dwell too much
on Matt leaving because it was a prospect which made all the
players uncomfortable. For whatever reason, Matt decided to
stay on at Old Trafford, but I don't think it was because he
had any burning ambition to retain the European Cup or win
the league again because he'd already achieved his dream.

Matt had turned fifty-nine on 26 May 1968. He was
knighted that summer for his services to football but he was
getting old and, privately after what he'd told me in the Cromford Club, I wondered how long he had left at United. I
believed he was the right man to stay in charge because I

173

couldn't pick a likely successor, apart from Jock Stein who was settled at Celtic, but I wasn't sure where the drive was going to come from and I was keen to see how he was once the season started. From a selfish perspective, I wondered what my own future would be under a new manager but rather than worry about what lay in store, I wanted to enjoy the summer and our new status of European champions.

The family and I went to Mallorca for a long break. Package holidays to the island were in their infancy and the island hadn't been overrun. I was a working-class lad with a middle-class income so we could afford to go there. Footballers loved Mallorca and Palma was the place. We used to drink around bars in the old town and you'd always bump into other first division players and talk football. George Best spent every summer in Mallorca and became friends with a lad called Felix who ran a bar there. When George started getting involved with bars in Manchester in the early 1970s he asked Felix to come over and he still lives in Manchester now, running a restaurant called Harpers which has stayed popular with the football community.

That summer, I also went to watch the cricket Test Match against the Australians at Old Trafford. Denis Law came along and we were taken into the England dressing room. We sat talking to Geoff Boycott and Basil d'Oliveira but we didn't learn much about cricket. It turned out that they were both United fans and all they did was talk about football. Interest in United was at an all-time high.

We'd won the European Cup and we wanted to retain it. That was the priority among the players and we believed that we were good enough to win the competition again, as well as mounting a challenge for the league. In reality, we were deluding ourselves as our league form dipped badly. We didn't admit it to ourselves, but a few of us were past our sell-by dates. Changes were needed, but they didn't happen on the scale they should have.

United were not a dominant team in the transfer market like they are today and Matt didn't always get the players he wanted. Chelsea may have more money than United now, but then there were five or six teams who were capable of paying more than United. Matt again tried to get Mike England – a defender who was good enough to play alongside the best of us. Jimmy Murphy had been manager of Wales and had smoothed the path for England to come to Old Trafford. He wanted to sign, but when it came to money Tottenham paid more for him and United got gazumped.

United did find the money for Willie Morgan. He cost a club record £117,000 from Burnley. Willie was a good player and Jock Stein tried to sign him for Celtic. He was about to sign for Leeds under Don Revie but then he changed his mind and signed for United. He said at the time that I was the biggest factor influencing his decision because I was an old Celtic hero of his. That was a nice thing to say.

Willie settled straightaway, making his debut at home to Tottenham Hotspur on 28 August 1968. United had lost the previous home game 4–0 to Chelsea and Tottenham were formidable opponents. Willie tore Cyril Knowles's side to bits and we won 3–1. It was a rare highlight from that season.

I landed Willie in trouble one day. Time keeping wasn't always my forte and I asked him to pick me up before one game. We were playing in Sheffield and the coach was due to leave Old Trafford at ten. He got to mine at ten to ten but I'd overslept. I opened the door and went back upstairs to get changed. He thought I'd gone back to bed. Then I came downstairs and made some breakfast. Willie was really worried because nobody misbehaved with Matt and we were going to be late. He crept on the coach hoping that nobody noticed but

175

just before we arrived in Sheffield, the gaffer pulled him over and quietly said: 'William, don't be picking up Patrick again.' Matt viewed my occasional tardiness as a misdemeanour, but he didn't want it infecting other players in the squad.

We didn't become bad players, but maybe subconsciously we were like Matt. What else was there for us to achieve? It was a confusing time and I wasn't sure whether Matt's or my own career had run its course, but I don't think any of us realized just how quick our decline would be in the league. We were letting people down week after week and given that we'd just won the European Cup that was a lot of people – over 61,000 saw our first league game. We won just four times in our first fourteen games and, looking back, Matt showed too much loyalty to those players who had served him so well. He was criticized for that when our form dipped and accused of being over indulgent in his treatment of wrong doers and lax in his discipline – but he could still be tough when he wanted to be, albeit in his own way. He'd get you in for a discussion and after a while you'd find yourself agreeing with him. You would then say that you accepted his judgement and sentence but by the time you had got home you'd think, 'My god, he's conned me again.' But one thing he never did was abuse you or dress you down in front of others, which we all greatly appreciated.

Very often, if he had you on the carpet for something or other, or was about to drop you from the team, you'd find yourself summoned during the week to the referee's changing room which was only a few yards down the corridor from the players' dressing rooms. Whenever we came back from training to have a bath or shower, we'd all run past that ref's cubby hole in case the door opened and Matt was there to request our presence inside. That was his punishment hole.

As well as focusing on retaining the European Cup, there was another big event for us in the 1968/69 season, the two unofficial matches of the World Club championships against Estudiantes de la Plata of Argentina. The game between the champions of Europe and South America had first been played in 1960 and it had a history of bad blood. In 1967, Racing Club of Buenos Aires played Celtic and I was at the Glasgow leg of the game, which was staged on a Wednesday night. Celtic won 1–0 and Billy McNeill scored with a header, but the Argentines kicked Celtic from pillar to post. I was about to drive back to Manchester the following day wc always got Thursdays off – when I stopped at the George Hotel in Glasgow for a spot to eat with Jock Stein, Neilly Mochan and some of the Celtic lads. I told them that they were going to face murder over in Argentina and that they had to be careful. I wasn't wrong. Celtic's game was almost abandoned over there after six players were dismissed after a big fight – although two refused to leave the pitch. Racing bullied Celtic throughout once more.

A year later and it was our turn, as European champions, to play the South American champions Estudiantes, with the first leg of the game in Argentina. La Plata is thirty miles south of Buenos Aires, but they chose to play the game in the capital at the home of Boca Juniors because their stadium was bigger. With the extra fans they were able to offer their players a win bonus of £1,750 per man, a fortune over there. We would have been glad of it at United as well.

We played Newcastle at home on Saturday 21 September and left for South America straight after the game. Without having had time for something to eat, we flew from Manchester to London. From London we flew to Paris, where we had another hour in the airport. By 11.30 pm, we were in Madrid. We were knackered, and that was before the longest flight, a ten hour overnight stretch to Rio de Janeiro. The feature film on the plane was *In Enemy Country* – and that's how we felt.

From Rio we flew to Buenos Aires, another three hours. The son of Billy Butlin, the holiday camp owner, was on the plane, and was a United fan – you remember daft details like that. We were shattered when we arrived, but it seemed like we were walking into a holiday camp when we saw a Union Jack flying above the terminal, not that it meant much to me. Everyone seemed to be really friendly as we left the plane, but then the mood changed as we walked through the airport and had to encounter a more hostile public.

A crowd had gathered to greet us and a loudspeaker announcement was made as each player walked into the airport. 'Bobby Charlton – El Supremo' the announcer said. 'George Best – El Beatle' and then 'Nobby Stiles – El Bandito.' The fans booed us relentlessly as we walked through.

Still, the country club where we stayed outside the city was beautiful, with two golf courses, a driving range, bowling alley, and tennis courts. The food was magnificent – the steaks seemed to be a foot long and three inches thick. I roomed with Alex Stepney, while David Sadler was with George Best. Nobby had been singled out at the airport and his day didn't get any better when he saw the room which he shared with Jimmy Ryan – we nicknamed it 'the dungeon' because it had no windows.

There were other attempts to make us feel welcome. A game of polo was organized for us to watch but we were working-class lads who easily got bored watching aristocrats play a toffs' sport.

Despite the efforts of the organizers, it was only two years after England had won the World Cup and the Argentine people hadn't forgotten that the England manager Alf Ramsey had called them animals. The fights between Celtic and Racing Club added to the ill-feeling and it was decided that the two teams would meet in front of the press the night before the game as a gesture of goodwill. Matt wasn't keen on us going – his players

178

spending a night travelling back and forward less than 24 hours before the game was not like how he liked to prepare – but he decided that we should do so in the name of goodwill.

Despite having a police escort wherever we went – from a training session at the stadium to a visit to church – it took us an hour to get into the centre of the city from our hotel. We were ushered into a smoky room where a couple of hundred media people were waiting for us. We waited for the Estudiantes players to arrive – and we waited. The crafty Argentines never turned up. Their manager Osvaldo Zubeldia said, 'This is a game for men. I see no point in the teams kissing each other.' If that was the case, why did he agree initially that his players would attend?

We had another hour's journey back to the hotel. Matt rightly felt insulted and was raging – we all were – but at least we got see much of Buenos Aires, a vast sprawl populated by three million. The centre of town was fine with boulevards, statues, and grand buildings, but it seemed to be encircled by shanty towns and the poverty which I saw from the coach window appalled me. People seemed to be living in chicken coops.

The bad blood continued on the day of the game. The official match programme had an article which called Nobby Stiles 'an assassin' and described him as a 'brutal, badly intentioned and bad sportsman'.

The atmosphere generated by the 60,000 crowd in the stadium before the game was easily the most hostile I've ever experienced in my career – far more extreme than a Rangers v Celtic game. Soldiers with helmets, batons, and tear gas stood behind the goals. Newspapers reports said there were 2,000 police and soldiers at the game, but they all seemed scared of the fans who jumped around on the terraces.

None of this ruffled Matt. As we were about to leave the dressing rooms he said, 'Don't let yourselves be intimidated ...

but don't allow yourselves to become provoked either. Go in hard and play your normal game and if you feel that you are going to get agitated, pull out.'

We walked out of the dressing room and emerged from the tunnel. A big bag of what appeared to be minced meat was thrown from the stand and exploded over Bobby Charlton's shirt. The police did nothing. A fire bomb was released which covered the pitch in a dense red smoke. The referee was used to the smoke, I saw him having a fag in the tunnel before we walked out. I seriously feared for our safety, should anything bad happen. And plenty did.

Their fans were loud. Deafening chants of 'Estudiantes! Estudiantes!' rang around the stadium.

From kick-off it was clear that Nobby was a marked man. Carlos Bilardo, a qualified doctor who went on to manage Argentina to success in the 1986 World Cup, head-butted him early in the game which left him with a gash above his eye and double vision. Estudiantes got their goal soon after, but that didn't stop the referee, who was from nearby Paraguay, from also targeting Nobby. He booked him for standing too close to one of their players at a throw-in. David Sadler scored an equalizer which the referee initially allowed but then changed his mind, saying that he was offside.

The pitch was terrible; the grass grew in clumps all over the place. It was far worse than what we were used to. At half-time Nobby and I spoke about how we could beat their offside trap which kept catching us out. We said that if our forwards came back as their defence ran out then Nobby should make some runs from midfield to try and catch them off guard and going the wrong way.

They were kicking us and getting away with it. They had ability, but they were nasty. Bobby Charlton needed two stitches in his shin after Bilardo caught him, and Nobby –

after intense provocation and some filthy tackles – finally snapped with ten minutes to go. Nobby did what we agreed at half-time but he was given offside and raised his arms angrily, like most players would. It was nothing, but the referee issued a straight red card and sent him off, meaning that he would miss the second leg in Manchester.

The headline in the *Manchester Evening News* screamed 'SAVAGERY', but FIFA said that if there was any retaliation from United in the second leg then the club would be punished heavily.

The United fans chanted 'animals' at the Estudiantes players back at Old Trafford, but they shocked us by taking the lead through Seba Veron's dad Juan Ramon after five minutes, putting them 2–0 up on aggregate. We were not helped when Denis Law had to have four stitches in a gashed knee and had to go off. Without him and Nobby we were well under strength.

The game really came alive in the last ten minutes. George Best was tackled viciously by Medina and retaliated with a punch which floored the Argentine. Both players were sent off. Three minutes before the end I hit a free-kick into the box which Willie Morgan smashed past their keeper Poletti. We chased an aggregate equalizer which would have meant a play-off game in Amsterdam. Brian Kidd scored from a Willie Morgan cross and 64,000 inside Old Trafford went wild. Except that the referee had already blown the final whistle a couple of seconds before the goal. The Argentines had been vicious in the first game, but far better in the second. It was the early goal that killed us.

The games against Estudiantes took attention away from our poor league form. Between mid-October and mid-January we won just three league matches. We were European champions, but sat six points off the bottom of the table.

Rumours began to circulate that Matt was on the verge of announcing his retirement. He said nothing to the players, but in January 1969, with the team sixth from bottom of the league, United issued the following statement: 'Sir Matt has informed the board that he wishes to relinquish the position of team manager at the end of the present season. The chairman and directors have tried to persuade him to carry on and it was only with great reluctance that his request has been accepted. The board fully appreciates the reason for his decision and it was unanimously agreed that Sir Matt be appointed general manager of the club which he is very happy to accept.'

The same day that the statement was released, Matt gathered us around after training at The Cliff and explained that he was quitting. 'I'm getting too old to do this,' he said. 'I've been here for over twenty years and it's time for someone else to have a go.'

Matt kept it brief and even though we were expecting the news, the reality hit us hard. I looked around and the faces of my team-mates were full of sadness.

'I don't want this announcement to detract from the rest of the season,' Matt continued. 'We've still got a lot of work to do.'

No successor was mentioned immediately. Matt's decision proved what we knew, that the European Cup had fulfilled his ambitions and that he wanted to hand over the reins. Matt later said that he felt United had ceased to become a football club and had become an institution and he felt that he was spending less and less time on the playing side – the most important aspect of any football club. It was ironic then that he accepted the position of General Manager which would entail spending virtually no time on the training field. But the change would not come until the end of the season and there was still a lot more football to play.

By the middle of March, our league record read: Played 31, Won 8, Drawn 10, Lost 13. That was relegation form. Can you imagine the reigning European champions being relegated? Bobby Charlton had been out injured for a time, and there were three or four players who just weren't good enough to play for Manchester United, but we were going over the hill. In some ways, our success had worked against us. There wasn't a squad system and players were maybe reluctant to join United because they didn't think that they would get a game.

We had to get our league form together and we started that in March with an 8–1 victory over Queens Park Rangers in which Willie got a hat-trick. The crowd was just 36,638 that day – a drop of almost 30,000 on the crowds we had been enjoying at the beginning of the season. Between that QPR game and the end of the season we played eleven matches, winning seven, drawing two and losing two. That run hauled us up to eleventh position, a failure by United's standards, but far better than where we had been two months earlier.

We still had a hunger, but we only seemed to find it in the cups. Our main aim was to retain the European Cup, but we also reached the FA Cup sixth round, going out to Everton by a single goal at Goodison in front of 63,464, the biggest crowd to watch us in England that season. For much of my United career, the biggest crowds to watch us play were frequently at Goodison Park. The crowds in the FA Cup that season were huge. Watford had 34,000 at home to us, Birmingham City 52,000. And the two replay games we played at Old Trafford against those teams were both 63,000 sell-outs. As European champions, we were the star performers, no matter how much we were fading.

Our best performances came in the European Cup. We had drawn the Irish champions Waterford in the first round. They switched the game to Lansdowne Road in Dublin, which staged its first ever football game, a correct decision as 48,000 turned up. We stayed in the Gresham hotel. The Garda – the Irish police – came into our dressing room before the game and we couldn't get them out. They were there to protect us and all they wanted to do was talk to us and get autographs. There was no control. The kick-off was held up because there was a crowd of people trying to get George's autograph – on the pitch. United were hugely popular in Dublin and still are.

Waterford played well and their goalie had a blinder, but we still beat them 3–1 with a hat-trick from Denis Law. Denis went one better in the return leg, scoring four in a far more convincing 7–1 victory at Old Trafford. We had too much quality for them.

The Belgian champions Anderlecht were our opponents in the next round, the team United had beaten by a record 10–0 score line in the club's first ever European tie in 1956.

Tension ran through our team during the first leg at Old Trafford. Denis Law missed a penalty and they hit the post. Two second half goals from George Best, and one from Willie Morgan meant we won 3–0, but Anderlecht had impressed us and we applauded their players off the pitch. We thought we were safe going to Brussels, but it turned out that we had only just done enough.

We didn't have George Best and adopted a defensive formation in the away leg. It seemed to be working when we took the lead. I threw the ball to Carlo Sartori, a twenty-year-old red-headed Mancunian-Italian midfielder who was doing well for us, and he put us 1–0 up. We were 4–0 up on aggregate and given that UEFA had introduced the away goal rule for the first time that season, extremely comfortable.

Then Anderlecht just decided to go for it. They threw everything at us and made us feel very, very uncomfortable. An equalizer after eighteen minutes gave them confidence and they attacked in waves. Bergholtz scored two and suddenly the aggregate score was 4–3 with twenty minutes left. They thought they had us and the crowd did too. What an achievement it would have been for any club, let alone a Belgian club, to knock the holders out of the European Cup. They needed to score twice to win but we held out.

There was still speculation about who would succeed Sir Matt. We all read the newspapers and it was causing uncertainty among the players. Then the club issued another statement:

'The board has given further consideration to the changes which will occur at the end of the season and has decided to appoint a chief coach who will be responsible for team selection, coaching, training, and tactics.

'Mr Wilf McGuinness has been selected for this position and will take up his duties as from 1 June, and in these circumstances it is not necessary to advertise for applications as we first intended. Sir Matt Busby will be responsible for all other matters affecting the club and players, and will continue as club spokesman.'

From the outset I wasn't convinced that Wilf's appointment was the right one, but I put my worries to the back of my mind as we focused on retaining our European trophy.

We met Austrian champions Rapid Vienna in the quarter-finals. We had drawn our match against Birmingham in the fifth round of the FA Cup but, rather than see sense, the idiots at the Football Association ordered us to play the replay two days before the first leg of the European Cup quarter-final. We cruised past Birmingham 6–2 in the replay, but it wasn't as easy when we met Rapid at Old Trafford. Despite our tiredness, we threw everything into building up a decent lead in the first leg and won 3–0. A 0–0 draw in Vienna saw us progress to the semi-final and a tie against Milan, who had overcome Celtic in the quarter-finals.

The first leg was in front of 80,000 in the San Siro. A further 23,000 watched the game on a screen at Old Trafford. Matt had been forced into making two crucial changes to our defence. Jimmy Rimmer, our twenty-one-year-old reserve goalkeeper, was picked ahead of Alex Stepney, who hadn't been playing so well. Jimmy had only made five first team appearances but he did superbly as Milan attacked us. But other United players were not up to the job. An injury to Bill Foulkes meant that the young defender Steve James was supposed to play. He was a kid and nerves got the better of him before the game, something which Matt witnessed and which made him decide to risk a half-fit Foulkes instead.

Milan went ahead after thirty-four minutes. I mistimed a clearance and the ball rebounded off the hand of Angelo Benedicto Sormani, their Brazilian striker. We all stopped and waited for the referee to blow, but he didn't as Sormani turned to lash the ball past Jimmy.

Sormani missed an open goal just after half-time but after fifty minutes Kurt Roland Hamrin, Milan's Swedish striker, who is still sixth in the all time Serie A top scorers' chart, made it 2–0. We were gutted, absolutely gutted. Ten minutes from time John Fitzpatrick was sent off for kicking Hamrin off the ball. Their fans let off fireworks after the game and threw missiles at us as we left the pitch.

The defeat was hard to take, but we still thought we could put two past Milan at Old Trafford and force a third game, which had been pencilled in for the Heysel stadium in Brussels. There was a three-week gap between the two legs and we were allowed a week off before having some warm up games in Waterford and Dublin. I needed the time off because Noreen gave birth to our third child, a son we named Danny.

The Italians were cocksure before the second game. Their coach Nereo Rocco said, 'When we played Celtic in Glasgow, we went out with nothing to lose, and hoping for a miracle. The match against Manchester United is very different. The Italians and the Italian press expect us to win. And if we resist for twenty minutes at Old Trafford, you will see a great Milan.'

That comment angered us and we were full of fight and spirit as we walked out in front of 63,000. We'd come back against Real Madrid a year earlier away from home so we thought we could do the same on our own turf, despite their goalkeeper Cudicini not having conceded more than two goals in a game for two years.

Milan were equally up for us, though. They had players like Gianni Rivera, who succeeded George Best as the European Footballer of the Year. Giovanni Trapattoni, who became a great manager with Juventus and Internazionale, played as a defensive midfielder alongside the more creative Rivera and Giovanni Lodetti, another Italian international.

The Italians had two very good chances in the first half, which, if converted, would have killed the tie. Just before half-time, some idiot in the Stretford End threw something from the crowd which hit Cudicini. He was knocked unconscious and the game was held up for five minutes. I didn't realize that he was unconscious. I just saw him go down like a sack of spuds like the other Milan players had been doing throughout the first half when we tackled them. They would lie there feigning injury and wasting time.

United played well. We came close four times in the first half, but it took until the seventieth minute before Bobby Charlton scored. Then I hit a cross from the byline which Denis Law prodded over the line before Mario Anquilletti, Milan's right-back, scooped it back into play. We knew it had crossed the line. And even if it hadn't been a goal, it would have been a penalty because Anquilletti used his hand to pull it back. But the French referee Roger Machin waved away our furious protests and allowed play to continue. We ended up going out 2–1 on aggregate. We thought there was something going on.

In my view, the official's refusal to allow a United equalizer was part of a dark and disturbing pattern that resulted, in the summer of 2006, in Milan being punished for an attempt to influence the selection of referees for their matches in the Italian league.

The Italians have got history with referees. In 1973, Brian Clough's Derby County were denied a place in the European Cup Final by a Juventus team whose general manager was later exposed, thanks to investigations by Brian Glanville of *The Sunday Times*, as having attempted to influence referees. The 'Golden Fix', as it became known, led to no serious investigation but its echoes were to be detected in scandals of later years.

Milan destroyed Ajax 4–1 in the 1969 final in Madrid and went on to play Estudiantes in the World Club championship game. Three Argentinian players ended up in jail for their behaviour on the pitch in Buenos Aires.

We played our final game of the season against Leicester City two days after the Milan game – it had been a month since our previous league match as the FA finally relented and allowed United to concentrate on retaining the European Cup.

The day before the game, Noel Cantwell, our former United colleague who was in charge at Coventry City, turned up with a bag of cash, saying that it would be ours if we beat Leicester. If we didn't, then his Coventry side would be relegated. I wanted to win against Leicester anyway, just as I wanted to win every game, but doubly so because I was mates with Noel.

I didn't want to see his team relegated and I agreed to take it, viewing it as an end of season bonus for me and the lads. Players accept money to win games in Spain all the time, but this was the first time I had been offered money in my career. I was doing nothing illegal in accepting money to try and *win* a game, but, looking back, ethically and professionally I was wrong to accept it. I told the lads before the match that there would be a treat in it for them if they beat Leicester, but I was deliberately vague and didn't let them know that I had bag full of used bank notes to share among them.

Leicester, managed by Frank O'Farrell, were a goal up at half-time and Noel was probably having kittens in the stand, but we came back and won 3–2 with goals from Best, Law, and Morgan. Coventry stayed up with thirty-one points, while Leicester went down with thirty. After the game I shared the money around the lads. They all accepted it as a gift from Noel, but I don't think Matt, managing us for the last time, knew anything of it.

That victory moved us from joint thirteenth with Manchester City to eleventh. It was nowhere near good enough for United, but few people were talking about our league position after the final game of the season.

After being in charge for a quarter of a century, Matt Busby stepped down as Manchester United manager. It truly was the end of an era.

NINE

Decline and Despair

Sir Matt's departure left a vacuum. I could understand why he stepped down and I even thought that it was the right thing to do, but he'd been manager at the club since the war. Nobody at Manchester United knew any different from Matt being in charge. It didn't take long for us to realize that nobody was up to the job of replacing Matt and the whole club suffered as a result.

Losing Matt as manager was particularly difficult for me because I'd always considered him a father figure and I valued that support. If I had a problem, whether it was with my football or something else, I could speak to him. It was always reassuring to know that he was there, like a security blanket, and I wasn't the only one who felt like that. A few of us were lost when he stopped being manager. Matt stepping down had other consequences. Jimmy Murphy, his long-time assistant, was cut out and was clearly very upset at his diminishing role in the club. It seems that no one at United gave much thought to what Jimmy would do and while he stayed on at Old Trafford, he didn't really have a role. He eventually retired in 1971 with a pay off of £20,000 and a scouting job which would pay him £25 a week, but he didn't want to retire as he still felt he had a lot to offer United. He should have been treated better by a club he had served so well. Jimmy had even camped outside players' houses, refusing to leave until their parents signed United's forms. Jimmy didn't drive and used to get a taxi to take him to Old Trafford, but the club suddenly stopped paying his taxi fares while he was scouting.

Wilf McGuinness became the chief coach of Manchester United in the summer of 1969. He wasn't given the full title of club manager because he had to earn the right to be called that, whatever that meant. I hadn't been surprised when Matt announced that he was going to step down, but I was when Wilf was named as his replacement. Experienced managers like the former United captain Johnny Carey who had managed Everton, Don Revie at Leeds, Ron Greenwood at West Ham, and Jimmy Adamson at Burnley were all talked about as Matt's replacement. Instead, the club appointed Wilf, a Collyhurst lad and one club man who understood United's values and had been senior coach for the previous season.

Wilf was Matt's choice. I think that Matt showed tremendous vision appointing someone from within the club, because that hadn't been done before, and in theory the idea was right. Wilf had done a great job looking after the youth team, the reserves, the England Under 23s and he'd been involved in coaching England in the 1966 World Cup finals. He had talent and personality. I am quite sure that the United job would have been perfect for Wilf three or four years later and maybe with a different set of players. Familiarity was the problem. Wilf was only 31. He was considered one of us because he had grown up and played alongside many of the men he was now expected to take charge of. He'd been mates with people such as Bobby Charlton most of his adult life and suddenly he had to turn round and tell them that they were not playing.

Wilf did not inherit a great team, so it was no surprise that the 1969/70 season started badly. Eventual champions Everton beat us easily home and away in August. United needed to buy new quality players but it didn't happen. We were linked with Colin Todd from Sunderland and Mick Mills from Ipswich, but neither signed. The talk was that United were not prepared to pay the money, so you could hardly blame Wilf.

There were also stories in the press that the senior professionals at the club including myself were not playing for Wilf because we didn't respect him. That was nonsense from my point of view. We had pride and we never stopped being professional, never deliberately set out not to play. We weren't playing as well because we were getting old, simple as that. I was 31, Bobby 33, Shay 33, Bill Foulkes 37, and Denis was 30 in an era when players' careers didn't last as long as they do now.

One thing which did change is that Matt had given us freedom to play, something which was altered slightly under Wilf, who was more regimented. That went against the grain of the Manchester United way. We were renowned for having attacking, flair players. Matt would never demean somebody by telling them to play a role with which they were not comfortable. The great players didn't need to be told how to play because they knew already. That changed under Wilf and so did the mood in the dressing room.

Wilf was a great bloke and someone I respect deeply, but he promoted players who weren't ready for the first team. It must have been difficult for him. Not all the players saw Wilf as a manager and that wasn't always his fault – it was an almost impossible job to replace Matt.

There was one incident which really saddened me. Bobby had finished training early to go to London for a meeting. He showered and put his suit on, then Wilf demanded that all the players gather on the pitch at The Cliff for a team talk. Bobby suggested that it would be better to go under the stand by the side of the pitch as it was raining, but Wilf said no. The rain got heavier and Bobby turned up his collars and put his hands in his pockets. Wilf ordered him to do twenty press ups, as that's what you did if you were caught with your hands in your pockets. Bobby thought he was joking, but he wasn't. Bobby then got down in his suit and did the press ups. Bobby and Wilf had been great friends and they get on great today, but that showed how difficult the relationship had become for both parties. Wilf later said that he had been joking, but those of us stood there didn't see it like that.

You can read too deeply into disagreements and differences of opinion, but they happen all the time and are often healthy because they release tension. People assume that footballers are all best mates, that because we play together we drink together. Sometimes we did, sometimes we didn't. Some were better mates than others. A good team spirit is important, but that doesn't have to come from being friends off the field.

Manchester United's current team don't all socialize together, but the team spirit is superb. The manager instils a feeling that it's them against the world and they stick together on the pitch.

Nevertheless, Wilf's first season saw us finish eighth, an improvement of three places on our previous position. We also reached the semi-finals of the FA Cup and the League Cup. Champions Leeds United were our opponents in the FA Cup semi-finals in 1970. They had become a stronger force than us, they consistently challenged for honours, won the Inter-Cities Fairs' Cup twice in four years and the league title in 1969.

The Leeds winger Eddie Gray, who was from the Gorbals, later told me a story that the Leeds manager Don Revie used to tell the Leeds players before they played us, 'If you kick Crerand and Law, they'll lose it.' They always did set out to kick us deliberately and invariably we took the bait and hit back. We rarely beat Leeds.

We were the underdogs for that 1970 semi. We drew 0–0 at Hillsborough. Despite the 0–0 score line, it was a classic game, a rough, rough match, a fight from the beginning until the end of extra-time. It was always like that with Leeds United. The replay was set as an evening kick-off at Villa Park.

Just before that replay, we had lunch at a hotel in Worcester. George was eyeing a lady up at the bar, but there was nothing unusual with that. After eating, we went to our rooms for a sleep in the afternoon. We could have won the match that night (we drew 0–0 again) but George wasn't at his best and after the game we found out why. When we had all gone for an afternoon sleep, he had chatted up the girl in the hotel and taken her to his room.

Wilf had found out about it and gone charging off to confront George. We were raging with George because we had played well enough to win that game. You don't get many chances to reach Wembley in the FA Cup Final and our chance had been weakened by George's behaviour. George should have known better than anyone, having never played in an FA Cup Final. Words were had on the coach back to Manchester. George was told that he was wasting his great talent and sticking two fingers up to the rest of us of who were less gifted, but had a more serious attitude to our approach to training and preparation. I sat down next to George as the coach was getting near to Manchester.

'You are wasting your talent George,' I said. 'We all get a gift from God and yours is football. The reason it is talent is because you've never had to work for it. I do. All you have to do is keep yourself fit.'

The problem was that George would always agree with everything I said at the time. He promised to improve and seemed genuine in his desire to reform, but his conduct continued to worsen.

We lost the second replay by a single goal at Burnden Park. The three games were watched by 173,500 people, but United's interest in that season's FA Cup didn't end with defeat to Leeds. At the start of that season, the Football Association introduced a third/fourth place play-off game, between the losing semi-finalists, to be played on the eve of the Cup Final in London.

It was a largely commercial decision. The FA wanted a money spinning diversion for their members who were in the capital for the final. Previously, this had been provided by a match between an old England and a young England side, but interest had waned and the play-off idea was hatched at Lancaster Gate. It was a mistake. Instead of being a lucrative and consolatory exercise, it became an unpopular poor man's cup final and only lasted four years because it never caught the public's imagination right from the first game between United and the other beaten semi-finalists, Watford, at Highbury. We won 2–0 in front of just 15,000, but, for some reason, there was no coach to take us back to our hotel from Highbury. We tried to get taxis, but couldn't. It wasn't like the entire Manchester United team could just pop into the underground, so the police split the team into two vans and drove us back. They found it as amusing as we did.

The next day, Bobby Charlton and I were working at the Cup Final as television analysts, Bobby for BBC and me for ITV. We went to Wembley together on the morning of the game and were walking around the pitch when Bobby tripped on a cable that was being used for television transmission. He banged his head and lay flat out, unconscious. He was taken to hospital and missed the game, while I rang his wife to explain why he wouldn't be appearing on the nation's television screens that afternoon. It capped a surreal weekend.

Despite his misdemeanours, George Best was the player of the season, especially for his form before Christmas. And despite our strong words to him on the coach back from Villa Park, he had been the player responsible for most of our win bonuses. The incident with the girl showed that George was getting frustrated that no new players were being brought in, and his way of showing that frustration was to adopt a more cavalier attitude. George started to wane when Matt left and he started to drink more. He realized that the team was getting old, yet he was still our best player by a distance.

George had met a woman called Eva Haraldsted on a pre-season tour to Denmark. The pretty blonde came up and asked him for an autograph for her boyfriend. Ever the romantic, George thought she was the most beautiful girl he had ever seen and asked a newspaper to trace her when he got back to Manchester. She was found and flew over to Manchester. They hit it off and a week later George walked into Matt's office and proudly told him that he was going to get married. Matt's influence at the club was still immense. Matt flew off the handle with George and said, 'How can you marry her, you've only known her a week?' George protested and said that he was doing it because Matt wanted him to get married and settle down. Matt told him to wait a while. It was the right thing to say because in a short period the relationship fizzled out.

George and I went to a club he frequented one night called Blinkers French. Dave Thomas, the golfer who finished behind Jack Nicklaus in the 1966 Open was in there, as was the comedian Jimmy Tarbuck.

We were sitting in the corner when this lad who was with Eva Haraldsted (she had become a regular face on the

Manchester nightlife scene) had a go at George. He was there with his brothers and I was with Noreen, but I got up and told him to push off and leave George alone. About two in the morning we went to pick our cars up as we'd not really had a drink. As we left the club, three of them were waiting to have a go at George.

I sized them up, before laying into the three of them. One of them got a broken jaw, another took a whack. The third didn't want to know. I'm not pretending to be harder than I was, but I was a young, fit man who barely drank. And I could handle myself. I later found out that one of them was in the British army.

The incident was in the Sunday papers. It was reported that 'someone' had broken the lad's jaw. Beneath that, it said, solemnly, 'Pat Crerand was present.' On the Monday I got a phone call at The Cliff telling me that the police were coming to arrest me.

I went to see my solicitor after training. He got in touch with the police and we arranged to meet two of them at his office in Manchester. The attitude of one of them left me in no doubt that he was determined not to make things easy for a football star. For starters he addressed me as 'Crerand', which made my hackles rise, but I wasn't going to take his disrespect. I told him straight, 'You either call me Mr Crerand or Pat; otherwise I'm not talking to you.'

He responded by accusing me of breaking this lad's jaw. Before I could answer, my solicitor started earning his fee and butted in. 'Do you have evidence to back up your claim that my client broke this man's jaw?' The officer was forced to admit he had none, so my solicitor asked him to withdraw what he had said. When the policeman became more belliger-ent my solicitor said, 'Look, this conversation is being taped.' There was an immediate change of expression – both were very worried and the meeting came to an abrupt close. We then went to Bootle Street police station and made a complaint. The police were still being cocky, saying, 'We're going to get that bastard Best as well.' George hadn't even done anything. One of the coppers was all right but the rest of them were nasty sods. Still, the whole thing ended up with me in court facing charges of assault.

I knew that I would have to tell Matt, but as I thought about the best way of breaking the news to him, I met his wife Jean who was shopping in Sale. Lady Jean was very pally with everybody. She was like a support network for the wives and given that we would go on tour for up to six weeks at a time, the wives needed that.

I explained my predicament and Jean told me a story about a fight in Belshill, Glasgow, years earlier when someone had a go at Matt, who responded by punching his lights out. Matt was arrested but released after pleading self-defence. I was made up at hearing this story ahead of seeing Matt, who was in hospital having a minor operation. Armed with this knowledge, I was feeling a bit cocky when I went into his room, but his reaction was not what I expected.

Matt sat up in bed and started giving me a right going over for fighting. I was saying that I lost my temper, that I was only sticking up for George and that these things can happen to anyone. He was having none of it. Then I told him that I had seen his wife and that something similar had happened to him years earlier. He started sliding down the bed and his whole attitude changed. He said that he could understand why I had done it, but that it still wasn't a good reflection on Manchester United. He said that negative headlines would hurt the name of the club. I accepted that.

I went to court a few weeks later and I was shaking inside because I thought that I was going down. The place was packed with friends, family, and fans. Just as the proceedings were about to start, guess who walked into court and plonked himself down beside me? Matt Busby. The court erupted and everyone applauded. I was cleared from any charges, which was obviously a big relief.

Although George had done nothing wrong, the issue which caused the problem was his relationships with girls. And he was very, very popular with them. For instance, I met the actress Joan Collins through Michael Parkinson. She was in Manchester doing a programme with Parky and I went for something to eat with Michael, who was a big football fan. He was a Barnsley lad and had been pals with Tommy Taylor before he died at Munich. Maybe he was always very pro-United because of this. We went to Slack Alice's, a bar George part-owned. Joan Collins came along too and she told me that she was a big fan of George so I introduced her to him. She was a very good looking girl and George's eyes lit up when he saw her. They hit it off immediately and went to the bar for a drink together. I left soon after by myself as George looked very happy receiving Joan's attentions. And Joan looked equally content with commanding the attention of a heart-throb thirteen years her junior.

You could get away with a lot in those days because the press were not as intense as they are now. George was a horrific gambler and he had a bigger problem with gambling than drinking, but that was barely reported. He was a well known face around the casinos of Manchester, but money meant nothing to him. If he had a good win then he would share his winnings. George wasn't one for playing poker or cards, but dice, which was very popular in the Manchester casinos. They banned it because people used to cheat by loading the dice or sliding it. George started to gamble because he got bored. He was a single fella who could get any girl he wanted. He used to turn up with one absolute stunner after another, but it was easy come, easy go, and he became bored and found a bigger buzz from losing money gambling.

George had other troubles. He often received death threats and, given the political situation in Northern Ireland, they were treated seriously, especially as his sister had been shot in the leg after leaving a Belfast dancehall. Another time, he was told of a threat at a game against Newcastle. He responded by not stopping moving for ninety minutes. If there was a gunman in the crowd, he would never have got him. I think George got more threats from boyfriends than from any other group, though.

I received several threats myself when I played, both at Celtic and Manchester United. They were usually in the form of an anonymous letter, the abuse being sectarian. They would threaten to beat me up, but there were never any names or addresses and I didn't lose too much sleep over them.

Politics was never far away in my life. I frequently returned to Donegal for holidays with my family in the early 1970s. The Troubles had intensified after the events in Derry on Bloody Sunday and tension was high. Cars were routinely stopped and searched as they crossed the border, and on one trip we were not surprised to be ushered to the road side check-point by two British soldiers. As I've said, I was used to the border being a problem from my childhood days. I didn't like the way the British soldiers used to steal our eggs and chickens, but my life had changed a lot since being a kid in the Gorbals.

One of the soldiers recognized me and started talking in a friendly manner. He was about 18 and a United fan from Wythenshawe. I was with an uncle and we had to get out of the car so that it could be searched. While we waited, the soldier asked me about United's chances in the league. I just chatted along being friendly, but I could see that my Uncle Hughie, who was driving the car, was absolutely raging with anger. He called me over and asked what I was doing talking to a British soldier. I told him that it was just a kid from Manchester.

'I'm not bothered about the kid from Manchester,' he replied. 'I'm bothered about the snipers in the hills over there who are after the soldiers. I'm bothered that they might miss him and get you.' I got back in the car, sharpish.

In the summer of 1970, I was asked to be on a television panel for the World Cup. I was offered £1,000 for three weeks' work – about twice what I was on at United. The television people told me that they had asked me because I always had opinions which I wasn't afraid to express. I joined the ITV panel with Malcolm Allison, the Manchester City coach, the Wolves player Derek Dougan, and Bob McNab of Arsenal, who didn't make the squad for the Mexico World Cup. Brian Moore and Jimmy Hill held the panel together. Although expert panels are commonplace now, the formula hadn't been tried on British television before. It was a big success. Nobody had seen people arguing about football on television. You were supposed to be staid and speak when the presenter asked you a question, so we changed all that. Malcolm was fantastic. He was really blunt and always thought that he was right. We'd argue like hell. Derek was eloquent and Bob was shy, probably because he was much younger than us, but he was astute and knew the game well.

Mail poured into the studios for all four of us. Some asked football questions, others complained, but the vast majority were fan letters, asking anything from fashion queries to marital status. Two ladies from Gloucester wrote to the production team saying, 'Will you send us Bob McNab when you've finished with him?' Then they wrote the word 'please' 1,300 times. Another ardent female Bob McNab fan invited him to her home for the weekend and included the return rail fare.

The critics loved it too. Writing in the *Sunday Times*, Michael Parkinson said: 'Crerand, Dougan and Allison is the most entertaining trio since Wilson, Keppel and Betty or Curly, Larry and Mo, depending which pleases you most.'

What the critics didn't know was that we ran up a hotel bill over the three weeks of £3,500, which was an obscene amount in 1970. Malcolm used to invite any girls he met back to the hotel. In fact, he invited anyone he met to the hotel and ordered drinks for them. I looked out of my window one day and he was having a picnic on the lawn, with two police-women sitting alongside him. I went out with him in his car another afternoon before filming. He said that he just had to stop at a friend's house and when we pulled up outside a flat in West London, I saw the former model Christine Keeler, who had been headline news for her affair with the government minister John Profumo, open the door. Malcolm wasn't seeing her, but I think he was trying to.

I said from the outset of the World Cup that Brazil would win. I had seen a Santos side which contained six or seven of the Brazil team including Pele play a friendly in Stoke a few months before the competition. Their skill and passing was only comparable with the great Real Madrid sides of the 1950s and 60s.

Jairzinho was the powerful winger who scored in every game in 1970 – he remains the only player to score in every game in a World Cup finals. Rivelino – the midfielder with a giant moustache – had a lethal left foot and provided danger from free-kicks, as did Tostão the captain, an intelligent forward and the perfect foil for Pele, who is right up there with Denis Law as my greatest player ever. I met Pele at Old Trafford when he opened the club museum in 1995. I was surprised to find he was a tiny fella who wore size four shoes. I wanted to have my picture taken with him but I was too embarrassed to ask.

Malcolm fancied Russia, but after watching Brazil he changed his mind. That year, we saw probably the greatest team ever win the World Cup. After the final, the Brazilian Embassy in London phoned the television station and invited us to a party at the Ambassador's house. It seemed like every Brazilian in London was there and they carried on celebrating all night. The one shame about the panel was that nobody in the North West saw it because there was a strike at Granada TV.

Back at United, Wilf entered his second season, 1970/71, in charge of the team. Again it didn't start well and United slipped well below the standards expected. By the Christmas of 1970, just two and a half years after winning the European Cup, we were close to the relegation zone.

I was dropped for John Fitzpatrick for most of the games around Christmas. Wilf never explained his decision to drop me and I felt left out; any footballer would be the same. I didn't agree with the decision, but when does a footballer agree with being dropped? I wasn't annoyed, though; it was Wilf's judgement and he was trying to do what was best for the team. But it didn't help the team's form, and you could see that Wilf was feeling the strain. His excitable nature had gone and he aged visibly. The change in his appearance was unbelievable. He'd come in on a Monday morning and his eyes had big bags underneath. He looked like he had the world on his shoulders. Wilf had the extra pressure that he was a United fan. He couldn't just move to another club because being at United was all he had ever known. Wilf's attachment to United went back before Munich and, had it not been for a knee injury, Wilf would have been on the plane which crashed.

Wilf was relieved of his duties on 28 December 1970. The final straw came when third division Aston Villa knocked us out of the League Cup a couple of days earlier. I wasn't surprised when Wilf was sacked. He was asked to go back to looking after the reserves, but declined. I think he felt humiliated and I felt sorry for him – football can be very cruel and unfair.

Matt took over for the final few months of the 1970/71 season and results improved almost straightaway. George Best was superb and scored thirteen goals in the second half of the season after getting just five in the first half. I was back playing every week and we moved away from the relegation zone, finishing eight for the second year in succession.

Our penultimate game of that season was against Blackpool away. Matt invited the comedian Frank Carson into the changing rooms and he was laughing and joking with us. The mood was good, but it wasn't in the stands as United fans ran on the pitch before the match and pulled the goals down. United used to take upwards of 15,000 travelling fans when we played Blackpool and they used to spend the weekend causing all kinds of problems.

Blackpool legend Jimmy Armfield was given a guard of honour by the players before his 569th and final game for the club. I applauded Jimmy, a Mancunian, because I always respected him as a player and a person, but from the minute the game started, Blackpool's right-back John Johnston started abusing me. In all the time that I played for Celtic against Rangers, there was never any religious abuse between players on the pitch. Yet Johnston, a protestant from Belfast, religiously abused me by calling me a Fenian bastard. I wasn't in the best frame of mind as I made a mistake which led to Tony Green scoring Blackpool's goal (the match finished 1–1) and the next time Johnston had a go I landed a right hook in his face. We started fighting and when another player, Blackpool's big captain John Craven, intervened I smacked him one too, and the referee sent the pair of us off. I nearly killed Craven in the tunnel after the game but a couple of security lads got in the way and held me back. The guy ran for his life. I never did get Johnston.

I played the following week against Manchester City and we won 4–3. I wasn't to know it at the time, but it was my final league appearance for Manchester United. I did play one other game in the ill-fated Watney Cup – an early 1970s preseason competition contested by the highest goalscoring teams from the four divisions who had not been promoted or got into Europe – on 31 July 1971. We lost 2–1 against Halifax Town at The Shay and I was substituted for Francis Burns. I trudged off the pitch wearing a United shirt for the last time at what was generally agreed to be the worst stadium in the Football League. What an end to my United career. I was 32 years old and had played 392 games for Manchester United, scoring fifteen goals.

TEN

Troubled Times

Frank O'Farrell was appointed as Manchester United manager in the summer of 1971. The talk had been of recruiting someone who was 'big enough to manage Manchester United' and a few months before Frank was given the job, Matt – in his capacity as general manager – asked me about Jock Stein. Matt's job was to oversee all the football-related business at Old Trafford without ever taking to the training pitch. He didn't pick the team or interfere with team selection, but he retained the manager's office and managers like Wilf could go to him for advice or talk about transfer targets.

'Jock would be under contract at Celtic, wouldn't he?' Matt asked.

I said that no Celtic manager had ever had a contract.

'Do you think Jock would come to Old Trafford?' he continued.

I told him that I was going up to Glasgow on Wednesday to watch Celtic against Ajax at Hampden Park and that I'd speak to Jock about it. Jock lived just across the road from Hampden Park and I remember Bill Shankly's brother being at the house when I arrived.

When I told Jock that Matt wanted him to become the manager of Manchester United, he looked a little bit shocked. We went upstairs to his bedroom so that we could speak privately. I reiterated what I'd said to George, Jock's son, who was also in the bedroom. George liked the idea. Not only did he idolize Denis Law, but he'd won a place to study at Manchester University. Jock's daughter came in and I told her about Manchester United – she thought it was great. Then Jean, Jock's wife, came up the stairs. She gave her husband a right going over, saying that it was the height of ignorance to spend time upstairs when they had other guests downstairs. I explained to Jean that Matt Busby wanted her husband to be the next manager of Manchester United. She stood there totally shocked. Then she said, 'I'm not going, I'm a Celtic supporter. I can't go, I support Celtic.' That wasn't a good sign.

Still, I went back to tell Matt that Jock had been sounded out and that he was keen.

Matt and Jock met a week later in secret at a petrol station in Haydock, between Manchester and Liverpool, in April 1971. They had both been to see Leeds beat Liverpool in the Inter-Cities Fairs' Cup semi-final at Anfield. They spoke for forty-five minutes in the back of Matt's Mercedes.

I knew that the two of them would get on. They came from very similar backgrounds in the Lanarkshire coal fields, but I wasn't expecting the reaction that I got from Matt a few days later. He wasn't happy and said, 'He's some man, that pal of yours.' I asked him what he meant.

'Jock Stein has turned down the job,' he said. 'And he's probably used us to get more money from Celtic.'

I didn't think that was true, because Jock's wife probably made the decision. Jock did go to England a few years later, joining Leeds United, but he only stayed for a couple of months.

Jock would watch any game of football that he could. While he was at Leeds, Morton played Oldham in some daft competition and he came to pick me up before driving to Boundary Park. We heard on the radio that the Scotland manager Ally Macleod had been sacked. I said to him, 'You'll get that job.' He shook his head. Jock dropped me off at home that night and then drove back to Leeds. He was offered the Scotland job the following morning and took it. It was a shame that Jock never came to Old Trafford. Had he replaced Matt, I'm sure that Jock would have done a great job and prevented the slide which ultimately led to United being relegated.

Instead, United went for O'Farrell. An intelligent Irishman from Cork, he had done well at Leicester City. He seemed like a nice man and my first impression was a positive one, but I doubted that he had the mental strength to be Manchester United manager. Frank gave me the extra responsibility of looking after the kids at Old Trafford, which was probably his way of nudging me to one side because I didn't feature in his long-term playing plans. I enjoyed working with the kids. There were some talented players, but it was so tough to get in the first team that hardly any of them made it. I think they enjoyed their time with me because they looked up to me as a senior player.

I got a new player's contract in the summer of 1971 – we were still working on a season to season contract – but because of the Blackpool sending off, I was suspended for the opening two games of the season. Alan Gowling played instead. He was a bright lad with a degree in Economics from Manchester University. We used to give him loads of abuse, saying that his degree was actually in reading comics. Fair play, he went along with it.

Alan played in a team which did exceptionally well, winning ten, drawing three, and losing one of the opening fourteen league matches. United were top of the league and my grounds for inclusion in the team were hardly strong. Frank O'Farrell achieved this without a single signing, but by reorganizing the existing players and giving a few young ones, including Belfast-born Sammy McIlroy, their debuts. By Christmas 1971, with United five points clear at the top of the table, Matt wrote in his *Express* column that Frank O'Farrell was probably the best signing he had ever made. Bookmakers made United odds-on favourites to finish as champions.

The bookmakers didn't have the players' inside knowledge that the results were an illusion, though, that some of the players' reputations were better than their performances. George Best was still a genius, however, easily the team's best player and had scored seventeen goals by Christmas. Denis Law had eleven.

The team still needed strengthening and Everton's Alan Ball was the target. Alan wanted to sign. He lived in Bolton, came to games at Old Trafford with his dad, was a friend of George and made it clear to everyone that he wanted to join. But United stalled and Arsenal got him for a record fee of £220,000. Again the talk was that United wouldn't pay the money.

So O'Farrell turned closer to home. He increased Best's wages to give him the financial parity with Denis Law and Bobby Charlton that he had been lacking. George repaid O'Farrell by frequently absconding from club duty as his private life became ever more overindulgent. In the first week of January 1972 he didn't turn up for training once. George was dropped on more than one occasion and he would invariably score two goals on his return.

George kept doing disappearing acts. What he really needed was to have married the right type of girl who would have made him a home and given him some stability, companionship and something worthwhile to hang onto. He built a big house, with just one bedroom, in Bramhall and was lonely as hell in it by himself. Every man and his dog was at the house warming party from the world of football and showbusiness. It was designed by an architect, but everyone thought the house looked like a big toilet.

Frank suggested that George move in with my family and me. He thought that if George lived with me then he wouldn't go out and he'd behave himself. So George moved into the box room of our semi-detached house in Chorlton. The newspapers got hold of it and I was quoted as saying that a stable environment would be good for George.

Noreen and I had the best intentions as George parked his E-Type Jaguar outside the house and came in with a single suitcase, which contained some clothes and a wash bag. I sat him down in the kitchen and explained that he had to get fit. It was a chat I had had with him a million times and he nodded along in agreement like he had done many times before. I knew I had my work cut out. If Matt Busby couldn't get George to alter his lifestyle, then what chance did I have? It was frustrating because whatever promises George made were never kept. I wondered if he was taking in what I was saying, because he used to pretend to listen to Matt, while at the same time counting the flowers on the wallpaper in his office.

George wasn't drinking a lot at the time; otherwise Noreen would not have allowed him in the house with the kids around. And if George thought he was moving into a hotel then he was wrong. We didn't even wash George's clothes for him – he took them to Mrs Fullaway's, his old landlady. I showed George up to his room. It was my son Patrick's bedroom. Patrick adored George. His last prayer every night was that God would let him wake up with black hair like George Best. We didn't tell Patrick that George was moving in, nor that he'd be sleeping in his bedroom. When we had guests Patrick shared another bedroom with Danny and Lorraine, but the following morning he woke up early and went in his own room. All he could see was a strange man in his bed, because George's face was buried in a pillow. He wasn't happy and got his younger brother and sister for support. The three of them attempted to drag George out of his bed in order to reclaim his bedroom. Patrick was eight. George saw the funny side. When Patrick realized it was George he was stunned. He then wouldn't leave his bedroom and started trying on George's hipster trousers.

All the neighbours knew that George had moved in and the doorbell started going, with kids asking for autographs. It was not ideal for George, or us. That night, George was out of the door and he came in about 1 am. He didn't bring any girls back – I didn't even have to explain to him that it wouldn't be acceptable because he was a well brought up lad.

Noreen had asked George what he wanted for breakfast the night before. George replied: 'Two eggs and bacon.' The next morning, Noreen left two eggs and two rashers of bacon on the table with a tomato.

George said: 'Noreen, you haven't cooked them.'

She replied: 'I've got enough to do without cooking for you as well.'

Noreen didn't give him a key because she was frightened that he would keep bringing girls back to the house – as he had done when he used to baby-sit for us with Mike Summerbee.

George went out in Manchester the following nights while he stayed at our house. He didn't get home early and he woke me up in the middle of the night. One of the most important things about being a professional footballer is keeping fit. If you lose your fitness then you are knackered. And George had lost his.

We didn't ask George for rent, but he was very generous with the kids and would give them a couple of quid, which was a lot of money then. The kids were delighted to have him stay. They told all their mates at school and didn't want him to leave. It was difficult for him though, coming into a house with three kids, a husband, and wife. We cramped his style. He was only 26 and United got him to see a psychiatrist, but it was no good. George left after just five days and Patrick cried for the next three because he missed him.

Matt and Frank O'Farrell had tried to get George's parents to move over from Belfast so that he could have a settled home life in Manchester, but they didn't want to leave Ireland. Without any close relations around him, George was always hanging out with the in-crowd and couldn't get out of that way of life which involved going out all the time.

Unlike George, I still felt in good condition and wanted to play. I spoke with Frank O'Farrell about my position and he said that he wanted me to focus more on training the kids, with the option of my being available to play in the first team if needed. I trained well and was always prepared to play, but the call never came.

Crystal Palace approached me and asked if I would be interested in joining them, but I was reluctant to leave Manchester because my kids were settled at school. It sounds big headed, but I didn't like the idea of playing with lesser players either. If I was going to stop playing then I wanted it to be at the top.

Maybe I should have carried on, because there was a void in my life when I stopped. Quite simply, playing is the best thing about football. Not playing, especially after doing it for so long, hit me hard, although it was always in very subtle ways. Newspaper billboards would remind you about a forthcoming game and you would think, 'This time last year I would have been playing there.' Or anniversaries would crop up – five years since we won the European Cup, that kind of thing. But you can't turn back time. I know of players who started to despair and saw their lives crumble. Relationships broke down, alcohol took over and they lost their shape and drive. I've never had the type of personality to let myself slip. I've always been driven in my own way – if you weren't in the Gorbals then you were going to have a pretty rough life.

I believed that I still had plenty to offer at United, even if it was as a youth trainer, and so did the people at the club.

United's form began to dip alarmingly halfway through Frank O'Farrell's first season in charge. The players knew we were punching above our weight but few expected United to lose seven league games on the trot as we did in January and February 1972. Among those defeats was a humiliating 5–1 score line at Elland Road.

George later went AWOL from training, claiming to be with his parents in Belfast and terrified about the safety of his family during The Troubles. Unfortunately for George, Frank O'Farrell was in Belfast discussing the idea of George's parents moving to Manchester so he was clearly somewhere else.

What was clear was that an ageing United side needed radical changes, especially in front of goal. O'Farrell sought to solve United's scoring problems by importing the prolific forward Ted MacDougall from third division Bournemouth, but although he had a great career later with second division clubs such as Norwich, Southampton, and West Ham, he struggled at a higher level at Old Trafford. Wyn Davies from Manchester City did no better. Ian Storey-Moore's career was truncated by injury. But O'Farrell did spot one gem, buying young Martin Buchan from Aberdeen for £125,000.

United finished eighth in O'Farrell's first season, the third in succession that the club had finished in that position, but the early form in the following season, 1972/73, was disappointing.

The atmosphere around the club was negative. Frank was an honest and personable man, but he was totally lost and working with ghosts, players who were past it. Frank later claimed that Matt Busby had interfered with his team selection and that senior players had undermined him by going to Matt with their problems, but I do not believe Matt was responsible for his demise. Matt did have an office at Old Trafford, but it wasn't the manager's one that he had kept when Wilf was in charge of the team. Frank had made sure that Matt moved out of there when he took charge. In all of Frank's time at the club, we only saw Matt on three occasions at the training ground – and that was because his wife was having treatment for her back.

Frank's problems with George Best continued. On one hand George was the finest talent at the club, on the other he was frequently missing training and messing around when he did turn up. In the spring of 1972, George decided to quit football and go and live in Spain. I heard that he was at the airport so I drove there and managed to find him – Manchester airport wasn't so big in those days so it was easy. I pleaded with him to stay in Manchester and followed him all the way to the departure gate, but he was adamant that he was going. For his part, George was tired of carrying the rest of the team. He didn't live like a professional, but he played like one and was top scorer five seasons in a row. When I realized that I couldn't get him to change his mind, I shook his hand and wished him all the best, saying that I was always there for him if he needed me. Seventeen days later George returned to United, having decided to come out of 'retirement'.

The final straw for Frank came with a 5–0 defeat to Crystal Palace on 16 December 1972 and he was sacked shortly afterwards. I met Denis Law, who came on as a substitute in that game, back in Manchester that same night and he just shrugged his head when he saw me. 'Crystal Palace were awful,' he said. 'And they beat us 5–0. What does that say about us?' Palace were bottom of the league before the match.

Frank, the assistant manager Malcolm Musgrove and the Chief Scout, John Aston Snr, were sacked. George Best was also told by the directors that his United career was finished.

I was put in temporary charge of the United team for a couple of days until Tommy Docherty was appointed manager in December 1972. Docherty arrived from his post in charge of the Scotland national team, with Willie Morgan and Denis Law playing a part in him getting the job. Morgan had been on tour with Docherty as a Scotland player and when Matt asked what he thought of him he said, 'Great.' Matt asked for his phone number and the Doc was soon on board.

Docherty appointed Morgan captain and even described him as the best winger in the world, but the relationship between the two would end in acrimony. I didn't know Docherty, but he had called me at my mum's in the Gorbals in 1961 when I was at Celtic and offered me £100 a week to play for him at Chelsea. I wasn't on a fifth of that at Parkhead, but I didn't want to move because I was a Celtic supporter.

My first impressions of Docherty were that he was ebullient, effervescent, and full of life. He had been very highly rated as a player for Preston and Scotland and as a manager he was a breath of fresh air for a club that had been stagnating. In the beginning I thought he was all right, but I always held reservations because Jock Stein had warned me that he was a Glasgow corner boy. If you hung around corners in Glasgow then you were a layabout. But there can be a lot of jealousy in football so I decided to form my own opinion.

What was clear was that the 1968 hangover was now at its most obvious. Best had been discarded as a liability, Denis and Bobby were nearing the end of their careers: Charlton retired at the end of Docherty's first season, Law was sold on to

Manchester City. But in truth the entire club was living on reputation.

Tommy Docherty made me his assistant manager, probably because Matt had suggested the idea, but it was a grey area because I had to look after the reserve team too. Why did Matt put me forward? It was said by others that he hoped I would manage Manchester United one day, but he never said that to me.

In January 1973, myself, Matt, Tommy Docherty, and a United director called Bill Young went to Anfield to watch Liverpool play Burnley in a cup tie. Docherty's son Michael was with Burnley at the time. When we arrived there were only two directors' passes so I offered to sit in the stand. I ended up sitting next to Sean Fallon, by then assistant manager at Celtic, and Lou Macari. The pair were guests of Bill Shankly. I asked Lou what he was doing and he said that he had come to sign for Liverpool. I took him to one side and asked him if he was interested in signing for United. He said he was so I said that I would speak to Docherty. I did that in the car after the game and Docherty was delighted. A few days later the pair of us went up to Glasgow to sign the Scottish international for £200,000. We went in Docherty's three-day old Mercedes which cost £5,000. We picked Lou up in Glasgow and were heading back to Manchester in the fog near Gretna when a heavy lorry struck the car. It thumped into the boot and kept coming, ripping the side. The lorry had been hit from behind itself. The three of us were unhurt, but we were very lucky – especially Lou in the back. He got a jolt but he was all right and passed the medical the next morning. Lou was United's fourth Scottish signing in three weeks and I think the number of Scots at the club was the reason he signed for United.

I would go to a lot of games in a scouting role, watching forthcoming opponents or checking out players United wanted to sign. I went to see one player at Shrewsbury, but it was another who caught my eye. Jim Holton was playing at centre-half for Shrewsbury and I loved centre-halves who were good in the air and frightened the lives out of forwards. Harry Gregg, my former United team-mate, was manager at Shrewsbury. I went to see him in his office after the game and enquired about Holton. Harry said, 'You'll like him because he's Scottish and a Celtic supporter.' I went back to Tommy Docherty. Harry battered the Doc over the transfer fee, getting £80,000 out of United when he should have been paid £40,000, but that didn't matter because Jim turned out to be a great player. He was one reason why United stayed in the first division and weren't relegated, but we didn't play well and finished in eighteenth position.

In Docherty's second season in charge, United were relegated. He and I argued about formations frequently and our relationship deteriorated. He favoured 4–3–3, while I favoured the traditional United one of 4–4–2, with two wingers. Matt agreed with me. The only other person with input was Tommy Cavanagh, a senior coach who went on to be Dave Sexton's assistant's manager. I didn't value his opinions on football and he was not popular with many of the players.

Seven seasons on from winning the European Cup, United were engaged in Division Two fixtures with Hull, Cardiff, and Bristol Rovers. United took thousands of fans to every away game. Doc's Red Army, as the supporters styled themselves, caused problems wherever they went as English football had entered its hooligan period. Lads could prove themselves harder than their peers by professing an affection for United. Match day coaches brought Reds up from Bournemouth, Basingstoke, and Bangor – distance was a mark of pride, back then, and I'm still proud that United have fans from everywhere. Liverpool might have been winning all that was on offer, but United offered glamour. Even in their season in Division Two, the Reds had the highest average home gate of any team in England.

During that relegation season, I had begun to lose my trust in Docherty. He hadn't treated Denis Law in a manner such a great servant to United deserved. The way Docherty would have seen it, he was getting rid of a lot of the former players who were living on past glories. He would have thought he was doing a difficult job for the good of the club, but he didn't do things in the right manner. Aged 33, Denis was coming to the end of his career and Docherty promised him a testimonial in return for him bowing out gracefully. Docherty never kept his word and instead gave him a free transfer to Manchester City. Except he didn't bother to tell Denis, who found out about it while watching television.

Denis's last kick in football was a goal against United at Old Trafford in April 1974, a goal he didn't celebrate. It's remembered as the goal that sent United down, but other United results ensured United were already relegated. The only thing that pleased Denis about that goal was the damage it caused Tommy Docherty.

Just before the relegation, Docherty wanted to sign Peter Osgood from Chelsea for daft money, about £400,000. Osgood was a great player. At 16 he looked like he was going to be one of the best in the world, but he broke his leg and this affected his performances; in my opinion he was finished. Matt Busby was then a director who basically held the purse strings and Docherty told me to tell Matt about Osgood. I phoned Matt at home and Lady Jean told me that he playing golf at the Mere – the beautiful course in Cheshire which remains popular with today's players – with Willie Morgan. I drove down there and, as luck would have it, could see them just coming up to the ninth hole. I walked over. It was a rainy day and my shoes got ruined. Matt was about to tee off with a pipe clamped between his back teeth. Without removing it he said, 'Hello Pat, what are you doing here?'

'Docherty wants to buy a player.'

'Who?'

'Peter Osgood.'

'How much for?'

'About £400,000.'

Matt's pipe fell out of his mouth before he gathered his thoughts and said, 'No. I've accepted that we are going to go down and we will need that money to get us back up.'

We signed Stuart Pearson instead in May 1974. I was sent to watch Stuart a few times at Hull and liked what I saw. He was a great centre-forward who brought people into the game. He ended up moving round the corner from me in Sale and my kids used to drive him mad for autographs.

By the start of the 1974/75 season, my trust in Docherty had completely evaporated. I was his assistant, but he showed so little confidence in my ability that I began to feel undervalued and unwanted. In hindsight, I should have raised the issue with him, but instead I let it fester. I wasn't the only one who wasn't on good terms with the Doc. Martin Buchan, the club captain, was so tired of the manager that he wanted to leave the club. He stormed out of the Old Trafford offices one day and I followed, before catching him up in the car park and persuading him not to ask for a transfer. Matt didn't trust Docherty either, but Docherty was a wily character well versed in football's politics. He could be charismatic and he made sure that he had the chairman Louis Edwards on side. I think Docherty wanted Matt out of Old Trafford because he saw him as being a figure from the past, not the future.

One reason I was asked to tell Matt about Osgood was because Docherty wouldn't front up to anybody. If he wanted to claim his expenses he would send me with his form to Les Olive, the club secretary.

Docherty was popular with fans because they liked the type of football the team played. He wasn't blamed for the relegation in 1974 because it wasn't seen as his team. With United in the second division, fans were happy to judge him by what they saw on the pitch. And what they saw was a decent, young and attacking United side which stormed the second division.

But behind the scenes I didn't like what was happening. I was stunned when Matt had a go at me one day about drinking too much and not being punctual. I couldn't believe what I was hearing and I suspected Docherty to be the cause. Docherty was trying to get rid of anyone who he considered a threat – and he clearly saw me as just that.

Apparently I was drinking in the club each afternoon. In reality, after training each day I would be at Old Trafford for a cup of tea. The physiotherapist Laurie Brown and I would sit in the boardroom. Docherty, who ended up having an affair with Brown's wife, was nowhere to be seen. Paddy McGrath would come down for a cup of coffee at half past three, every day without fail. He had the Playboy club in Manchester and we'd talk football. Me having a few cups of tea and coffee each day had been reported to Matt as me laying into the booze. I suspected that Docherty had told him, but I could never prove it.

On another occasion, Docherty arranged to take the playing staff to watch a big game between Derby County and Real Madrid at the Baseball Ground. Everyone was told to report at Old Trafford at three o'clock. Then Docherty asked his secretary to contact everyone and tell them that the coach would now leave Old Trafford at 2 pm. Everyone except me. The Doc apparently told his secretary that he would contact me himself. He never did. I arrived at the ground at three o'clock and the coach had left an hour earlier. He then told me that he had notified me of the correct time and that I was in the wrong.

I can remember a party at Paddy McGrath's one night when Docherty was there with his wife. She had the needle with me and said to him, 'Pat thinks he's more important than you.' Paddy McGrath told me about that afterwards. I knew everyone in Manchester because I had lived in the city for eleven years, which I don't think the Doc liked. I also think he was wary of me because of my relationship with Matt.

In the second division, Docherty, to his credit, went for wingers and by 1975/76, Steve Coppell and Gordon Hill were rampaging down the wings, Lou Macari and Sammy McIlroy were scuttling around the middle, while Martin Buchan, signed by O'Farrell, was solid in defence. He ensured goalkeeper Alex Stepney, by now the only survivor of 1968, could keep his reputation intact.

I was assistant manager of Manchester United, yet I didn't go to most games. Whereas Sir Alex Ferguson's assistants sit by his side on the bench and they swap ideas, I was sent to scout players or forthcoming opponents most Saturdays. When I did go to United games I was rarely comfortable. I felt humiliated when Docherty asked me to leave the dressing room during half-time in a League Cup game against Manchester City that we lost 4–0. I wanted to hit him, but what could I do? He was the manager and if he didn't want me in there then it was his decision. I went to sit on the bench by myself. He came out for the second half as if nothing had happened. In my mind, that was the end.

I don't know why he had such a problem with me but I suspected it was partly jealousy. In 1974, I worked again on a panel that covered the World Cup for television. It was very popular, with people such as Brian Clough on it, and this time it was broadcast in the Granada region. It was more interesting for me because Scotland were in the finals in Germany. There was a threat made to the Scottish team by the IRA, which understandably made some of the players very nervous.

A day later, a phone call came in to me at the television studios. I didn't take the call because I was on air, but a message was left, supposedly from the IRA, saying that there was no threat to the Scottish team and there never had been. Two policemen came up to the studio and notified me of this. The news was relayed to the team and I spoke to big Jim Holton, the United player, about it in Germany. '*You'll* be all right,' I said. 'But tell the Rangers players in the squad to move quickly on the pitch.' I was joking, but for a minute he believed me.

By 1975, my position at Old Trafford had become untenable. For the first time since the Glasgow shipyards, I hated going to work each morning. Matt decided that I should have a testimonial before I left the club and I appreciated that. I hadn't really made any money from football so when Matt told me I was happy. A few weeks later Tommy Docherty came rushing up to me to tell me that he had negotiated me a testimonial match. It was as if he had done me this big favour and it wasn't even true – Matt had got me the game. If you tell lies then you have to be good at it. You have to have a good memory and Docherty didn't, so he frequently undid himself.

My testimonial was held at Old Trafford on 26 November 1975. Three hours before kick-off, George Best called to say that he had been delayed by a bomb scare in London. He assured me that he would make kick-off and this time George didn't let anyone down.

Liverpool had been considered as opposition because of the friendship I had with Bill Shankly and Ian St John. The manager Bob Paisley offered to bring a team for free, but the police suggested that it probably wasn't a good idea. Celtic were considered because of my obvious links, but in the end the Manchester United team of that time took on the 1968 European Cup winners.

Over 38,000 turned up and I played for the 1968 team. We held our own for a while, before the younger lads started to hammer us as we tired. Matt Busby, Jock Stein, and Tommy Docherty wrote some nice words in the programme, even if Docherty and I were barely speaking. The chairman Louis Edwards repeated a line which a lot of people had said about me over the years. 'When Pat Crerand plays well, United play well.' That was always very flattering, even if not always accurate. He also wrote, 'Many people have recently expressed their opinion that, in these days of high rewards for soccer players, testimonials are unnecessary and undesirable, but I might point out that the major part of Pat's playing career was the period prior to high wages.' He was right; I had virtually nothing to show for my football, except a nice house in Sale. That's different today and I don't agree with testimonial games for very wealthy players, unless they give the money to charity. My accountant Reuben Kaye then gave me a great bit of advice, when he told me to pay my mortgage off with my testimonial money. I had £32,000 in savings, most of it from the testimonial game and I paid off the house, which was worth about £22,000.

The Manchester City chairman Peter Swales was a patron on my testimonial committee. I liked Peter and his wife. He got a lot of abuse from City fans in later years, but he was City through and through. Fans are entitled to give stick out if your team is not successful, and he got a lot of stick for City's failings.

I didn't want to leave Old Trafford but I disliked Tommy Docherty so much that I had to get out of the place. I told the club of my intentions and the news came out. The headline in the *Sun* was 'Crerand Quits United!' with a line underneath claiming, 'I want to be a boss, he says.'

The journalist Peter Fitton reported the news at length. He wrote, 'Pat Crerand is set to quit his £8,500-a-year job with Manchester United ... to look for work. The former Scottish international yesterday publicly revealed plans to turn his back on Old Trafford after thirteen years and put himself on the managerial market. Crerand's decision to seek a new future comes after three years as assistant manager during Tommy Docherty's dramatic revival of Britain's biggest club.

'The 36-year-old former midfield star has been unhappy in his recent scouting role. But he rejected ideas that a back room conflict was behind the move.

'Crerand explained: "The reason for my parting is ambition. I want to be No 1 and my only chance is to leave. I'm going without hard feelings and there is no question of me being pushed out. This decision is mine."

'Crerand – one of the European Cup heroes eight years ago – first discussed his future with The Doc and the directors at the time of his November testimonial. The issue was again thrashed out over the weekend.

'"I am willing to listen to offers from any club in Britain, although I don't want to go abroad," he said. "Tommy Docherty and the chairman have promised me all their help. I can stay here until I land a new job, but I'm hoping to get fixed before the end of the season. When I finished playing I had a few offers but I wasn't ready."

'Docherty said: "Pat is a great bloke and has been a tremendous servant. He wants a manager's job and the best way is to let everyone know he is available."'

Very little in this piece was the truth, as Peter Fitton understood. He would have known that the relationship between

Docherty and I had completely broken down, but he couldn't write that when publicly we were saying otherwise.

Matt Busby told me that he wasn't happy about my leaving, but he wasn't prepared to say anything. Matt's own position had been marginalized. He wasn't the all-powerful figure that he once was and it was symbolic that his office was now a tiny windowless room under the main stand. Matt had to put himself first rather than speak up for people like me who were considered 'Busbyites'.

Thirteen years after joining Manchester United, I left Old Trafford, in August 1976. I had played for the greatest club in the world, alongside some of the best footballers the game has ever produced. Playing for a man I idolized, United had been England's pre-eminent side at the peak of my career. We'd become the first English team to lift the European Cup and United had become renowned throughout the world for brilliant attacking football. Even though my time as assistant manager had ended in disharmony, I was dreading not being involved with Manchester United any more. But I had to leave, not only because my position had become untenable, but because I'd accepted the offer to join Northampton Town as manager. I was unsure of what I was doing, but what other options did I have?

ELEVEN

A Brave New World?

Northampton Town had done exceptionally well in the 1960s, rising from the fourth division to the first in five years. I played against them at the County Ground in 1965 and they gave us a tough game – we drew 1–1. We beat them 6–2 back at Old Trafford and they were relegated immediately, despite losing fewer games than six other teams. They could be proud of their achievement as there are not many small clubs which get to play in football's top division like Northampton did, even if it's only for a season.

The Cobblers (they owe their nickname to the town's shoe-making history) are famous for another game against United. George Best scored six goals against them in an 8–2 victory for United in the 1970 FA Cup.

So I knew a bit about Northampton when I joined the club as manager in 1976. They had just been promoted to the old third division and while it seemed strange that a manager who had just taken them up should leave the club, Bill Dodgin Jnr did just that, apparently having tired of the job.

While at Old Trafford, I'd started to believe the noises I'd been making in the press about becoming a manager in my own right, but deep down I wasn't convinced that I wanted to go into management. I said what I said in the papers because it was the right thing to say. I'd been a successful footballer at two big clubs and the natural step is to attempt to become a successful manager. People who were respected in football had me down as good management material: I had a never-say-die attitude, I always put the team first and I was popular with the other players. But I just didn't have what it takes to become a good manager.

It only took me weeks to realize that management wasn't for me. I was barely over leaving a club I had loved dearly for thirteen years when I found myself at the County Ground, a small old fashioned lower league stadium with three sides because it doubled up as the cricket pitch for Northamptonshire.

When I played at United I always felt that I was a well grounded person who was firmly in touch with reality. Yet when you're at a club like United you take things for granted which you shouldn't – like the high quality of the players. The Northampton players were a great set of lads. I bonded well with them, but I just couldn't get to grips with their inability to do things with a football which I considered simple. My standards were high and I got frustrated, but I was the one with the problem, not them.

My mind wasn't clear for the job. I still dwelt on the rejection that I felt after leaving Old Trafford. I knew that I had a lot more friends at the club than the manager Tommy Docherty, but I was the one who was travelling up and down the M6 to manage a small club and he was in charge of Manchester United. I know he earned the right to get there by working his way up in football, but it was something I just couldn't get my head around for a while.

It was no surprise then that I wasn't successful at Northampton. You hear the stories about how driven Sir Alex

Ferguson was in his first days of management and how he would argue over £20 with the club chairman. He lived and breathed the job twenty-four hours a day, just as Jock Stein had done at Celtic. I tried it and found it hard – I had no time to myself.

The change from being a player to a manager really hit me at Northampton and life was a continual struggle. When you are a player you look after yourself. When you are a manager you spend every week-night trawling the country to see players. When I found one I wanted, it was very, very difficult to sell Northampton Town to them, mainly because the money was so tight that we couldn't offer more than they were on already.

I saw issues as black or white. Things were either right or wrong. That had always got me by as a player, but as a manager life wasn't like that. Players had different personalities and they reacted differently. Some needed their confidence lifting all the time, some needed to be treated with strict discipline. My 'one rule for all' style was lost on some of them.

My right-back John Gregory, later to be Aston Villa manager, was easily Northampton's best player. I thought John was good enough to play for Manchester United but I disliked Tommy Docherty so much that I didn't want to help him out so I never mentioned John's name. I was wrong to do that, because United should have come before a personal issue. John ended up leaving Northampton for Aston Villa in 1977, where he won the first of his six England caps.

I didn't want to be one of the lads, but I was probably a bit soft on several individuals. If they played badly and the fans were on their back, I would side with the players, even if they *had* played badly. I was still seeing things from a player's point of view – that no player goes on the pitch to play badly and if they did under perform I would be sympathetic. Fans who paid their money saw things differently. I felt under pressure at

Northampton to do better than I was doing. That was at a small club, so imagine what it's like for Sir Alex Ferguson.

I remember an FA Cup game against Leatherhead. They had a reputation for being giant killers in the 1970s and had reached the fourth round in 1974/75. The following season they beat a Cambridge United side managed by Ron Atkinson and in 1976 Northampton were drawn against them at their place in the first round. We got off the team coach and saw the TV cameras at the ground. I told my players that the television crews were there because they sensed an upset, which wasn't the best way to inspire confidence, was it? Sadly, they were right and they got one as Leatherhead won 2–0.

On a personal level, I really missed my family. They stayed in Manchester and the intention was for them to follow me down when we had found a nice house in which to live. I lodged in Northampton during the week – sometimes staying over at Noel Cantwell's house as he was manager at nearby Peterborough United – and would drive back to Manchester on a Sunday to see the wife and kids. That wasn't easy, nor was the fact that deep down I knew they didn't want to leave Manchester.

My sons Patrick and Danny were going to United matches, with Patrick watching United home and away from the age of 13. He still does and United is a huge part of his life. Years later when Patrick got married, his wife Patricia complained to me that he was going to every single United match and that it was too much, so I said to her, 'You're a very lucky girl. Patrick is going out every week watching eleven fellas chase a ball around. Other guys go out and chase eleven girls.'

'Well, I've never thought of it that way,' she replied.

Back in 1976, my three kids were settled in school and had close Mancunian friends. It troubled me that I was planning to uproot them to take them somewhere where I wasn't even happy, but I just kept my thoughts to myself. After all, I was expected to be a success at Northampton and move my way up the managerial ladder once I'd proved myself at a smaller club. If only.

I found it hard to cope without my family over Christmas 1976, so that probably contributed to an incident over the New Year which made me decide to resign. We played Preston North End, who were managed by another former United team-mate Nobby Stiles. Nobby had a good team who were top of the league and it looked like they were going to be champions.

I wanted to take the Northampton lads to a hotel ahead of the game on New Year's Day – my idea being to get the team together so that they wouldn't go drinking and I could keep an eye on them. The club refused to pay for a hotel so, in frustration, I paid for it myself. It wasn't much – about £3 per room for the night – but I took it as a sign that the board's hearts weren't in it. In fairness to them they could probably see the same signs in me.

A few weeks later, I offered my resignation after a 2–0 defeat against Brighton. It was accepted. I wasn't thinking about what I'd do next, but it wouldn't have looked good in football. I had marked myself out as a failure, someone who threw the towel in because I couldn't hack it. And I couldn't. I never thought at the time that I wouldn't manage another team, but that proved to be the case.

I went back home to Manchester and enjoyed being around my family. It was a week or so later when I woke up one morning, read the *Daily Mirror* and had a cup of tea. And then it hit me. I was out of football for the first time in my life and, worse, I had no obvious prospects of getting back into it.

I didn't go to any United matches while Tommy Docherty was still at Old Trafford, but still followed the club and despaired at the stories I heard from my contacts there. Stan Flashman, the big ticket tout, came up from London before the 1976 FA Cup final. Touts are inevitable, but Matt Busby would have made people like Flashman stand outside in the car park, not brought him up to the directors' lounge as Tommy Docherty did. Flashman was buying tickets off a player. It was wrong that a player should sell tickets when fans were missing out on them, but unfortunately that happened a lot. Matt heard about Flashman being at Old Trafford and ordered him to be taken out of the club.

I was outraged when the story about Tommy Docherty's affair with Mary, the wife of the United physio Laurie Brown, came out in the summer of 1977. United had just beaten treble chasing Liverpool to win the FA Cup. I got a phone call at home the night before the story broke. The caller said, 'There will be a story in the *News of the World* tomorrow about Tommy Docherty having an affair with Mary Brown.' That was the first I knew and it surprised me, although nothing should have surprised me when it came to Docherty.

Matt had gone away for the weekend, but I knew he was staying in Dowanhill Hotel in County Mayo with his golfing mates. I rang the hotel, but the lad on reception said that Matt wasn't taking any calls. One of Matt's friends was passing by and heard this. He asked the receptionist who was calling. He told him, 'Paddy Crerand from Manchester.' Matt came to the phone.

His first words were, 'What has he done now?' He didn't even need to ask that Tommy Docherty would be the subject of my phone call.

'He's only gone and got off with Mary Brown, Laurie's wife,' I said.

'My God almighty,' Matt muttered. 'I'll be in Manchester tomorrow.'

Meetings were held at Old Trafford over the coming days. Docherty claimed that he was punished for falling in love and the chairman Louis Edwards wanted Docherty to stay. Matt then interjected and said, 'So does that mean that Laurie Brown will lose his job as well as his wife?'

It must have been horrible for Laurie because he didn't have a clue what was going on. Docherty is still with Mary so their feelings were genuine and the unfortunate thing for Laurie is that these things do happen in life, but Matt always thought that the club was bigger than anybody and his morals were very high. Matt was a Holy Joe, a very religious man, and like him I felt that United's name was being dragged through the mud.

Docherty was dismissed, but he was rarely out of the newspapers. Willie Morgan had been on Granada television and described him as the worst manager he had ever had. Docherty contested this and the pair ended up in court for a libel trial. It was ironic, because Willie had helped get Docherty the United job in 1972.

Willie spent two years preparing his defence and drew up twenty-nine allegations against Docherty to support his claim that he was 'about the worst manager there has ever been'. Along with Lou Macari, Alex Stepney, Laurie Brown, Denis Law, and Ted MacDougall, I was one of Willie's witnesses prepared to stand up in court against Docherty. I wasn't alone in hoping that the court would put matters straight with Docherty, but in the end none of us had to testify. The case collapsed before prosecution had even finished its argument, when Docherty accepted that not telling Denis Law about his free transfer 'was very wrong'. Willie's barrister then put it to Docherty that he had told a 'pack of lies' and Docherty admitted that he had.

Docherty had to pay Willie's costs as well as those of Granada TV. The failed libel action cost Docherty £50,000 and he described it as the biggest mistake of his life. A few years later, a jury at the Old Bailey cleared Docherty of two charges of perjury relating to the Willie Morgan case. They accepted that his lies were not deliberate.

For the third time in succession, I was invited back to be on the ITV panel for the 1978 World Cup finals in Argentina, this time with Johan Cruyff, who didn't travel to South America because threats were made to kidnap his family. The story at the time was that he was injured, but that wasn't the truth. I hated what the military dictatorship stood for in Argentina and took the opportunity to abuse them every night on television.

Cruyff is one of the best players ever and I got very pally with him. After the tournament he offered to send a case of Spanish red wine to my house. I told him that while I loved red wine, I just didn't like Spanish red wine. He looked at me like I was a bit stupid, which I probably was, but I just don't like Spanish wine.

My old friends Malcolm Allison, Jack Charlton, and Brian Clough were also on the panel. Brian was even more critical than me on television – I'd never met someone more left wing than me until I met him.

Because England didn't qualify for the competition, Kevin Keegan made some guest appearances, and the comedian Frank Carson was included to lighten the mood whenever Brian Clough paused for a moment from slaughtering Argentina's military dictator.

I played squash every day with Kevin and really liked him. Players have been gifted with more natural talent than him, but the work he put into becoming a player who was good enough to twice be named European Footballer of the Year drew my admiration.

As I was in London for three weeks working on the panel, my family came down to the capital at weekends to see me.

My kids were fascinated by the ice machines in the hotel – they couldn't believe that you could get free ice, and used to take it. I never did work out what they did with it.

After one programme, we went back to the hotel, where we found Denis Roche, the football agent, criticizing players for being thick. I didn't agree with him and told him that he made a good living out of footballers and he wasn't being fair slagging them off. He disagreed, so I became livid and accused him of being a hypocrite. We were sitting at a table, but rather than argue my point, I jumped up and leapt over the table towards him. I tried to punch him, but people intervened. Denis looked petrified and he cowered behind his hands. It's not the right way to make a point, but he never said a word afterwards.

After the World Cup had finished I needed to find some work. I didn't have much money to my name, but I had the advantage of not having a mortgage. Ernie Kearns and Tim Kilroe, two friends of mine who were involved in the construction industry in Manchester, gave me some public relations work which involved meeting their clients. A lot of the Irish immigrants who arrived in Manchester with nothing went into construction and made good through hard graft. They looked after each other and many of them were United fans who bought boxes at Old Trafford. It's nonsense when people say that the people who sit in the executive seats at Old Trafford are not genuine supporters because some of them contain the biggest Manchester United fans that I know.

I also started doing some sportsmen's dinners. Vince Miller, a local singer, comic and a great host, got me involved. He was very talented and should have been far more famous than he was. His idea was that he would compere an after-dinner function at the Acton Court Hotel in Stockport and that I would stand up and speak about my experiences in football. I told him that I couldn't do it, that I was petrified of standing up in front of 300 people. The money was good, though, and with three kids to get through school, I needed it. A compromise was reached, where I agreed to answer questions from the audience. I felt much more comfortable doing this, as the onus wasn't on me to speak all the time. I still do the after-dinner circuit, maybe one night a week. I can be in a working men's club in Sunderland one week and a football club in Kettering another. There's never a shortage of questions from the audience – and most are usually about Best, Law, or Charlton. 'What was George Best really like?' someone might ask. There's no shortage of material – I could take all night to answer that question alone.

I rarely get asked questions about the political and religious aspects of being a Scottish Celt footballer during The Troubles – that sort of material is a bit heavyweight for those evenings when the wine is flowing. But politics has always been a massive part of my life

In March 1972, internment had been introduced in Northern Ireland and I was outraged that suspects could be held in custody for months at a time without being charged. John Hume, later a Nobel prize winner for his efforts in bringing peace to Northern Ireland, used to rent the house of my aunt every summer in Donegal. I had met him for the first time in 1960 and he struck me as an impressive figure, one who was committed to improved human rights and civil liberty.

In 1975, members of the republican movement organized the 'rents and rates' strike, in which they said that no rents or rates should be paid to their landlords – ultimately the British government – while they lived in oppressive conditions. I disagreed with the strike because ordinary people were suffering. Because they weren't paying their rents and rates, their electricity, gas and water supplies had been cut and there was real hardship. John Hume spoke to me about trying to do something about it. He said that the republican movement wouldn't listen to him or deal with him, so I spoke to Jim Harkin, a pal of mine who knew all the influential people.

I'd met Jim in Donegal one summer too. Jim arranged for us to drive into Derry for a meeting with members of the republican movement. We finished up in a safe house in Glenfada Park in the Bogside with ten of the most wanted men in Ireland. I sat down in a room with the lads around me and the mood was serious. I said: 'The biggest problem you lot (nationalists) have got is that the unionists will always put disagreements aside and get together when they need to. But you lot are always arguing among yourselves. You need to find some common ground and have one voice because that will have a lot more power.' I told them that they needed to become political and renounce violence if they wanted to achieve their aims and that the only way of solving their problems was by dialogue and not by shooting each other, which years later they did. They were working-class lads in their twenties with a left wing outlook. I wasn't that different, nor was I scared about the situation I was in. But my brother-in-law, who had driven us there, was in a complete state.

I was under no illusions. They didn't meet with me because they thought I was some kind of inspirational figure, a master of political dialogue with contacts in high places. They spoke to me because I had been a well-known footballer and most of them were football fans, many of them United fans, and they wanted to talk about football as well. One of the republican lads showed me a letter he had written to Matt Busby congratulating United on winning the European Cup. Matt had written back to him and he had that letter too. Yet just as they wouldn't listen to John Hume, they wouldn't listen to me either. They were unmoved and just saw the strike as a means towards a United Ireland. For them it was all or nothing.

I called John Hume and told him that I had tried my best, but the lads were not going to change their minds. I told him that I had tried to arrange a meeting between them and John but they didn't want to know. John was disappointed.

It's great that Manchester United's support in Northern Ireland transcends the political divide. I've met groups of Catholics and Protestants for a drink after a game at Old Trafford. They have Manchester United in common, and yet the only time they spoke to one another was when they were in Manchester for a game. I'll never forget seeing news footage a few years ago of young kids throwing rocks across the dividing wall in Belfast. The Catholic ones were wearing Manchester United shirts, and so were the Protestant ones on the other side.

I went back to Derry when United played a friendly game against Derry City in 2000. Derry wanted to raise money and they attracted Barcelona to the Brandywell. None of the people in the United party knew it, but seven miles outside the city, the police escort was very discreetly handed over to republicans. The Bogside, part of the scene of Bloody Sunday in 1972, was not a place where the police tended to go. The republicans took charge of our security thereafter.

Back to 1978, there was some speculation linking me with the manager's job at Parkhead. The former Celtic player Bertie Auld said that I was in contention, but I never heard anything officially. Unofficially, I was told that someone in football had told them I was a member of the IRA and that had done my prospects irreparable damage. That was ridiculous – I have never been a member of the IRA in any shape or form, in fact I've been a peacemaker. Billy McNeill was appointed Celtic manager in 1978, where he enjoyed a successful five years at the club. He was an obvious choice, having managed at Clyde and Aberdeen.

I remained friends with Billy and stayed at his home while I was in Glasgow in 1983 to watch his Celtic side beat Rangers to win the Scottish League Cup. I was at the after match party in the Grosvenor Hotel and Billy asked me how my mother was doing. I mentioned that she wasn't in the best of health.

He knew that she was a mad Celtic fan and suggested that we go and show her the League Cup to cheer her up. I was in no fit state to drive, so Billy's wife Liz offered. We were soon waking my mother up in her maisonette in the Gorbals. She opened the door wearing her dressing gown and curlers, to be greeted by the sight of her son, the Celtic manager and his wife, plus the Scottish League Cup trophy. News travelled fast, lights started coming on and we were soon surrounded by neighbours having their photos taken in the courtyard with the cup.

I used to go to Glasgow from time to time in the 1980s, usually to watch Celtic. One bloke whom I knew from the Gorbals sent me the *Celtic View* magazine for years. I did one newspaper article where I opined that Celtic needed to step up a gear because they hadn't been playing well. It was a harmless opinion I've offered a million times before, but the guy who sent me the *Celtic View* didn't see it that way. I was in a pub in Glasgow a few weeks later when he came charging up to me and accused me of being a Rangers fan. He stopped sending me the Celtic magazine after that and started sending me *Rangers News* instead. It must have killed him to buy that.

My sons say that I change when I go back to Glasgow. If I do, it's not a conscious thing. When Sir Alex Ferguson goes back to Glasgow he is not 'Sir', he's just 'Alex'. The one thing you cannot be in Glasgow is big-headed. I got a letter recently from my old school asking me to attend an awards ceremony. There was no pandering to my ego or comments to big me up – it just told me that I had been invited and asked for a yes or no response. I like that black and white, no nonsense approach.

Unfortunately my no nonsense approach to conflict isn't always the best policy. In 1982, we went on holiday to Mallorca as usual. My son Danny got in a spot of bother. Some American sailors were being a bit smart with my daughter Lorraine and Danny threw a bottle at them. He was only 14, but a sailor chased after Danny and punched him a few times. I was having a drink with Paddy McGrath when Danny came running up telling me what had happened. Paddy told Danny off and lectured him about avoiding trouble. While he was having a word, I went in search of the sailors. They were pointed out to me and I gave it to the one who had hit Danny good and proper. There was a bit of a commotion and I remember some cockney holidaymakers coming along and shouting, 'Blimey, it's Paddy Crerand!'

You have to look after your kids. I wasn't right to hit that guy; it wasn't a good reflection on my character. It takes a lot for me to lose my temper, but when I do I go mad. And I lost it that night.

On that holiday, I saw an old friend from Manchester called John Hart. He wasn't married, but had a different girlfriend every time I saw him. He introduced us to his latest girl and she seemed very pleasant. Noreen had a necklace with my European Cup winners' medal hanging off it. John's new girlfriend said, 'That's lovely, what a wonderful idea. I'd love to be able to do that.'

Noreen was very proud and a little bit cocksure and said, 'That's a European Cup winners' medal that is,' the implication being that it would be impossible for the lady to do it.

'I know,' replied John's girlfriend, 'My ex-husband has got three.' She had only been married to Wim Suurbier, the legendary Ajax full-back. Noreen wanted the ground to open up and swallow her.

In 1982, I had the chance to start running a pub, The Park, in Altrincham. I needed to earn a more secure living than picking up bits and bobs here and there so I decided to go for it. Noreen was not convinced, but we were hardly flooded with offers of work. It was a gamble when I became a landlord because I had to pay for all the fixtures and fittings, despite not owning the building.

I was lucky because Martin Roarty, a relation of mine, had run my uncle's pub in Donegal and he was a great barman. I asked him to come over and be the main man at the pub. He agreed. He was football mad – a Liverpool fan believe it or not – and he used to wind everybody up in the pub. He was a great mickey-taker and superb at his job. He could hold four different conversations at the same time and serve four other people at the other end of the bar while he was talking. Martin could lie through his teeth and get away with it. He once convinced regulars that the German tennis player Boris Becker was Irish because he had red hair.

The pub opened for business at the start of the 1982 World Cup finals. I had an early baptism of fire – a fight on the first night after a bloke started giving me sectarian abuse. I was livid and punched him a good few times before throwing him out. I was told that he had been a regular, so I don't know whether he was testing out the new landlord or not, but his wife came back two hours later. She wasn't looking to have a go at me, but politely explained that her husband's false teeth had been knocked out and that she had come to retrieve them because he was too scared. The lad came back eventually and became a regular again – he was a nice guy as it happened, one of many characters.

There was an old Irish fella with a thick accent called Billy Neary who was always in there and he never shut up about the actress Grace Kelly. He used to sit at the bar and go on and on about her. He wrote her a letter once and she replied to him. He treasured that reply and showed it to everybody who came near him in the pub.

My son Danny once found Billy drunk in a street nearby, struggling on all fours. Danny helped him back to his hostel in Altrincham. Bill thanked him by inviting him in for a nip of poteen – a form of whisky that they distil illegally in Ireland. It was so strong that it would take paint off a gate. Danny declined.

There was another guy called Ronnie who looked like Dracula. He was a lunatic after a few beers and used to say to people, 'Yer effing bastards, eff off.' He once said to Bryan Robson, 'And what the hell do you do?'

'I play football,' replied Bryan.

'Who the eff for?'

'Manchester United.'

'Eff off,' was Ronnie's answer.

The pub became a big success and so many people would come in on a Saturday night that we had to lock the doors. I was putting Irish music on there when it was unheard of and every member of the Irish Parliament came into that pub at some point or other. Several of them were in one Sunday in the autumn of 1982 when Bryan Robson walked in. He'd not been at United too long and wasn't put off by drunken Ronnie, so he sat at the bar having a few pints of Guinness. After a while he asked to see my medals so I went upstairs and got them – the FA Cup Winners' one, the League Championship, and the European Cup Winners' medal. He looked at them and said, 'I'm going to win them with United. You are nothing in football without medals like that.'

I was close to Bryan. He came to ask me for advice when there was interest in him from Italy. I could see he was tempted and there had been offers from Sampdoria, Milan, and Juventus. I asked him if he was happy at Old Trafford. He said he was. I asked him if his family were happy in Manchester. He said they were. So I asked him why he wanted to go somewhere else for a few quid when there was a chance that a lot of things could go wrong. I said the same thing in 1998 when Brian Kidd was offered the Blackburn Rovers job. But I didn't realize that he was on such poor money at Old Trafford when I said that.

Someone kept grassing Bryan Robson up for drinking. It used to annoy him because he would come in and only have two or three pints. He was considered a local and people didn't pay him special attention, but word would get back to Old Trafford that he had been steaming drunk after downing sixteen pints in my pub. The other locals found out who had been spreading rumours and the lad had a hell of a time in Altrincham. He was considered a grass of the worst kind, one who was telling lies. The lad was punched a few times when he went out and it got so bad for him that he had to leave the area.

The United lads used to come in most weekends on a Saturday after the game. By 6.30 pm most of the team were in the pub and the atmosphere was brilliant. In that period after a game, players are still pumped with adrenalin and want to remain active. I knew that from when I played. I can remember coming back late from an away game in London and making bacon and eggs for Denis Law in my kitchen because neither of us wanted to go to sleep. It wasn't like you could stay up watching television because that usually finished about 11 o'clock.

Footballers are always giving each other abuse and mickey taking so they created a buzz. They didn't want to go home and relax. It was mostly men in the pub, with maybe the odd wife of a regular. It wasn't a place where women came to try their luck with a famous footballer. The lads would stay for a couple of hours before going out, either into Manchester or around Altrincham, Wilmslow, or Hale.

Mark Hughes used to come in and I can remember him sitting at the bar, having signed a contract to leave United for Barcelona, saying, 'I don't want to go to Barcelona, I don't want to go.'

Peter Reid and Alan Hansen came in one night. People didn't realize that Alan had been a big United fan who wanted to join the club. He had been at the 1977 FA Cup final as a United supporter.

In 1984, United beat Dundee United 3–2 away in the UEFA Cup. On the same night, Celtic had to replay a game against Rapid Vienna at Old Trafford because there had been trouble in the original tie at Parkhead, with a bottle being thrown. They lost the game 1–0 at Old Trafford, but the pub was packed with Celtic supporters. The United lads came back straight from Dundee and walked into a pub packed with Celtic fans. The fans loved it and we had a great night.

We did some wind ups in the pub. Colin Gibson, the United defender, was convinced that he was good enough to play for England and kept pestering Bryan Robson to have a word with Bobby Robson. Bryan set up a sting. While the lads were having a beer in the pub, I called the pub from an outside phone and got one of the barmen to shout that it was Bobby Robson for Bryan.

'Is Colin Gibson with you?' I asked, pretending to be the England manager.

'He is gaffer,' answered Robson, as solemn as a judge.

'Well, tell him that he's getting a call up.'

Robson duly relayed the good news.

Colin Gibson shouted, 'I knew it, I knew I was good enough. I knew I was better than Kenny Samson!'

All the United players were in the pub the day after beating Everton in the 1985 Cup Final. They used to board their open top bus at St Margaret's church in Hale, before heading down the Chester Road and into Manchester, so they came in for a few beers. The pub was rammed and the atmosphere was absolutely brilliant. Everyone was singing United songs, including the players. Little Gordon Strachan, who hardly drank anything, was standing on the chairs singing when someone shouted, 'Stand up when you sing.'

'I am stood up,' he replied. Two pints and he was anybody's.

Our eldest son Patrick loved the players coming in and as he became older he became good friends with a lot of them. In later years he became mates with Roy Keane. Roy took him to Barcelona as his guest for the European Cup Final in 1999. He went to the players' party after the game and was fascinated by the European Cup and the fact that it was silver on the outside and gold on the inside. Patrick took Roy to Parkhead to watch Celtic one game. Roy wore a hat and kept his head down, but some Celtic fans recognized him.

I got to know Roy Keane very well too. I was in Dublin in 1993 when Roy had just signed for United. Alex Ferguson and I were guests of honour from the Football Association of Ireland, when Alex said, 'Can you do me a favour Pat and go to say hello to Roy Keane's family over there.' I went over and made his family feel welcome.

I was out with Roy not long after he joined United in Mulligans, a pub in a hotel close to Manchester which was a favourite with the players in the 1990s. Roy could be hot headed when he was younger. I had to step in to prevent him and Bryan Robson coming to blows. It was as if Roy wanted to prove that he was as important to the Manchester United team as Bryan.

Another time in Mulligans, two Manchester City fans had a go at Roy. These things happen when you are a United player and you have to walk away. Roy wanted to take the pair of them on when I got hold of him.

'If you hit them then it will be you in the papers, not them,' I said. 'Just think about it and ignore them. Tell them to come back in a few years to see your medals, because no current City player will be able to show them any.'

Roy went on to become a Manchester United legend and he's had an excellent start in management at Sunderland too, winning the Championship in his first season after joining them when they were at the bottom of the table. I'm not surprised at how well he's done because he's so determined and driven. As I found out myself, playing in midfield for a successful Manchester United side doesn't make you a great manager, but Roy could be different. Players listen to him because they respect him, but also because he is very concise and doesn't waste words. There are no clichés and waffle with Roy, that's why the United players were almost in awe of him. He's a perfectionist who sets incredibly high standards for himself and those he works with.

Roy changed when he stopped drinking. He used to spend more time hanging around with my son Patrick than anyone in Manchester, but Patrick wasn't even mentioned in his 2002 autobiography. I think Roy associated time spent in Patrick's company with drinking.

If Roy can keep Sunderland in the Premiership it will be a great achievement. If he can get Sunderland at the top end of the Premiership then I would see him as an eventual replacement for Alex Ferguson. The fans would be delighted if Roy took over from Alex, as they would be if Mark Hughes, another ex-Old Trafford legend, took over. Both men understand what Manchester United is about and appreciate the size of the club and the demands of its fan base. Of the former players now in management, I think those two would be favourites to one day be in charge at Old Trafford. Mark has really surprised me because he was so quiet when he was a player. He used to come into my pub and would barely speak, but now he comes across as articulate and measured when interviewed.

A lot of Irish people who came in the pub were big hard lads who made sure that there were never any problems. A big crowd of my Irish customers had travelled to watch United play away at Queens Park Rangers one Saturday tea time in December 1987. The pub started filling up with lads I didn't recognize. We were going to have a band on that night called 'Cross Fire' and they were setting up their equipment as these lads I didn't recognize started to mess about. There were about forty or fifty of them and they started getting loud and abusive. Then I received a call from the landlord of another pub who told me that Manchester City's hooligans were coming to my pub to cause trouble.

These blokes were clearly the hooligans and soon things started to get ugly. One of them took the charity box and while some of the older lads in their group told them it was out of order, they were making a right nuisance of themselves. My son Patrick told me that there was going to be trouble and he was right. Before long, Tom Whitty, one of the regulars was going toe to toe with about eight of them. He had told them to stop acting like kids and they didn't take too kindly to him. They started throwing bottles and all the windows were smashed. I was livid and went to get a baseball bat that I kept in case of any problems. I walked back through the bar and towards them. Apparently I was shouting, 'I just want one, I just want one.' I started whacking any of them that I could and they began rushing for the doors, desperate to get out.

I was fuming and wanted revenge. I left the pub, leaving the bat behind, and started jogging towards Altrincham town centre with my two sons and Tom Whitty. We soon caught up with one lad, a fat kid who had been left behind by the others. He was out of breath and he got a whack straightaway, before he started protesting his innocence, shouting that he was just walking to the bus station.

'Where are you going?' asked one of our lot.

'Urmston,' replied the lad.

Unfortunately for him, we had family in Urmston and knew the bus routes well.

'Which bus are you going to catch?'

The lad didn't know. His face dropped and he got another whack. My kids were trying to drag me back, but I had completely gone. I rushed off to catch up with the rest of them, leaving the fat lad behind. He had somehow mustered enough energy to shout, 'City, City'.

We arrived at The Grapes pub in Altrincham, where they had been causing problems with the bouncers. I didn't want to go inside and start a fight on another landlord's property, so we told the City fans to come outside. I was completely off my head. None of them would come out, so I went inside and tried to drag three of them out. They were bricking it. There was plenty of bravado when they had been in a big crowd of their mates, but now they were frightened. The police then turned up and made arrests. A few of the troublemakers went to court and had their wrists slapped. I'm not proud of what I did, but I was fuming that they came to my pub and broke all the windows. They never came back to give us problems again.

I left the pub in 1989. Noreen rightly felt that we weren't just working as landlords, but as social workers, too, because everyone came into the pub with their problems. Even though we had people like the head barman Martin working with us, I found it very tough having a family and running a pub. I thought football management was bad, but the pub was my first twenty-four-hour occupation.

The only time I had some free time was to go and watch United on a Saturday. Since the mid-1980s I had been doing corporate hospitality work at Old Trafford. I enjoyed that and I still do it. I meet fans in the executive boxes before matches and we talk football. I like meeting new people. Twenty years ago there was just me, a former player, meeting business people. These days, that's a valuable source of income for ex-players.

It was a change in the licensing laws which made it impossible for me to continue as a publican. Longer opening hours meant even less time with the family. I had already made the mistake of moving the family into the pub, while keeping our family home in Sale empty for eight years.

In 1983, one of the directors of Manchester City asked me about Billy McNeill. I put a good word in for him, and it must have done some good because he got the job. There was a lot of talk about me being Billy's assistant, but that would not have been the done thing given my association with Manchester United. I've always had a lot of good friends who were City fans and I never shared the hatred of the club that some United fans feel, but I couldn't have gone to Maine Road. I'm stunned that City haven't won a trophy for so long. When people talk about the great football cities of the world they don't mention City. Yet more people watch live football every week in Manchester than Liverpool, Glasgow, Milan, or Madrid. The problem is that City haven't kept their part of the deal because they haven't won anything for so long. City should be playing in Europe every season, not playing a subservient role to Manchester United.

I helped Billy and his family settle into Manchester and introduced him to people. He kept inviting me to City games and I kept declining. I thought that I would get a bit of abuse there with my United links, but one day I just thought 'what the hell' and went along. I knew half of the City fans there and Billy realized this and asked me to run the hospitality in his manager's office while he got down to the serious business of managing the team. After a while in Manchester, Billy said, 'I'm amazed you're not a millionaire Pat because you know everybody.'

I did and do know a lot of people in Manchester because I'm sociable and like to get out and about. I do people favours and don't expect anything back in return. Paddy McGrath did things for people, but he always got things back in return.

Besides, I've had enough luck in life. I was invited to Dubai in the mid-1980s to watch Celtic play Liverpool in a game to decide the unofficial British champions. I was part of a threesome with Denis Law and George Best brought over to speak on the eve of the game. Both teams flew on the same plane along with the media.

I travelled on an Irish passport, but the morning after the game the customs man at the airport stopped me. He explained that I didn't have a visa and so couldn't leave the country. British passport holders didn't need a visa, Irish ones did. I explained that I wasn't an Arab.

'Look at me,' I said, 'I'm not an Arab. I look different. I'm not trying to leave the country without a visa.'

He wouldn't budge and I missed my flight. I didn't know what to do. One of the lads who worked in the airport was an Irish fella. He must have heard about my plight because he approached me and offered to help me out. He rang the Irish embassy, who arranged for me to stay in a hotel – all paid for. They also booked me on a flight home the next day in first class. It was wonderful. But I made sure that I had the right visa next time I travelled.

My family life, enjoying watching my kids grow up, has given me great pride and pleasure. I'm not sure that they always appreciated me, but I always had their best interests at heart.

My second son Danny was quite a good footballer. He started out at United in the 1980s, just after Mark Hughes had come through the ranks. In one game for the 'A' team, he came on against Formby away and changed the match. He reckoned that he understood the rivalry between Mancunians and Liverpudlians when all the other players didn't.

Danny ended up at Rochdale and broke into the first team under the former Leeds player Eddie Gray, whom he really liked. I remember watching him against Middlesbrough in a pre-season friendly and spotting a big centre-half for Middlesbrough who looked like he could play. That was Gary Pallister.

My Danny was a good passer of the ball, but like his father he couldn't run. Danny sometimes felt that it went against him that he was my son. It must have been difficult for him.

Danny worked at United between 1993 and 2000 in the merchandise division under Edward Freedman. Edward doesn't get the credit he deserves because he realized the potential of merchandise at Old Trafford. When Martin Edwards asked him to join from Tottenham in 1991, Tottenham had a bigger turnover than Manchester United. Edward changed that. He was a bright bloke who could sell sand to the Arabs. That money from merchandising allowed United to buy Roy Keane.

My daughter Lorraine told me that I was a tough father to please, that I described any boyfriends she had as being either 'a total idiot' or 'stupid'. One of them came and introduced himself, saying, 'I think we've met before.' He must have recognized my face. 'I don't we think we have,' I replied. He was a fool.

Lorraine got married to Neil, a good Irish lad. Moya Ní Bhraonáin, the singer from Clannad was at the wedding. She is the eldest sister of the singer Enya, who was also briefly a member of Clannad in the early 1980s. Clannad put Irish traditional music and the Irish language on the world stage and paved the way for many other Irish artists. As I've said, the band was from Gweedore like my family and Moya was a big United fan. Clannad once played in Manchester and Moya came back to the pub after the concert because she wanted to meet Bryan Robson.

Lorraine's kids are called Saoirse and Ursula. Paddy McGrath's daughter was called Ursula – named after the sister who looked at Matt Busby in the Munich Hospital.

Patrick was the first of the kids to get married. He planned his wedding for 19 August 1989, thinking that would avoid the football season. He didn't count on 1990 being a World Cup year and it clashed with United against Arsenal, the day that Michael Knighton, who thought he had bought the club, ran on the pitch dressed as a red devil, juggling the ball. Patrick has two lovely children, Nicholas Patrick Catona and Jade.

Danny was the last one to get married, to Faye in 1993. His wedding clashed with Newcastle's visit to Old Trafford, when Andy Cole scored in a 1–1 draw. We went from the church to the reception in a fancy carriage and I felt a right fool with a top hat on. The wedding was at the Copthorne Hotel in Salford Quays. They have four kids, Chelsea, not named after the football club, Scarlet, Enya and Danny. I dote on them like I do with all my grandchildren.

TWELVE

Red Eyed

Since giving up the pub, I've almost always made my living from the media, and continue to do so. I have a good standard of living and I enjoy my current occupation, following United all over the world. People think I am stinking rich when I am not, but I'm just happy to have been involved in professional football for almost five decades.

The majority of my work is for MUTV, the in-house Manchester United TV station, and I take particular pleasure in commentating on games. I like to be honest, but I suspect some people may see me as being a little bit biased towards United. I don't see it quite like that. I think that United get a bad deal from the media and I consider the club needs support at times. I don't criticize players either because no player goes out to have a bad game on purpose. Fans have the liberty to criticize them because they pay their money and they are entitled to their opinions, but fans expect players to be world beaters every game and football isn't like that.

My advantage is that I can say what I want because it's my opinion and I'm not in the position of managers or players where they could be fined for bringing the game into disrepute if they speak their mind.

Sticking up for Eric Cantona after he jumped at that idiot at Selhurst Park in 1995, when so many didn't, made me a marked man. Unlike so many who were quick to condemn Eric, I was at the game and I'd watched him get kicked for the full match. I see it every week when Cristiano Ronaldo gets fouled, but he doesn't react because he doesn't have Eric's fiery temperament. Alan Wilkie, the referee that night, gave Eric no protection. I know that it is not easy to referee a game when it is under so much scrutiny, but with extensive television coverage, officials can come to believe that they are the stars in games. Wilkie seemed to be enjoying the annoyance his decisions were causing United players – such as when he didn't punish defender Richard Shaw for catching Cantona on his ankle. I was raging in the press box because I could see how the Palace players were trying to wind Eric up.

Shaw then directed a tackle at Eric's Achilles tendon as he twisted, back to goal, to try to lay off a pass to the running Andy Cole. There were other less blatant efforts like shirt pulling to push him Eric over the brink. The longer the game went on, the more he seemed to be seething inside, ready for revenge when the opportunity came. As soon as Eric made a bad tackle on Shaw, Wilkie sent him off. When the Palace fan Mathew Simmons rushed towards the front of the stand to abuse Eric, the Frenchman really lost at and did his famous kung-fu kick. The only mistake Eric made was not aiming it higher so that his studs connected with Simmons' head.

I was prepared to take the flak which came my way for defending Eric, even though Eric and I were hardly best friends. I probably spoke to him for about three minutes in all his time at Old Trafford, when I told him that he should go on television more so that people could see the real Cantona. He refused point blank.

The criticism didn't bother me one bit because it came from people who were not involved in Manchester United. Their opinions were worthless as far as I was concerned. One problem, however, was that I was not faceless. Since 1989, I had been doing match commentary for practically every United game for local radio in Manchester. I loved it, I was effectively being paid to be a supporter and I travelled home and away, mixed with Reds and enjoyed the banter with away fans. I was never afraid to give my opinion, to defend United when others were ready to have a go. United sell the most newspapers so the press are always looking for stories, good and bad. You can see newspaper billboards with United stories in London, but you'd never see boards in Manchester with Chelsea or Arsenal stories.

People would have a go at the fact United fans come from far and wide. As I've said, what's wrong with that? I think United should be proud that there are fans who love the club all over the world. It's not like United don't have a huge support in Manchester because they are by far the most popular team in the city.

Yet as Manchester United became more successful in the early 1990s, so the levels of jealousy crept up. When United started winning the league with regularity from 1993 onwards, people started to loathe their success, completely failing to recognize the magnificent achievement of Alex Ferguson in turning the club around.

Away fans would abuse me because they saw me as a redder than red United fan. They couldn't get to Alex or the players, but I was an easier target given that I sat in the press boxes at away grounds and they tended to be located in main stands, surrounded by home supporters. Fortunately, I had heard this all before when I was a player.

The abuse after the Cantona 'kung-fu' incident didn't just come from fans. I went to a game at Everton's Goodison Park a few weeks later, where I bumped into the former Liverpool hard man Tommy Smith, whom I like. He didn't waste much time having a go.

'That effing Eric Cantona,' he said. 'How can you defend that French nutter?'

'Tommy,' I said calmly, 'we all lose our head on a football pitch. You've done that yourself a millions times.'

'I've never jumped into the crowd and hit anybody,' he replied.

'So you're telling me that you've never had a go at a fan?' I asked.

He went quiet, then grinned, and I thought, 'I've got him here.'

'There was the one time at West Ham,' he went on. 'When a fan was calling me every name under the sun. So when I left the pitch at the end of the game I jumped up, punched him then ran into the dressing room.'

'There you go,' I said. 'None of us are perfect.'

'Yes, but the television cameras were not there at West Ham,' he declared, like that had anything to do with it. I think I changed his mind on the Cantona incident. Others were less willing to listen.

I think United fans appreciated my support of Cantona when so many other people were quick to admonish him. Peter Boyle, who starts many of the songs at Old Trafford, even wrote the following song dedicated to me. To the tune, of 'Maggie May', by my good friend Rod Stewart, he called it 'Paddy Eh'.

Ay up, Paddy,
I think I've got something to say to you,

It's late September and Eric's coming back to rule,
We know he was abused,
We're glad you aired your views,
Oh Paddy, you couldn't have done anymore.

You support us away from home,
Defend us but rarely moan,
Oh Paddy, I guess that's what friends are for.

The tabloid *Sun* when it's in your house,
It really makes you rage,
But that just makes me proud of you,
Each and every day,
I laughed at one of your jokes,
Well the room was full of blokes,
Oh Paddy, you couldn't have done anymore.

You gave me a lift from town,
Held my daughters and watched them frown,
Never forget your roots,
And that's what it's all about,
Oh Paddy, you couldn't have done anymore.'

Brilliant, eh? I didn't even have a song like that when I played. Peter does a good job trying to kick-start the atmosphere inside Old Trafford. My mother's maiden name was Boyle and our families are from the same part of Ireland, but I can state quite categorically that I'm in no way related to that mad man.

Sometimes Peter has his work cut out and the noise inside Old Trafford is really flat. I think all-seater stadiums are to blame and it saddens me because I remember what Old Trafford used to be like. It's not just at United either; Celtic Park is nothing like it used to be unless it's for the really big games. All-seater stadiums mean that mates who stood together have been split up, so it needs crazy United fans like Peter Boyle and I wish more people were like him. That said, the atmosphere at United's away games is fantastic. Usually there are 3,000 or so hardcore United fans and the support they give the team makes a difference when there's so many home fans wanting to see United fail.

I'm not in favour of a return to standing areas inside football grounds. I realize that they exist in Germany, but I think that terracing is inherently unsafe. I'm amazed that more people weren't seriously injured or killed when I watched Celtic as a lad or when I played. The Ibrox disaster in 1971, which killed sixty-six, was horrific and conditions needed to improve. It wasn't right that fans were hemmed in with iron bars. The change only came following the publication of the Taylor Report after the Hillsborough disaster. By that time football was changing and attracting more middle class fans, but, if anything, the abuse I received at grounds got worse.

Against Arsenal at Wembley in the 1993 Charity Shield, I left the press box at half-time and went beneath the stand to get a cup of tea. This Arsenal fan started having a go at me, calling me an 'effing Man U wanker' and using other phrases that I don't want to repeat. He was with a few mates and thought he was being brave because he had a couple of drinks inside him. As I queued for my cup of tea, it occurred to me that there was no way that I should have to put with that kind of abuse. So I walked back over to him and there weren't so many of them this time. I was raging with him and he didn't even respond. But this time he listened in silence, with a sheepish expression and I couldn't understand why, because a few minutes earlier he had been so vocal. Then I saw the four lads standing behind me. They were members of a very hard North

Manchester family. They said nothing, not even to me, but their presence had clearly spooked the lad.

A few months prior to that incident, I caught the train from Manchester to London to watch United play against Wimbledon in the final game of the 1992/93 championship-winning season. The crowd at Selhurst Park was 30,000 and 23,000 of them must have been United fans. Peter Boyle took all his clothes off and ran across the pitch at half-time. I wouldn't have done that if I was him, because it wasn't even cold that day! I travelled with Danny and Patrick and for some reason we caught a train that went via Coventry, where a load of Leeds United supporters boarded. I think they were a supporters' club of southern based Leeds fans and they weren't too happy that they had just lost their league title to Manchester United. One of them saw me and started the abuse, making sick references to the Munich air disaster.

Danny and Patrick were big lads, so I was never going to make the first punch, but the lad who was having a go soon shut up when he realized that we were not going to sit there and get abused. That's the thing; people think that because they see you on television they have a right to abuse you without any comeback. The more famous someone is, the worse it is. I was at Newcastle in the press box, when, twenty minutes before kick-off, this Geordie walked past and started saying the most disgusting things about David Beckham and his wife. I watched him closely and saw him go and sit down next to a girl. I went over to him.

'Is this your wife?' I asked. He said yes.

'I would not like to repeat what I have just heard your husband saying about David Beckham and his wife.'

The fan's wife went potty and had a real go at him. She was screaming, 'What did you say? What did you say?'

I carried on talking to the lad.

'You think you can come to football and say what you like. Yet if someone said the same thing about you and your wife you would hate it.' I walked away with his wife still going mad at him.

Some grounds are worse than others, and you'd be surprised at the abuse you can get at smaller places.

At Coventry in 1993, Denis Irwin scored the only goal of the game as United pushed for their first championship title for twenty-six years. It was a huge result, there must have been 10,000 United fans in the crowd of 24,248 and I was delighted that United won. My feeling of elation was not shared by some of the Coventry fans around me in the main stand. Two or three of them looked at me in the press box and started hurling abuse, calling me a 'red bastard'. Without saying anything, I left the press box and went to confront them. I said, 'If you want to hit me, go on and hit me. I've come down to save you the trouble of coming to me.' Their attitude changed quickly and they kept their hands by their sides. The stewards then intervened. There were three of them and I started having a go at the stewards because I was sorting it out with these lads personally and there was no need for them to butt in. The security soon came in and stood in between us. It's that Glasgow thing. Somebody will beat me up one day, but I won't stop challenging people if I think they are out of order.

However, as I've said earlier, I've been to Anfield many times and had no problems whatsoever. I love going to Liverpool for football matches. Liverpudlians are football aficionados and I've got a great deal of respect for genuine Liverpool fans. Each year before United play at Anfield, I have a chat with a group of older fans close to the Hillsborough memorial. I like them and we have the banter and talk about games from years past. I was talking to them a couple of years ago when one Liverpool fan recognized me and steamed into me, calling me a 'Manc bastard'. I wasn't angry, just embarrassed. The Liverpool fans must have felt the same because they gave him the biggest verbal going over he'd had in his life and he scuttled off towards the Kop.

I've had some notable run-ins with other members of the media, notably the BBC commentator Alan Green. I actually get on very well with him and consider him a great commentator, but we've had our moments. I had a row with him after he called Roy Keane 'a thug' in 1995, after Roy had been sent off for making a bad challenge on a Crystal Palace player. Roy was in the wrong, but we all lose our tempers at times and I felt Green went too far calling Keane a thug and told him so.

Matters turned more serious between Green and me in 1997. He wrote an article in the *Daily Post*, a Liverpool-based newspaper, ahead of a game between United and Liverpool. In it, he described me as a 'would be commentator'. Ian St John pointed it out to me. I've got no problem with criticism and people a lot bigger than Alan Green have had a go at me, but I was interested to see what he meant by the phrase 'would be commentator'. I felt that it was implying that I was some kind of amateur who didn't know what I was talking about, when I have played football to a very high standard.

A few days later I saw Green at Old Trafford before a game against Blackburn. I went to approach him, but he scarpered, telling stewards that he was about to be assaulted. I was still fuming and determined to catch up with him when United played in Turin a few weeks later. I was in Italy working for Piccadilly Radio and when I arrived at the Delle Alpi with the press lads one of the first people I saw was Glenn Hoddle, who was there co-commentating for ITV.

'Have you seen that so-and-so Alan Green?' I asked him.

'Get behind me, there's a big queue,' he joked.

I couldn't find Green anywhere, but five minutes before the game started I saw Green try and sneak into the press box. I went over and started having a go at him as he passed nearby. I wasn't very professional because we were on air and the radio programme cut to an impromptu break.

'Paddy, you don't intimidate me,' Green said.

'Nobody likes you,' I said.

Then a message came through that we were about to go back live on air.

On another occasion, I had a go at the *Daily Mirror* journalist Oliver Holt because he wrote that Rio Ferdinand should be punished more severely than he was for missing a drugs test. I disagreed with that. Rio had been stupid, but he's not into drugs. The next time I saw Oliver was in a crowded press room at White Hart Lane. I shouted across the room to him, 'Loved your article in the paper the other day.' It had showed a photograph of him with Don King, the American boxing promoter.

'You slaughtered Rio Ferdinand for missing his drugs test and took the moral high ground and yet you were happy to be pictured with Don King, who was convicted of manslaughter after killing two men.'

The place went deadly quiet and Oliver didn't say a word. He's a very good journalist whom I read all the time, but newspaper writers like Oliver only offer an opinion. Their opinion is no better or worse than anyone else's. They might be able to write properly, but some columnists think they know everything just because they write in a newspaper.

Henry Winter of the *Daily Telegraph* is another one. I have a lot of respect for him, he's a superb writer, but he also absolutely slaughtered Rio Ferdinand for his poor memory. So when Henry turned up at an airport, only to discover that he had forgotten his travel tickets I was happy to remind him that we can all be forgetful sometimes. He didn't write about that incident in his newspaper.

I seem to attract controversy away from football, too. In 2001, I was involved in an argument with another car driver near my home in Sale. I had gone to pick my granddaughter up from school, when this car started beeping and flashing its lights behind me. The driver followed me all the way back to my house. I pulled into the driveway, with my granddaughter still in the back of the car. I could see that the other driver was ranting and raging. He accused me of cutting him up and jumped on me, attacking me and punching me on the lower jaw. I grabbed a golf club out of the car to try and protect myself and he got hold of it. I got my hands on it and we were both wrestling. I acted in self defence on my own property with my four-year-old granddaughter present. The police were called and I was arrested outside my home. I was taken to the police station for seven or eight hours – it was a harrowing experience and I was in a very agitated state.

I was charged with wounding with intent to cause grievous bodily harm – an offence which has a maximum sentence of three years imprisonment. After attending Trafford magistrates, I was bailed to appear at Crown Court. The other driver said that I attacked him with a golf club and had several stitches on the right hand side of his forehead, and bruising to his left eye and cheek. I maintained that I acted in self-defence.

I was worried when I went to court. I confirmed my name, address and date of birth and said that I understood the charge during a three-minute hearing in front of a packed court of sixth-form students on work experience.

The trial was set for Manchester Crown Court in May 2002. I was nervous, but I knew I had done nothing wrong. Bryan Robson came to court and gave me a good character reference, saying that I 'had always offered a deaf ear and turned away from trouble', while Mike Summerbee, who was also part of my defence, said, 'Patrick was like the peace-maker. He came in to calm any trouble down, he calmed the situation down.' The jury found me not guilty of wounding with intent to cause grievous bodily harm and not guilty of unlawful wounding. The verdict was unanimous.

In his closing speech, defence counsel Anthony Rumbelow QC, said the other guy 'was not telling the truth. Mr Crerand believed he was being followed, when his car turned, the other car turned, not once, but twice.' He told the jury, 'You are dealing with a mature man who was taking care of his grand-daughter,' and in reference to my performance in the witness box Mr Rumbelow said, 'Mr Crerand will never have had a more important ninety minutes on the pitch in his life.' I was a relieved man when I walked from court free and we held a party that night as thanks to all the people who had helped me.

My United television work has introduced me to a genera-tion of new fans. Steve Bower is someone I enjoy working with at MUTV. He's a passionate, talented lad who will go far. I don't think Manchester United television realize how good he is, because he should be working for the BBC or Sky. Steve is a proper football fan, he and his dad have been season ticket holders at Tranmere Rovers for years, but he's covered United for so long that he's got a great affection for them. Steve's great advantage is that the manager and the players like and trust him. Steve did the famous Roy Keane interview in 2005, in which Roy was allegedly very critical of certain team-mates. The interview was never broadcast and led to Roy leaving the club a few weeks later. I've asked Steve a million times what Roy said and he still won't tell me. He's never told anyone, in fact.

We have a good partnership on screen, but I think he sees me as being slightly mad, because I can't get my head round what an email is. He also thinks that I've got no concept of time. He'll ask me for directions to a ground and I'll say something like, 'Just get on the motorway.' He'll then point out that because I've always been driven everywhere in a coach I've got no sense of direction.

I'm lost with technology. I had a mobile phone once but I couldn't work it out. People complained that my phone was never on and I had no idea what they were on about – I thought your phone was only on when people rang you. I wanted to throw it in the River Mersey near my house, but it went in the bin instead. I really can't understand the point of a mobile phone. I couldn't use one to contact my friends anyway, theirs are always switched off, too.

Steve had a surprise when he started working with me for Piccadilly Radio in 1996. Our first game together was the Charity Shield match between United and Newcastle. Before the game, a Newcastle fan caught my arm with a cup of tea which went all over me, so I hit him. Apparently Wilf McGuinness, who was also doing media work, walked into the press box and shouted, 'Paddy Crerand's only gone and knocked a Geordie out.' Steve thought, 'What am I doing commentating with this lunatic?'

We worked together at Piccadilly until 1998, before Steve left to join MUTV. I followed him a year later and since the 2000/2001 season we've commentated together. From 1999, we've done *The Crerand and Bower Show* which goes out every Monday. It's the most popular show on the channel so we must be doing something right. The viewers ring in and we talk about anything to do with United. Some of them comment on my jumpers and have a bit of fun. They don't think that they are the most fashionable apparently, but there's nothing wrong with them and they keep me warm. My favourite one is a green one which Brian Kidd and his family bought me for my 60th birthday. I don't let Noreen buy me jumpers because her taste is awful.

Steve and I went back to the Gorbals in 2006 because United played Celtic in a pre-season game. I'd been to Glasgow many times, but this was my first return to the Gorbals for over twenty years. The place had changed beyond recognition and I didn't have a clue where anything was. Streets didn't exist and there were not many people around. I was walking along with Steve Bower when we heard a big bang. He thought it was a gunshot and nearly passed out, but I think it was just a car backfiring. It was funny to see his face.

We've had a few bloopers on MUTV. Unbeknown to me, in 2004 MUTV sold footage of a United v Celtic game that Steve and I were commentating on to the Hollywood film company which made the science-fiction movie *The Day After Tomorrow*, where a giant wave sweeps over Manhattan. One of our readers saw the footage and rang in the show to say that we were in *The Day After Tomorrow*. It was being hyped at the time, but neither Steve nor I paid much attention to that kind of thing.

'What is *The Day after Tomorrow*?' Steve asked the viewer.

'Friday,' I replied.

I travel to European games with the players and I get on with them, but I'm older than most of their parents so I have more in common with their mums and dads. A surprise 60th birthday party was held for me in 1999 and David Beckham's dad Ted was there. He is a United fan and the players he idolized were the lads I played with. Ted said that the last thing David had said to him was, 'Don't go annoying all the old players.'

I get on very well with Alex Ferguson too, but it hasn't always been so during his time at Old Trafford. In 1990, when the manager was under serious pressure and there was talk about him being sacked, the *Daily Mirror* ran a piece in which it used comments I had made out of context, so that the article read as if I was having a go at him. Alex and I have never spoken about this, but I don't think he appreciated what I was supposed to have said and it took a few years before we got to know each other better.

Alex reminds me of Matt, and not just because he is so driven. It's often the attention which he pays to detail – he is very strict on appearance, for instance. He thinks that players should be clean shaven and wearing a suit because they are representing Manchester United. I like that because Matt was the same. I'm not in Alex's company all the time, but when we chat he often relates back to his time in Glasgow and we talk about the various characters. I would never speak to Alex about team selections, about whom he should or shouldn't sign. He's done a magnificent job and greatly enriched my life, so why should he listen to my opinions? I go on television all the time and offer my opinions. Not once has Alex collared me for what I've said.

Football people, and by that I mean people who have played the game, often share similar opinions. Fans can be a million miles apart. They make snap judgements and write players off easily. They'll describe a player as rubbish – how can he be rubbish if he's in the first team of Manchester United? It's easy for me to have an opinion. I can react with the benefit of hindsight and I don't have to go out and play in front of 76,000. What sometimes happens is that journalists take my comments out of context and make out like I am slagging off Alex's decisions when I'm not. But Alex is not a fool, and he knows how journalists work, although I once thought that I was due for the hairdryer treatment from him.

I was standing at Manchester Airport before one European game with a bad headache. The press and the team were there and I could see Alex out of the corner of my eye. He was fuming and he was coming towards me. I wondered what I had done wrong as he steamed up. But he walked straight past and ripped into two young journalists stood behind me. Their newspaper had written a story that David O'Leary was being lined up to be the boss of Manchester United, and the manager was not happy.

'My name is on that story, but I didn't write it, the editor wrote it,' replied one of the journalists. That didn't matter to the manager.

I try and stay out of the Alex's way on European trips. He has a job to do and so do I, but our paths inevitably cross as I travel on the same plane as the players. In the summer of 2002 Alex and I were among the invited guests to see Sean Fallon, my old coach at Celtic, receive the Freedom of Sligo. Sean was a great help to Alex when he started in management. Everybody had a drink after the ceremony and people started singing 'You'll Never Walk Alone' because it is a favourite with Celtic as well as Liverpool fans. I hate that song, I absolutely hate it because I associate it with Liverpool, but I looked across to see that one other person wasn't singing. Alex was stood leaning against a wall looking mildly appalled.

We had a round of golf the day after the ceremony, but Alex was continually distracted because Rio Ferdinand was just about to sign for United. Alex confirmed that Rio had just signed for a British record fee of £30m just as a young local reporter from a radio station was coming to interview some of us after golf. Alex told him that United had just signed Rio Ferdinand. The kid didn't know what to do.

'You have just got a huge scoop there lad,' I said to him. 'You could make a fortune from that if you do your job properly.' He was lost for words.

I went back to the airport with Alex after the golf. It was like a small house and we were just about the only people there. The conversation slipped back to Glasgow in the 1950s and 60s. We talked about games and players. Alex's memory was staggering. I would recall a game which I was convinced Celtic had won 2–0. Alex could tell me that the result was actually 2–1 and name all three goalscorers.

I never trust Alex when he gives me team news, even though as MUTV's representative I'm supposed to get preferential treatment. I can have a quick chat with him about what team he is going to play and then talk with assurance on television about United's line-up, only for Alex to pick different players. He's very cute, the manager, and I can see where he is coming from. He doesn't want anyone to know his team, even though I would never pass on any information that he told me in confidence.

My main role is as a pundit, working alongside a commentator. I accept that as a United fan I may occasionally see things through red tinted spectacles, but I would like to think that I am redressing the balance. I am very complimentary about United but the club have won nine Premiership titles since 1993, several FA Cups and the European Cup so there has been plenty to be complimentary about.

I love watching *Match of the Day* for the quality of the punditry, which I think is superior to anything on Sky. Not only could people like Alan Hansen play the game to a very high standard, but they can articulate their thoughts especially well. I know that Eamon Dunphy, the great Irish writer and broadcaster who used to play at United, has been critical of people like Alan Hansen and Alan Shearer for sitting on the fence and not being controversial, but Eamon is the type of fella who would say that black is white and white is black just to get a reaction. I know he appears on a hugely popular show on RTE in Ireland with two other great football brains Johnny Giles and Liam Brady, but I think part of their attraction is that they court controversy. *Match of the Day* works because it offers analysis rather than generating controversy.

I cover the first team games which are broadcast on a delayed transmission and I also do a lot of the reserve and youth team games. I've been fortunate to see many young players well before they have broken into the first team, but Wayne Rooney is one who sticks out. He was only 15 when I first watched him play for Everton Reserves against United Reserves at Goodison. Before the game, I spoke to a few Everton people and they were raving about him, saying how he was the best young player they had seen. One of them took me to meet Wayne. He looked up at me and said, 'Have you got a programme?' I didn't have a match programme, but he just wanted to see his name in print.

The game was two minutes old when he tried to chip the United goalkeeper from the half way line. United's Reserves had four or five players who had won the European Cup, but Wayne was completely unfazed by reputations.

The only other young player who has impressed me as much was Cristiano Ronaldo. In the summer of 2003, I travelled with the team on the long pre-season tour of America. It was a success and huge crowds came to watch United in Seattle, Los Angeles, New Jersey, and Philadelphia, despite the star attraction David Beckham having just left the club for Madrid. A friendly game against Sporting Lisbon, staged to open their new 50,000 seat stadium, was tagged onto the end of the trip and there wasn't much enthusiasm about going to Lisbon after such a long tour. I settled into the commentary box and watched this young lad shred the United defence. He was quick, strong and very, very skilful. That was the first time I saw Cristiano Ronaldo.

The 2006/07 season has been a remarkable one for United in many ways, as they have confounded the expectations of many who predicted that Chelsea would continue to dominate the domestic competitions. When Wayne Rooney and Paul Scholes were given ridiculous three-match bans for being sent off in a pre-season game in Amsterdam, I told Alex after the game that, knowing what the Football Association is like, they would probably ban Scholes and Rooney in the Premiership. He didn't believe they would. A couple of weekends later I was watching one of the young United teams at Carrington with Alex when his mobile phone went. It was someone calling to tell him about Scholes and Rooney being banned and he was furious.

In August 2006, when the bans came into place, United appeared to have even less chance of winning the league. That month in Amsterdam, the manager came to talk to a few of us in the team hotel about the season ahead. He was very confident that United could take the Premiership trophy, certainly far more than I was. United and Chelsea were like two heavyweights going at it for twelve rounds. By the time both teams reached the semi-finals of the European Cup they had nothing more to give. United's magnificent performance at home to Roma in the previous round had given the fans confidence, but some of the performances in Europe in 2006/07 were poor.

It was great for United to draw Celtic for the first time in the competition and I enjoyed going back to Glasgow again, but I got a right going over when I came out of Celtic Park. A Celtic fan overheard me say, 'I can't believe that United have just lost to a Celtic team as bad as that.' The Celtic fan said that it was a disgrace that a former Celtic player should say such a thing, but I didn't mean to be disrespectful to Celtic. I just couldn't understand how United had lost. When Louis

Saha stood up to take a penalty, my son Danny clasped his crucifix and prayed that he scored. Then he realized that 58,000 Celtic fans were likely to be doing the same, hoping Saha would miss. He didn't score. I supported United in those games, but I'd support Celtic against anyone else.

I'd never compared any United player to George Best until Cristiano Ronaldo, although when Ryan Giggs burst on the scene he was often tagged the 'new George Best'. Ryan was a remarkable talent, but it is Cristiano's impudence and sheer daring which reminds me so much of George. I don't think Ryan will receive the recognition he deserves in this country until he has retired. There seems to be little appreciation of what it takes to play at such a high level for so long. I get to see United play all over the world, and the one player people in other countries consistently praise is Ryan. Giggs had a superb season in 2006/07, as did Paul Scholes. If he didn't try and tackle he would be the perfect midfielder. Watch Paul closely and you'll see that he bounces around. He never stands still on his feet, he always moves and he knows where he'll play the ball before he receives it.

Gary Neville is a great United captain. I watched Gary a lot as a kid and I didn't think he had what it took to be a Manchester United player. His crosses weren't strong enough and he didn't have that 'wow' factor which marked out the likes of David Beckham. I was convinced that his brother Phil was going to make it, not Gary, but Gary has proved me wrong. His commitment is exceptional and is only matched by that of John Terry at Chelsea. Rio Ferdinand is another player from the current team who I'd pick out. In my day centre-halves headed the ball out – or kneed it in the case of Jock Stein – but Rio has the technical ability to play in a more advanced position. The football played at United in 2006/07 was like it was in the mid-1960s – attack minded and brilliant.

271

We had players of individual brilliance like George, Denis, and Bobby, just as the current team have Wayne, Ryan, Paul, and Cristiano.

United have gained a magnificent reputation around the world because of their style of play. I never fail to be amazed at how popular United are in countries you might not expect. After the World Club championship game in Brazil in 2000, I was on the team's private plane back to Manchester. We stopped in Senegal in West Africa to refuel in the middle of the night. We were supposed to stay on the plane, but I wanted to say that I had been to Senegal. I got off the plane and walked onto the tarmac. Four airport workers came over to me.

'Is Dwight Yorke on the plane?' one asked in perfect English.

'Roy Keane?' said another.

I went to tell the lads back on the plane, but when I got back on board the head air steward said to me: 'Paddy, you were my favourite player, my hero.' That was nice. A bottle of very expensive red wine was brought to me.

The one thing that has changed from my day is diving. A player had to be hit by an axe before he went down back then. We used to say that George had double-jointed ankles and couldn't understand why he never got injured. Opposition players would try and take him out because they knew he was such a threat. He rode some very strong tackles, usually by turning 180 degrees instantly. Today, a player goes down too readily and it's even worse on the Continent.

One of the hardest things for me was covering George's death on television. I'd played a bigger part in George's life than most and I asked myself a few questions. Could I have helped in a different way? Should I have done more? There was an element of guilt, but when I considered things rationally I realized that the only person who didn't help George was George himself. I spoke to the Irish politicians Martin McGuinness and David Irvine at the funeral at Stormont, Belfast. They agreed that George had brought people together in the north of Ireland.

There's always a story with Manchester United and my home phone rings all the time, whether it's radio or television stations calling up for a comment about United or family members in Ireland calling for team news. It's always football.

Lots of the family come to Manchester to watch United, but the cost of watching football means that their trips are becoming more limited. I'm privileged to watch United as part of my job, but the ticket prices are too expensive to watch top class football and it's the working-class people who are starting to struggle. That saddens me greatly.

Today, I'll have a break from the phone calls for a little while because I'm off to the hospital. I had a minor operation recently and when they checked me over the doctor said my heart was beating too fast. They gave me a blood thinning drug called Warfarin. It's actually rat poison – that's why the rats have been doing a runner when they see me recently. If the Warfarin doesn't work then they might have to put a clamp on my heart to get it beating right. It's nothing serious. Gordon McQueen had it done to him but it didn't work, that's why he's so mad.

To get to Trafford General I drive past Carrington, where United and City train. United wanted to build accommodation for the young players at Carrington. Do you know why they couldn't? Because the land has to be used to grow food in the event of a third world war. Can you believe that? We used to train in Salford at The Cliff. We were the biggest team in the country but the facilities weren't great – amounting to one outside pitch, a small gym and an indoor pitch. Our manager Matt Busby was a believer that fans should be able to watch their heroes train. There used to be thousands of kids in the summer holidays and it's a shame it's not like that now. Clubs could create a good bond between them and the fans. United have an open day once a year which is a good idea, but it's not really the same.

Trafford General was the first NHS hospital in the country. The media give the National Health Service a bad name, but I think it's wonderful. The nurses say 'hello' to me when I walk into the hospital and take me straight into a room, where they take a pin prick of blood from my finger for analysis. I came last week and an old fella started talking to me about football. That happens a lot and I like meeting people, but I was in a rush and he wouldn't let me go. He grasped my arm and kept going on and on. He wanted to go through my career game by game. I played over 600 games so it was going to take a while. What can you do?

Manchester's a village. Everyone knows everybody. I'd hate not to be able to walk through Manchester with my head held high and not to be able to look people in the eye. When you're a footballer you meet all kinds of folk and you've no idea what they do in life. Most are into football and they want to know footballers. I was once sent a hand crafted plaque from the Maze prison in Belfast.

People are attracted to footballers and you have to be wise enough to know who is a hanger on and who isn't. And when you are on television, like I am a lot now, people think that they know you even if they don't. They come up to you in the street and talk to you about football. I don't mind that because I think it's important for players to have a good relationship with fans. The only thing that changes as you get older is that they call me Mister Crerand rather than just Paddy.

City fans come up to me, too, and have a laugh. Always have. I remember being at some traffic lights twenty years ago when a Rolls Royce pulled up alongside. The driver beckoned for me to wind the window down, so I did. He shouted: 'Eff off, you red bastard!' and then drove off. It was the comedian Bernard Manning. I knew Bernard and I just sat there laughing. I'm friends with lots of City fans, people like Tudor Thomas. He's a Welshman who been going to City long before I moved to Manchester. He came to my 60th birthday and he took a little bit of a turn and fell down. He panicked a little bit and a few of us went to pick him up. He looked up and said, 'Get me out of this place. I don't want to die in front of all you red bastards!'

When I'm going to the city centre I park in Vinny's used car yard in Ancoats on the northern edge of Manchester. He's an old face and we've been friends for years. I pop in for a cup of tea and we talk football, often for hours. I never intend for it to be that long, but Vinny loves his football like me. Brian Kidd and Alex Stepney are often in there too, always talking football – and maybe a bit of politics or boxing – with the characters that come along to the yard.

Vinny's a man's man, a well known Mancunian character. He's a big City fan but, like many of his generation, he wants United to do well and travels to European games with United. Vinny used to try and get me to join City and flatter me with comments such as, 'If we had a passer like you in the middle of the park we'd win everything.' City did well enough without me in the 1960s and I'd never have gone there anyway. Vinny says that I'm a professional moaner but we have great banter and the odd time that City beat United he's on the phone to me straightaway. It's almost as if he still thinks that I play in United's midfield and I'm able to do something about it if we lose.

I like to walk into town from the yard and, despite Ancoats being one of the poorest areas of Manchester, I know that my car's safe with Vinny. Nobody messes with him and his mates. People say they were supposed to be in the Quality Street gang, Manchester's mafia if you like, in the 1960s, but they were just the boys around town.

Vinny and I walk from his yard to the Midland Hotel, where we both go to the gym together three times a week. I've been going to the gym with him for twenty years. We used to train in a little boxing gym in Ancoats. The junior boxers used to say, 'Here's the over the hill gang.' Ancoats has changed over the last decade and the cotton mills which were built in the industrial revolution are being turned into fancy new flats. The little gym has been upgraded, and the Ancoats kids can't go there any more because they have been priced out. It would be easy to slag the council off, but Manchester's got a good Labour council and they do a decent job with various schemes to keep the kids off the streets.

We pass by the art deco *Daily Express* building and then walk down Tib Street into Piccadilly and see all kinds of characters. I get a great deal of pleasure from that walk through town. Manchester is a melting pot and you see every different nationality and hear different languages. What I love about Manchester is that it's a tolerant immigrant city with little bigotry. I'm an immigrant and so is Vinny. His family on his father's side were Italian and Irish on his mother's side. Lots of Italians moved to Ancoats, along with the Irish. There's a church, St Michael's, near his yard that the Catholic diocese is going to close down. The people are up in arms so Brian Kidd and I have been on marches to keep it open. I like that sense of community.

I know all the barrow boys who sell fruit and veg on the streets in Manchester. Sometimes they give me so much fruit and potatoes that I can hardly carry it. One of them is a City fan and he always tries to wind me up. On our walk we pass

Rafa's hairdressers, where we often see Rio Ferdinand and Wes Brown. We have a rabbit with people along the street as we go through Piccadilly. We usually see the former United captain Martin Buchan or Gordon Taylor from the PFA getting their sandwiches at lunch time. It winds you down, that walk. We go through Chinatown where Vinny knows everyone. All the Chinese are football fans and they love talking about it. We pop into one or two of the restaurants for a chat and they won't let us leave the place. I try to look after myself, but I can't resist the food, so we try and go through Chinatown after the gym.

I was born in Scotland and consider myself Irish, but Manchester is home. It's the city where Noreen and I have lived since 1963 and raised a family, the city where our eight beautiful grandchildren are growing up. I've been blessed with a great life, playing for two of the biggest football clubs in the world. I'm still involved in football as I near my eighth decade. And I'm proud to say that I've stayed true to the principles that were drilled into me in the grinding poverty of the Gorbals. I've always tried to give my best, and never did turn the other cheek.

The Crerand Career

Born: Glasgow, 19 February 1939
Married: Noreen Ferry, 24 June 1963
Children: Patrick, Lorraine and Danny
Education: St Luke's Ballater Street Primary School,
    Holyrood Secondary

Clubs
Duntocher Hibernian
July 1957–August 1958

Celtic
August 1958–February 1963
Celtic debut: v Queen of the South, 4 October 1958
Celtic career: 120 games, 5 goals

Transferred to Manchester United for £43,000 on
    6 February 1963

Manchester United
February 1963–July 1972
Manchester United debut: v Bolton Wanderers (friendly in Cork) 13 February 1963
Manchester United league debut: v Blackpool (h) 23 February 1963

Appearances for Manchester United

Season	League App's	Goals	FA Cup App's	Goals	Europe App's	Goals
1962–63	19	0	3	0	0	0
1963–64	41	1	7	1	6	0
1964–65	39	3	7	2	11	0
1965–66	41	0	7	0	7	1
1966–67	39	3	2	0	0	0
1967–68	41	1	2	0	9	0
1968–69	35	1	4	1	8	0
1969–70	25	1	8	0	0	0
1970–71	24	0	2	0	0	0
Total	304	10	42	4	41	1

Four more appearances in the Football League Cup and five in other games

Total Manchester United appearances: 396, 15 goals
Became Youth Team coach: 26 August 1971
Retired as player: July 1972
Appointed Assistant Manager: 2 January 1973
Left position as Assistant Manager by mutual agreement: May 1976
Northampton Town manager: August 1976–January 1977

Honours
European Cup winner: 1968
Football League Championship winner: 1964–65, 1966–67
FA Cup winner: 1963
Scottish Challenge Cup runners-up medal: 1960–61

Scottish international appearances
1960–61: v Republic of Ireland (twice), Czechoslovakia
1961–62: v Northern Ireland, Wales, England,
   Czechoslovakia (twice), Uruguay
1962–63: v Wales, Northern Ireland
1963–64: v Northern Ireland
1964–65: v England, Poland, Finland
1965–66: v Poland

Index

Adams, Gerry 15
Adamson, Jimmy 191
Adolfo 166
Albert, Florian 102
Allen, Tony 130–131
Allison, Malcolm
  Brown Bull pub 128
  Krays incident 72
  Manchester City assistant
    manager 121, 160
  TV analyst 201–203, 233
Amancio 152, 154
Anderson, Willie 104
Angus, John 91
Anquilletti, Mario 187–188
Armfield, Jimmy 204
Armstrong, Louis 168
Aston, John (junior) 98, 107,
    111, 166
Aston, John (senior) 98, 215
Atkinson, Ron 229
Augusto, José 116, 118–119
Auld, Bertie 47–48, 237

Baker, Joe 126–127
Ball, Alan 209
Banks, Gordon 69
Barnwell, John 127
Bassey, Shirley 71
Baxter, Jim
  footballing skills 38–39
  friendship with Crerand
    37–38
  Law's views on 64
  Old Firm derbies 45–46
  playing for Scotland 35, 36

prison visiting 44–45
Puskas incident 149
Scotland v England 1962
    39–40
Beckenbauer, Franz 127
Becker, Boris 240
Beckham, David 78, 107, 258,
    265, 269, 271
Beckham, Ted 265
Bell, Colin 159–160
Bergholtz, Gerard 185
Bernabéu, Santiago 151
Best, George
  1966–1967 season 126, 129
  absconding from duties
    209–210, 213–214
  Bramhall house 210
  Brown Bull pub 128
  chicken bones incident
    156–157
  comparison with Ronaldo
    271
  Crerand fighting incident
    197–199
  Crerand's testimonial 222
  Crerand's views on 81–83
  death of 272–273
  death threats 200
  dress sense 91
  dropped by Busby 111
  European Cup 1966
    118–119
  European Cup 1968 149,
    155–156, 165–166
  European Cup 1969 184,
    187

FA Cup 1963 72
Footballer of the Year 1968
    157
footballing skills 91
friendship with Sadler 79
gambling 199–200
goal scoring 90, 98, 113,
    129, 204, 209, 226
Inter Cities Fairs' Cup
    1964–1965 99
Irish supporters 150, 184
knee injury 119
living with Crerands
    210–212
Mallorca holidays 174
Manchester derbies 159
match-day routine 106
memorial service 82
physical agility 272
Polish fans 144
public profile 12, 82–83, 85,
    139
public speaking 249
Riley portrait 157–158
sacked by Manchester United
    215
Summerbee's best man 160
support from fans 109
views on Irish politics 86
wing position 107
womanizing 88, 156–157,
    160, 194–197, 199–200
World Club championship
    1968 178, 181
youth football 61–62, 104
Bilardo, Carlos 180

Black, Cilla 82
Blanchflower, Danny 113
Boardman, Stan 82
Bower, Steve 263–265
Boycott, Geoff 174
Boyle, Hughie (uncle) 169, 200–201
Boyle, Peter 255–258
Boyle, Sarah 256
  see also Crerand, Sarah
Brady, Liam 269
Brand, Ralph 46
Brazil, Alan 18
Bremner, Billy 100
Brennan, Shay
  ageing player 192
  FA Cup 1963 68
  friendship with Bobby Charlton 87
  gambling 77–78
  Irish supporters 150
  replaced by Burns 139
  smoking 77
Briggs, Ronnie 92
Brown Bull pub 128–129
Brown, Laurie 220, 231–232
Brown, Mary 231–232
Brown, Wes 277
Bruce, Steve 64
Buchan, Martin 83, 213, 219, 221, 277
Burns, Francis 139, 162, 205
Busby, Lady Jean 65, 120, 198, 218
Busby, Sir Matt
  admired by Connolly 75
  admired by Crerand 36
  allegations of Crerand drinking 220
  approaching Stein to be Manchester United manager 206–208
  arguments with Setters 85
  bag of cash incident 189
  Best misbehaving 196, 210, 212
  Brown Bull pub 128–129
  Catholic faith 150, 162
  Checkpoint Charlie incident 114–115
  complemented by Murphy 136
  Crerand appointed Manchester United assistant manager 216
  Crerand fighting incident 198–199
  Crerand leaving Manchester United 225

Crerand's testimonial 222–223
Crerand's views on 66–67
disciplinarian 66–67, 130, 175–176
Docherty appointed Manchester United manager 215
Docherty's affair with Mary Brown 231–232
Docherty's proposal to buy Osgood 218–219
dropping Crerand 123–124
European Cup 1966 113–115, 118, 120
European Cup 1968 139–141, 144–145, 152, 161–167
European Cup 1969 186
European Cup parade 171–172
European Cup Winners' Cup 1963–1964 95–96
FA Cup 1963 69–70
giving players freedom 192
good loser 66, 160–161
House of Commons dinner 96
interest from Real Madrid 73
Irish supporters 236
knighted 173
League championship 1965 101
League championship 1967 129–130
League Cup 1967 126
McGuinness sacked by Manchester United 204
missing penalties 46
Munich air disaster 137, 140, 153, 170, 251
players' lounge 83
players' wages 72, 74, 93, 125
poor morale among Manchester United players 58–59
post-match analysis 109
post-match banquets 121–122
post-season tours 138
praised in media 112
reaction to winning European Cup 166–168
Real Madrid v Manchester United 1968 151–156
rebuilding Manchester United after air disaster 54–57
respect for Shankly 105

retiring as Manchester United manager 182, 185, 189–191
Riley portrait 157
rivalry between Crerand and Bobby Charlton 88
role as general manager 206, 214
seeking players' opinions 64
selling Giles 89–90
signing Connelly 98, 104
signing Crerand 51–52, 54–55
signing Law 65
signing Quixall 89
signing Sadler 78
signings in 1964–1965 98
signings in 1968–1969 175
similarities with Ferguson 266
strategic planning 30
support for players 190
team talks 107, 152–154, 166, 179–180
testimonial dinner 60–61
The Beatles 82–83
thoughts of retirement 120, 173
training sessions 273–274
twentieth anniversary at Manchester United 114
views on Docherty 219
views on football hooliganism 110–111
views on gambling 77
views on Law 83–84
views on O'Farrell 209
views on playing formation 107, 217
views on smoking 77
views on ticket touts 231
Wagstaff incident 67
World Club championship 1968 178–180
Busby, Sandy 156
Butlin, Billy 178

Caldow, Eric 46
Callaghan, Ian 122
Cantona, Eric xii, 64, 253–256
Cantwell, Maggie 88
Cantwell, Noel
  appointed Coventry City manager 126
  bag of cash incident 188–189
  covered by Dunne 78
  Crerand's househunting 76
  Crerand's views on 88–89

Index

European Cup Winners' Cup
  1963–1964 93
FA Cup 1963 68
Irish supporters 150
leadership skills 94
leaving Manchester United
  126
Peterborough United
  manager 229
poor morale among
  Manchester United players
  58
post-match banquets 121
support for Crerand 59
Carey, Johnny 150, 191
Carroll, Bobby 34, 42–43
Carson, Frank 71, 204, 233
Cavanagh, Tommy 217
Celtic FC
  1958–1959 season 26–30
  1959–1960 season 30–34
  1960–1961 season 52–53
  1961–1962 season 48–49
  1962–1963 season 49–51, 53
  Crerand as supporter 11–13,
    19–20, 24
  Crerand's transfer to
    Manchester United 51–52
  European Cup 1967
    132–133
  European Cup 1969 186
  European Cup 2007
    270–271
  fans 33–34
  'Kelly Kids' 30–31
  losing Stein 31–32
  management problems
    29–31, 46–48, 53
  McNeill appointed manager
    237–238
  Old Firm derbies 34, 45–46,
    49–50
  professional contract for
    Crerand 25–26
  rumours of match fixing 29
  scouting Crerand 21–22
  signing Crerand 23
  Stein appointed manager 54
  Stein leaving club 53
  training regime 25, 53–54
  UEFA Cup 1984 243
  World Club championship
    1967 177
Charles, John 113
Charlton, Sir Bobby
  1966–1967 season 126, 129
  ageing player 192
  ambassadorial role for
    Manchester United 87

concussion incident 195–196
Crerand's temper 62–63
Crerand's views on 87
European Cup 1966 116,
  118
European Cup 1968
  165–170, 172
European Cup 1969 187
European Cup Winners' Cup
  1963–1964 93
European Footballer of the
  Year 1966 127
FA Cup 1963 59, 69
footballing skills 67, 111
friendship with McGuinness
  191, 193
gambling 77–78
goal scoring 90, 98, 129
injury 183
Inter Cities Fairs' Cup
  1964–1965 99
leadership skills 94
League championship 1965
  102
marriage 85
missing penalties 46
Munich air disaster 88, 169
pre-match whisky 108
press-ups incident 192–193
reaction to criticism 109
retirement 215
smoking 77
teamwork with Crerand
  87–88
wages at Manchester United
  209
World Club championship
  1968 178, 180
World Cup 1966 123–124
Charlton, Jack 85, 100, 233
Charlton, Norma 62
Chisnall, Phil 90
Churchill, Sir Winston 18
Clannad 16, 251
Clark, John 53
Clough, Brian 188, 221, 233
Cole, Andy 251, 253
Coleman, David 167–168
Colerain, John 169
Coll, Vincent (Mad Dog)
  15–16
Collins, Bobby 28–29, 90, 101
Collins, Joan 199
Collins, Michael 15
Colrain, John 48
Coluna, Mario 172
Connelly, John
  European Cup 1965 103
  European Cup 1966 118

Inter Cities Fairs' Cup
  1964–1965 103
League championship 1965
  101
signed by Manchester United
  98, 104, 110
Connolly, Billy 17, 75
Cooper, Tommy 164
Coppell, Steve 221
Craig, Bobby 53
Craven, John 205
Crerand, Anabella
  (grandmother) 2, 4
Crerand, Bridie (sister) 2, 18,
  38
Crerand, Danny (son)
  Best as lodger 211
  birth of 186
  bottle-throwing incident 239
  football career 250
  Manchester United fan 229,
    271
  marriage 251
  Paddy abused by fans 258
  Paddy as pub landlord 241
Crerand, Faye (daughter-in-
  law) 251
Crerand, John (brother) 2–3,
  11, 16–18, 138
Crerand, John (uncle) 2
Crerand, Lorraine (daughter)
  Best as lodger 211
  birth of 122
  Mallorca holidays 239
  marriage 251
  views on Paddy as father
    250–251
Crerand, Mary (aunt) 4
Crerand, Mary (sister) 2
Crerand, Michael (father)
  death of 1–2
  Irish background 2–3
  republican views 4, 15
Crerand, Noreen (wife)
  see also Ferry, Noreen
  bell-boy incident 151
  Best as lodger 210–211
  birth of Danny 186
  birth of Lorraine 122
  birth of Patrick 97
  Bobby Charlton's practical
    jokes 87
  brother in Australia 138
  chicken bones incident
    156–157
  Chorlton house 76
  European Cup 1968 151,
    168–169
  FA Cup 1963 70

giving sheets to Best 160
Krays incident 71
lack of interest in football 83
medal necklace 239–240
Paddy as pub landlord 240, 248
Paddy fighting 197
Paddy's jumpers 265
Paddy's post-season tours 134, 138
pail of water incident 128
phone conversation with Shankly 106
plate-throwing incident 141
Crerand, Paddy
1958–1959 season 26–30
1959–1960 season 30–34
1960–1961 season 34–36
1960–1961 season 52–53
1961–1962 season 48–49
1962–1963 season 49–51, 56–73
1963–1964 season 77, 90–97
1964–1965 season 97–103
1965–1966 season 104–122
1966–1967 season 123–131
1967–1968 season 139–172
1968–1969 season 174–189
1969–1970 season 192–195
1970–1971 season 203–205
1971–1972 season 208–213
1972–1973 season 213–217
60th birthday party 265
abuse from fans 257–260
ageing player 192
appointed Manchester United assistant manager 216
appointed Northampton Town manager 225–226
approached by Crystal Palace 212
approaching Stein to be Manchester United manager 206–208
arrested in Glasgow 27
bad temper 63, 94
bag of cash incident 188–189
Best as lodger 210–212
Best going to Spain 214
Best's womanizing 194–197, 199–200
bible-smuggling incident 142–143
birth of 4
birth of Danny 186
birth of Lorraine 122
birth of Patrick 97
Brown Bull pub 128–129

Busby contemplating retirement 173–174
Busby's retirement 182, 185, 189–191
Cantona incident 253–256
car accident 216
career statistics 278–280
Catholic upbringing 7, 10, 19
Celtic supporter 11–13, 19–20, 24
Celtic's training regime 25, 53–54
Checkpoint Charlie incident 114–115
chicken bones incident 156–157
childhood in Gorbals 4–11, 18–19
Chorlton house 76
coaching Manchester United youth squad 208, 212–213
confrontations with fellow commentators 260–262
corporate hospitality work for Manchester United 248
criticized by media xii
dating Noreen 42–44
death of Best 272–273
death of brother 16–18
death of father 1–2
death of White 97
debut with Celtic 26
deciding not to play for Scotland 146, 148
deteriorating relationship with Docherty 218–223
dislike of Docherty 223, 228, 230
Docherty's affair with Mary Brown 231
Docherty's proposal to buy Osgood 218–219
doubts about managerial role 226–227
driving test 94
dropped by Busby 123–124
dropped by McGuinness 203
Duntocher Hibs 20–21, 24
end of playing career 212–213
England v Scotland 1965 60, 80
European Cup 1965 102–103
European Cup 1966 113–121
European Cup 1967 132–133

European Cup 1968 139–157, 161–170
European Cup 1969 183–188
European Cup 1999 167
European Cup parade 171–172
European Cup Winners' Cup 1963–1964 92–93, 95–96
excused National Service 37
FA Cup 1963 68–70
FA Cup 1964 94–95
FA Cup 1965 100
FA Cup 1966 121
FA Cup 1967 127
FA Cup 1969 183, 185
FA Cup 1970 193–195
Falkirk five-a-side incident xii–xiii, 28
family life 250–251
fan mail 139–140
fighting 8–9, 196–199, 239
final games for Manchester United 205
first professional contract 25–26
football commentator 254–255, 260–261
football style 113
friendship with Baxter 37–38
Glasgow pubs 27, 32
Glasgow rolls 61
goal scoring 129, 205
grandchildren 251
heart problems 273–274
holidays in Ireland 14
hooligans in pub incident 246–247
hotel burglar incident 134–136
House of Commons dinner 96
Inter Cities Fairs' Cup 1964–1965 98–99, 102–103
Irish background 2–3, 15–16
Jack Ferry in Australia 138
jumpers 264–265
'Kelly Kids' 30
Krays incident 71–72
Kvasnak incident 35–36
League championship 1965 102
League championship 1967 129–130
League Cup 1967 126
learning from senior players 28

Index

leaving Celtic 49–52
leaving Manchester United 223–225
leg injury 113–114
love of reading 9
'Maggie May' spoof 255–256
Mallorca holidays 174, 239
management problems at Celtic 29–31, 46–48, 53
Manchester derbies 67
Manchester digs 62
Manchester United captain 94
marriage to Noreen 74–76
match-day routine 106–109
meeting Duke of Edinburgh 99
meeting Irish republicans 236–237
meeting Mandela 146
meeting Noreen 41–42
missing penalties 46
Morgan's libel case with Docherty 232
MUTV work 252–253, 263–265, 268–269
O'Farrell sacked by Manchester United 214–215
Old Firm derbies 34, 45–46, 49–50
pail of water incident 128
plate-throwing incident 141
players' union role 93
political awareness xiii, 3, 15, 18
poor morale among Manchester United players 58–59
post-match banquets 121–122
post-season tours 132–138
praised in media 69–70, 111–112
pressures of manager's job 227–229
prison visiting 44–45
pub landlord 240–248
public relations work 234
RanCel 19
reaction to criticism 109
Real Madrid v Manchester United 1968 151–156
red wine 70, 140, 233
relationship with media 112–113
resigning from Northampton Town 230

road-rage court case 262–263
running speed 32–33
sacking of McGuinness 204
Sale house 223
schooling 6–7, 18
Scotland debut 34–35
Scotland v England 1962 39–40
scouted by Celtic 21–22
scouting role 216–217, 219, 221
sectarian abuse 204, 240
shipyard worker 20, 24
signed by Celtic 23–24
signed by Manchester United 51–52, 54–55
spitting incident 130–131
sportsmen's dinners 234–235
support for Kidd 133
support from fans 33–34, 108–109
supported by Busby 190
swearing 28
teamwork with Bobby Charlton 87–88
teamwork with Law 57–58
testimonial 222–223
threats from fans 200
timekeeping 130, 175–176
transfer fee 55
TV analyst 195, 201–203, 221–222, 233–234
views on all-seater stadiums 256–257
views on Beckham 78
views on Best 61–62, 81–83
views on Bobby Charlton 87
views on Busby 66–67
views on Cantwell 88–89
views on current Manchester United team 270–272
views on Docherty 215
views on Ferguson 265–268
views on football pundits 268–269
views on Foulkes 79–80
views on Gregg 85–86
views on Herd 90
views on imperialism 3
views on Irish politics 3, 15, 18, 86, 200–201, 235–237
views on Kelly 47–48
views on Kidd 162–163
views on Law 83–85
views on Manchester 273–277
views on Manchester United team 1963–1964 77–90

views on Manchester United xi–xii
views on McGuinness 191–192
views on Murphy 107–108
views on national anthem 34–35, 165
views on new technology 264
views on players' wages 72, 74
views on playing formation 217
views on racism 158
views on Rangers 38, 45–46
views on religion 41
views on Scotland team 146–148
views on sectarianism 18, 20, 28, 65
views on Shankly 105–106
views on Stein 23–25
views on Stepney 124–125
views on Stiles 79–81
visa incident 249–250
visiting Auschwitz 145
visiting South African township 145–146
wages at Celtic 49
wages at Manchester United 55, 74, 125
Wagstaff incident 67
World Club championship 1968 177–181
World Cup 1962 qualifiers 34–36
World Cup 1966 122–123
World Cup 1970 201–203
World Cup 1978 233–234
youth football 5–7, 10, 18–21
Crerand, Patricia (daughter-in-law) 229
Crerand, Patrick (son)
  birth of 97
  fan of Best 210–212
  friendship with Keane 244–245
  hooligans in pub 246–247
  Manchester United fan 229
  marriage 251
  Paddy abused by fans 258
Crerand, Sarah (mother)
  birth of Mary 2
  Celtic supporter 11
  death of John 17–18
  death of Michael 1–2
  disowned by Michael's family 4

European Cup 1967 132
FA Cup 1963 70
Glasgow pubs 27
impoverished circumstances 4–5
Irish background 2–3
marriage to Charlie 16
Paddy leaving Celtic 50–52
Paddy scouted by Celtic 21–22
Paddy's Celtic debut 26
Scottish League Cup incident 238
strictness 9, 10, 16, 19, 44
telephone in house 37
Crompton, Jack
Best as youth player 61–62
booking hotels 161
European Cup 1968 156, 167–168, 170
Manchester United coach 101
Cruyff, Johan 233
Cudicini, Fabio 187
Cunningham, Willie 53

Dalglish, Kenny 85
Daly, Jimmy 37
Davies, Wyn 213
Davis, Harold 46, 48
Delaney, Jimmy 13
Di Stefano, Alfredo 48, 85, 149
Dienst, Gottfried 120
Dobing, Peter 130
Docherty, Tommy
affair with Mary Brown 231–232
appointed Manchester United manager 215
Crerand appointed Manchester United assistant manager 216
Crerand leaving Manchester United 223–225
Crerand's scouting role 216–217, 221
Crerand's testimonial 222–223
Crerand's views on 215
deteriorating relationship with Crerand 218–222
disliked by Crerand 223, 228, 230
libel case with Morgan 232–233
proposal to buy Osgood 218–219
sacked by Manchester United 232

shabby treatment of Law 218, 232
ticket touts 231
unpopularity at Manchester United 227
views on playing formation 217
Dodgin, Bill (junior) 226
d'Oliveira, Basil 174
Dougan, Derek 201–202
Duffy, Charlie (stepfather) 16, 70, 132
Duffy, Eddie 32, 101
Duffy, James 16
Duke of Edinburgh 99
Dunne, Pat 98, 103, 124
Dunne, Tony 78, 92, 104
European Cup 1968 152
Irish supporters 150
Dunphy, Eamon 268–269
Dyson, Terry 92

Edwards, Duncan 13, 170
Edwards, Louis 105, 111, 140, 219, 223, 232
Edwards, Martin 250
England, Mike 124, 175
English, Sam 86
Enya 16, 251
European Cup
1965 102–103
1966 113–120
1967 132–133
1968 139–157, 161–172
1969 183–188
1973 188
1999 244
2007 270–271
European Cup Winners' Cup 1963–1964 92–93, 95–96
Eusebio 69, 116–117, 127, 158, 165
Evans, Bobby 29–30

FA Cup
1963 68–70
1964 94–95
1965 100
1966 121
1967 127
1969 183, 185
1970 193–195
1977 231
1985 244
Fallon, Sean 49–50, 216, 267
Ferdinand, Rio 261, 267, 271, 277
Ferguson, John 9
Ferguson, Sir Alex 51, 123

achievements at Manchester United 254
Crerand's views on 265–268
disciplinarian 66
Drumchapel team 21
Glasgow background 238
good loser 66
Keane as potential successor 246
Kidd as assistant coach 163
management problems at Celtic 47
pressures of manager's job 227–229
role of assistant managers 221
Rooney and Scholes bans 270
seeking players' opinions 64
signing Ferdinand 267
signing Keane 244
Fernie, Willie 29
Ferry, Jack 138
Ferry, Noreen
see also Crerand, Noreen
beauty competitions 42–43
dating Paddy 42–44
Manchester digs 62
marriage to Paddy 74–76
meeting Paddy 41–42
Paddy leaving Celtic 51–52
Paddy signed by Manchester United 54–55
Finney, Tom 12, 113
Fitton, Peter 224–225
Fitzpatrick, John 123, 134–135, 186, 203
Flashman, Stan 231
Foulkes, Bill
1963–1964 season 96–97
ageing player 192
Crerand spitting incident 130
Crerand's views on 79–80
European Cup 1965 102
European Cup 1966 116
European Cup 1968 155
European Cup 1969 186
golf player 172
Foy, Johnny 65
Freddie and the Dreamers 82–83, 156
Freedman, Edward 250

Gallagher, Charlie 28
Gallagher, Moira 33
Garrity, Freddie 82–83, 156
Gaskell, David 68, 89, 124
European Cup Winners' Cup 1963–1964 92, 95

Index

Gemmill, Archie 21
Gento, Paco 48, 149, 152
Geo 95
Gerrard, Steve 145
Gibson, Colin 243–244
Giggs, Ryan
  2006–2007 season 271–272
  admiration for Kidd 163
  inspirational player 104
  hard worker 107
  missing out on World Cup
    122–123
Giles, Johnny 269
  FA Cup 1963 69
  footballing skills 89–90
  Irish supporters 150
  Leeds player 100, 123
Gillis, Billy 162
Glanville, Brian 188
Glass, Jackie 156–157
Gloria, Otto 165
Goldie, Willie 47
Goodwin, Mick 128
Gowling, Alan 208
Gray, Andy 21
Gray, Eddie 18, 193, 250
Greaves, Jimmy 93, 113
Green, Alan 260–261
Green, Geoffrey 111–112
Green, Tony 204
Greenwood, Ron 191
Gregg, Harry
  Crerand's temper 63
  Crerand's views on 85–86
  end of playing career 124
  FA Cup 1963 68
  friendship with Crerand 59
  Irish supporters 150
  Munich air disaster 88
  pre-match whisky 108
  Shrewsbury manager 217
Gregory, John 228
Grummitt, Peter 127
Guevara Lynch De La Serna,
  Ernesto (Ché) 9

Hamrin, Kurt Roland 186
Hansen, Alan 243, 268
Haraldsted, Eva 196–197
Hardman, Harold 65
Harkin, Jim 236
Hart, John 239–240
Hartford, Asa 21
Henrique, Luis 166
Herd, Alec 90
Herd, David 79, 89, 104
  Crerand's views on 90
  dropped by Busby 123
  European Cup 1966 116

European Cup Winners' Cup
  1963–1964 92–93
  FA Cup 1963 69
  goal scoring 98, 129
  Inter Cities Fairs' Cup
    1964–1965 98
  reaction to criticism 109
  teamwork with Law
    109–110
Heslop, George 159
Hill, Gordon 221
Hill, Jimmy 201
Hitler, Adolf 145
Hoddle, Glenn 260
Holt, Oliver 261
Holton, Jim 217, 222
Hughes, Mark 243, 246, 250
Hughes, Phil 82
Hume, John 235–237

Inter Cities Fairs' Cup
  1964–1965 98–99,
  102–103
Irvine, David 273
Irwin, Denis 150, 259

Jackson, Mick xii, 28, 37, 48,
  52
Jairzinho 202
James, Steve 186
Jennings, Pat 139
Johnston, John 204–205
Johnstone, Jimmy 53

Kaye, Reuben 91–92,
  143–144, 223
Keane, Mossy 59
Keane, Roy 24, 59, 80, 250,
  272
  aggressive player 260
  argumentative nature
    244–245
  European Cup 1999 172
  friendship with Patrick
    Crerand 244–245
  Irish supporters 150
  leaving Manchester United
    263
  Sunderland manager
    245–246
Kearns, Ernie 234
Keegan, Kevin 233
Keeler, Christine 202
Kelly, Bob 37
  arguments with Crerand 54
  Crerand leaving Celtic
    49–52
  Crerand's views on 47–48
  'Kelly's Kids' 30–31

Kelly, Grace 241
Kelly, Kitty 99
Kennedy, Bobby 55
Kennedy, Jim 74
Keyworth, Ken 69
Kidd, Brian
  Blackburn Rovers job 242
  Crerand's jumpers 265
  Crerand's views on
    162–163
  European Cup 1968 141,
    163, 165–166, 172
  frog incident 162
  living in Manchester
    275–276
  Manchester United
    apprentice 133
  World Club championship
    1968 181
Kilroe, Tim 234
King, Don 261
Knighton, Michael 251
Knowles, Cyril 175
Kvasnak, Andrej 35–36

La Rue, Danny 169
Law, Denis
  1966–1967 season 127, 129
  admired by Crerand 202
  adrenalin rush 242
  ageing player 192
  avoiding publicity 163–164
  Brown Bull pub 128
  Chortonville house 76
  Crerand signed by
    Manchester United 54–55
  Crerand's temper 63
  Crerand's views on 83–85
  cricket fan 174
  Docherty appointed
    Manchester United
    manager 215
  European Cup 1966
    116–119
  European Cup 1968 149,
    172
  European Cup 1969 184,
    187
  European Cup Winners' Cup
    1963–1964 92–93
  FA Cup 1963 68–69
  FA Cup 1964 94
  FA Cup 1965 100
  football skills 67
  Glasgow rolls 61
  goal scoring 90, 97–98, 113,
    129, 209
  injury 101–102, 144–145,
    163–164

Inter Cities Fairs' Cup
  1964–1965 98
Krays incident 71
League Cup 1967 126
Morgan's libel case with
  Docherty 232
O'Farrell sacked by
  Manchester United
  214–215
players' wages 125
playing in Italy 36
practical jokes 138
public speaking 249
reaction to criticism 109
retirement 218
Scotland caps 147–148
smoking 57, 77
support from fans 109, 207
teamwork with Crerand
  57–58
teamwork with Herd
  109–110
transfer fee 65
transfer to Manchester City
  215–216, 218
views on Baxter 64
views on Crerand 64
World Club championship
  1968 181
World Cup 1966 123
Law, Diana 54, 71
Lawton, Tommy 12
Lee, Francis 159
Liddell, Billy 12
Lodetti, Giovanni 187
Lowe, Jennifer 88–89
Lowry, L. S. 157
Lubanski, Wlodzimierz 141,
  144
Lynch, Benny 8

Macari, Lou 83, 216, 221,
  232
MacDougall, Ted 213, 232
Machin, Roger 188
Mackay, Dave 92–93, 113,
  147
Macleod, Ally 208
Manchester United FC
  1962–1963 season 56–73
  1963–1964 season 77, 90–97
  1964–1965 season 97–103
  1965–1966 season 104–122
  1966–1967 season 123–131
  1967–1968 season 139–172
  1968–1969 season 174–189
  1969–1970 season 192–195
  1970–1971 season 203–205
  1971–1972 season 208–213

1972–1973 season 213–217
1973–1974 season 217–218
1974–1975 season 219–220
1975–1976 season 221
2006–2007 season 270–272
ageing team 192, 213–214
atmosphere at Old Trafford
  255–256
big screen at Old Trafford
  128
Busby Babes 13–14, 30–31
Busby retiring as manager
  182, 185, 189–191
Busby's twentieth
  anniversary 114
corporate hospitality work
  248
Crerand coaching youth
  squad 08, 212–213
Crerand leaving club
  223–225
Crerand's final games 205
Crerand's testimonial
  222–223
development of Old Trafford
  105
Docherty appointed manager
  215
European Cup 1965
  102–103
European Cup 1966
  113–120
European Cup 1968
  139–157, 161–167
European Cup 1969
  183–188
European Cup 1999 167,
  172, 244
European Cup 2007
  270–271
European Cup parade
  171–172
European Cup Winners' Cup
  1963–1964 92–93, 95–96
FA Cup 1963 68–70
FA Cup 1964 94–95
FA Cup 1965 100
FA Cup 1966 121
FA Cup 1967 127
FA Cup 1969 183, 185
FA Cup 1970 193–195
FA Cup 1977 231
FA Cup 1985 244
fans 108–109, 217–218
hooliganism 110–111, 204,
  217
Inter Cities Fairs' Cup
  1964–1965 98–99,
  102–103

Irish supporters 150, 184,
  236–237
League champions 1965
  102
League champions 1967
  129–130
League Cup 1967 126
Manchester derbies 67, 159
match-day routine 106–109
McGuinness appointed
  coach 185, 191
merchandising 250
Munich air disaster 13, 55,
  56, 73, 88, 137, 140, 152,
  170
O'Farrell appointed manager
  206
players' lounge 83
poor morale among players
  58–59
post-match banquets
  121–122
post-season tours 132–136
potential successors for
  Ferguson 245–246
Real Madrid v Manchester
  United 1968 151–156
relegated to Division Two
  217–218
rules for players 57
rumours of match fixing 59
sacking Docherty 232
sacking McGuinness 204
sacking O'Farrell 214
signing Crerand 51–52,
  54–55
signing Law 65
signings in 1964–1965 98
signings in 1966–1967
  124–125
signings in 1967–1968 139
signings in 1968–1969 175
signings in 1974 218–219
supporters' club 110–111
team in 1963–1964 77–90
team uniform 170
UEFA Cup 1984 243
World Club championship
  1968 177–181
World Club championship
  2000 272
worldwide reputation 272
youth team 1964 104
Mandela, Nelson 146, 157
Manning, Bernard 275
Mannion, Wilf 12
Martin, Dean 32
Matthews, Sir Stanley 11–12,
  113

Index

McCartney, Sir Paul 83
McGoohan, Patrick 71
McGrath, Paddy 249, 251
  coffin incident 150
  Crerand's relationship with
    Docherty 220–221
  Cromford Club 65, 71, 173
  FA Cup Final 1963 70
  Mallorca holidays 239
McGrath, Paul 150
McGrory, Jimmy 26, 30–31,
  48, 52
McGuinness, Martin 273
McGuinness, Wilf
  appointed Manchester
    United coach 185, 191
  Best's womanizing 194
  Busby as general manager
    206, 214
  Crerand's views on 191–192
  dropping Crerand 203
  media work 264
  Munich air disaster 203
  press-ups incident 192–193
  sacked by Manchester United
    204
McIlroy, Sammy 150, 209,
  221
McIlvanney, Hugh 112, 121
McLean, Jimmy 21–22
McLintock, Frank 6, 71
McNab, Bob 201–202
McNeill, Billy
  Celtic manager 237–238
  Celtic's training regime 25
  esteem for Stein 53
  footballing skills 49
  friendship with Baxter 37
  'Kelly Kids' 30–31
  learning from senior players
    28
  Manchester City manager
    248–249
  marriage 76
  Scotland caps 34–35, 147
  signed by Celtic 23
  watching Rangers 38
  World Club championship
    1967 177
McNeill, Liz 238
McPhail, John 13, 54
McQueen, Gordon 273
Medina, Nicolas 181
Meek, David 112–113, 116
Mercer, Joe 159–161
Mihajlovic, Ljubomir
  120–121
Millar, Jimmy 46
Miller, Vince 234

Mills, Mick 192
Mitchell, Warren 169
Mitten, Charlie 46
Mochan, Neilly 177
Monroe, Marilyn 108
Moore, Bobby 34, 94
Moore, Brian 201
Moran, Kevin 150
Morgan, Willie
  appointed Manchester
    United captain 215
  European Cup 1969 184
  golf player 218
  hat-trick 183
  libel case with Docherty
    232–233
  signed by Manchester United
    175
  support from fans 108
  timekeeping 175–176
  World Club championship
    1968 181
Mourinho, José 105
Moy, Tommy 41–42
Moyes, David 21
Murdoch, Bobby 38, 54, 147
Murphy, Andy 23
Murphy, Jimmy
  coaching skills 136
  Crerand's view on 107–108
  European Cup 1968
    161–162
  Munich air disaster 137
  post-season tours 136–138
  retirement 190–191
  signings for Manchester
    United 104, 175
Musgrove, Malcolm 215

Neary, Billy 241
Neville, Gary 105, 271
Neville, Phil 271
Newman, Paul 75
Ní Bhraonáin, Moya 251
Nicklaus, Jack 196
Noble, Bobby 104, 125–126,
  128
Northampton Town FC
  225–230

O'Donnell, Jimmy 162
O'Farrell, Frank
  appointed Manchester
    United manager 206
  Best misbehaving 209–210,
    212–214
  coaching role for Crerand
    208, 212
  Leicester manager 189

sacked by Manchester United
  214–215
signings for Manchester
  United 213
O'Leary, David 267
Olive, Les 171, 220
Onassis, Jackie 99
Orosz, Zoltan 103
Osgood, Peter 218–219

Paisley, Bob 222
Pallister, Gary 64, 250
Parkinson, Michael 199, 202
Peacock, Bertie 28, 53
Pearson, Stuart 219
Pele 202–203
Peronace, Gigi 65
Pirri 152
Poletti, Gustavo 181
Pope John Paul II 157
Prinzip, Gavrilo 140–141
Profumo, John 202
Puskas, Ferenc 48–49, 149

Queen Elizabeth II 70
Queen, Tony 52
Quinn, Pat 46, 63
Quixall, Albert 89, 123

Ramon, Juan 181
Ramsey, Alf 13, 99, 178
Real Madrid v Manchester
  United 1968 151–156
Reid, Peter 243
Revie, Don 89, 100, 175, 191,
  193–194
Riley, Harold 157–158
Rimmer, Jimmy 104, 134, 186
Rivelino 202
Rivera, Gianni 69, 187
Roarty, Martin 240, 248
Robertson, John 21
Robson, Bobby 243
Robson, Bryan 241–245, 251,
  262–263
Rocco, Nereo 187
Roche, Denis 234
Rodger, Jim 51–52
Rodgers, Brid 16
Ronaldo, Cristiano 64, 253,
  269, 271–272
Rooney, Wayne 90, 269–270,
  272
Rumbelow, Anthony 263
Ryan, Jimmy 178

Sadler, David 78–79
  European Cup 1968
    154–155, 165

World Club championship 1968 178, 180
youth football 104
Saha, Louis 270–271
Samson, Kenny 244
Sanchis 155
Sands, Bobby 146
Sartori, Carlo 184
Scholes, Paul 163, 270–272
Schulz, Dutch 15
Scotland
  Crerand's debut 34–35
  England v Scotland 1965 60, 80
  Scotland v England 1962 39–40
  selection policy 146–148
  World Cup 1962 qualifiers 34–36
  World Cup 1966 148
Scott, Alex 46
Sellers, Peter 80
Setters, Maurice 76, 85
Sexton, Dave 217
Shankly, Bill 206, 216
  Busby's testimonial dinner 60–61
  buying Chisnall 90
  Crerand's testimonial 222
  Crerand's views on 105–106
  League Cup 1967 126
  players' wages 72
  respect for Busby 105
Shankly, Nessie 60
Shaw, Richard 253
Shearer, Alan 268
Shearer, Bobby 45–46
Silva (Lisbon player) 95
Simmons, Mathew 253
Sinatra, Frank 32, 99
Smith, Andy 10
Smith, David 110–111
Smith, Jimmy 21
Smith, Teddy 21–22
Smith, Tommy 255
Sormani, Angelo Benedicto 186
Speight, Johnny 169
St John, Ian 105, 122, 222, 260
Stalin, Josef 10
Stapleton, Frank 150
Stein, George 207
Stein, Jean 207
Stein, Jock 52
  appointed Scotland manager 208
  approached to be Manchester United manager 206–208

Celtic manager 49, 64, 174, 175
  coaching skills 24–25, 30
  Crerand's testimonial 223
  European Cup 1967 132–133
  Glasgow rolls 61
  leaving Celtic 31–32, 53
  Leeds manager 207–208
  playing career 23–24
  pressures of manager's job 228
  Scotland caretaker manager 148
  signing Crerand 23–24
  views on Docherty 215
  views on sectarianism 21
  watching Rangers 38
  World Club championship 1967 177
Stepney, Alex 104, 275
  ageing player 221
  Crerand's views on 124–125
  dropped by Busby 186
  European Cup 1968 152, 156, 165–166, 172
  hotel burglar incident 134
  Morgan's libel case with Docherty 232
  rooming with Crerand 140, 143
  signed by Manchester United 124
  World Club championship 1968 178
Stepney, Pam 151
Stewart, Rod 255
Stiles, Nobby
  Crerand's views on 79–81
  European Cup 1966 119–120
  European Cup 1968 154,172
  European Cup Winners' Cup 1963–1964 92, 95
  FA Cup 1963 68
  friendship with Bobby Charlton 87
  gambling 77–78
  League championship 1964–1965 102
  Manchester United youth team 90
  Preston North End manager 230
  reaction to criticism 109
  rivalry with Manchester City 161
  shortsightedness 80–81

World Club championship 1968 178–181
World Cup 1966 123–124
Storey-Moore, Ian 213
Strachan, Gordon 244
Summerbee, Mike 81, 88, 160, 211, 263
Suurbier, Wim 240
Swales, Peter 223

Tagliaferro, Father Hilary 140
Tarbuck, Jimmy 196
Taylor, Gordon 277
Taylor, Tommy 199
Terry, John 145, 271
The Beatles 82–83
Thomas, Dave 196
Thomas, Tudor 275
Thompson, John 86
Todd, Colin 192
Torres 117, 165
Tostao 202
Towers, Ian 91
Trapattoni, Giovanni 187
Tully, Charlie 12–13, 28–29

UEFA Cup 1984 243
Ure, Ian 64

Veron, Seba 181

Waddington, Tony 130
Wagner, Malcolm 82
Wagstaff, David 67
Walker, Dennis 58–59
Whalley, Bert 137
White, John 27–28, 97, 113
Whiteside, Norman 150
Whitty, Tom 246–247
Wilkie, Alan 253
Winter, Henry 261–262
Wiseman, Hugh 19
World Club championship
  1967 177
  1968 177–181
  2000 272
World Cup
  1962 34–36
  1966 122–123, 148
  1970 201–203
  1978 233–234

Yeats, Ron 122
Yorke, Dwight 272
Young, Bill 216

Zocco 152, 155
Zubeldia, Osvaldo 179